PIPE FITTINGS

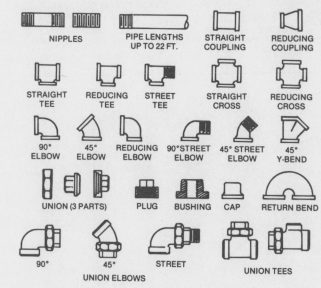

NIPPLES   PIPE LENGTHS UP TO 22 FT.   STRAIGHT COUPLING   REDUCING COUPLING

STRAIGHT TEE   REDUCING TEE   STREET TEE   STRAIGHT CROSS   REDUCING CROSS

90° ELBOW   45° ELBOW   REDUCING ELBOW   90° STREET ELBOW   45° STREET ELBOW   45° Y-BEND

UNION (3 PARTS)   PLUG   BUSHING   CAP   RETURN BEND

90°   45°   STREET   UNION TEES
UNION ELBOWS

COUPLING   NUT   CAP

90° ELBOW   90° ELBOW

REDUCING TEE   REDUCER

PLUG   45° ELBOW   TEE

Here are the common steel pipe fittings. Nipples are simply short lengths of pipe threaded on both ends. Reducing fittings join two different sizes of pipe.

Compression fittings of the flared-tube type are the easiest for the novice to handle when working with copper tubing.

STANDARD STEEL PIPE
(All Dimensions in Inches)

Nominal Size	Outside Diameter	Inside Diameter	Nominal Size	Outside Diameter	Inside Diameter
⅛	0.405	0.269	1	1.315	1.049
¼	0.540	0.364	1¼	1.660	1.380
⅜	0.675	0.493	1½	1.900	1.610
½	0.840	0.622	2	2.375	2.067
¾	1.050	0.824	2½	2.875	2.469

SQUARE MEASURE
144 sq in = 1 sq ft
9 sq ft = 1 sq yd
272.25 sq ft = 1 sq rod
160 sq rods = 1 acre

VOLUME MEASURE
1728 cu in = 1 cu ft
27 cu ft = 1 cu yd

MEASURES OF CAPACITY
1 cup = 8 fl oz
2 cups = 1 pint
2 pints = 1 quart
4 quarts = 1 gallon
2 gallons = 1 peck
4 pecks = 1 bushel

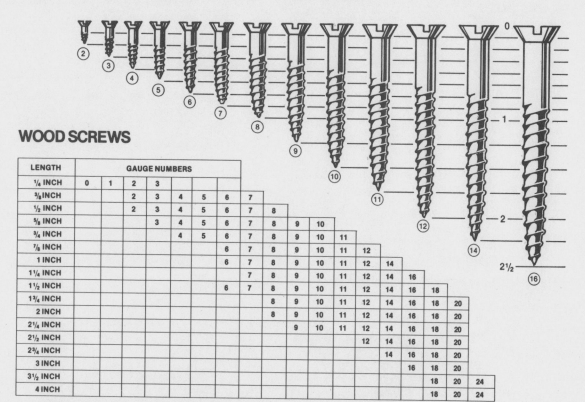

WOOD SCREWS

LENGTH	GAUGE NUMBERS													
¼ INCH	0	1	2	3										
⅜ INCH			2	3	4	5	6	7						
½ INCH			2	3	4	5	6	7	8					
⅝ INCH				3	4	5	6	7	8	9	10			
¾ INCH					4	5	6	7	8	9	10	11		
⅞ INCH							6	7	8	9	10	11	12	
1 INCH							6	7	8	9	10	11	12	14
1¼ INCH								7	8	9	10	11	12	14	16
1½ INCH						6	7	8	9	10	11	12	14	16	18
1¾ INCH								8	9	10	11	12	14	16	18	20
2 INCH							8	9	10	11	12	14	16	18	20
2¼ INCH								9	10	11	12	14	16	18	20
2½ INCH											12	14	16	18	20
2¾ INCH											14	16	18	20
3 INCH												16	18	20
3½ INCH													18	20	24
4 INCH													18	20	24

WHEN YOU BUY SCREWS, SPECIFY (1) LENGTH, (2) GAUGE NUMBER, (3) TYPE OF HEAD—FLAT, ROUND, OR OVAL, (4) MATERIAL—STEEL, BRASS, BRONZE, ETC., (5) FINISH—BRIGHT, STEEL BLUED, CADMIUM, NICKEL, OR CHROMIUM PLATED.

Popular Mechanics

COMPLETE

GUIDE

TO

PAINTING,

REFINISHING,

AND

WALLPAPERING

EXTERIOR PAINTS
INTERIOR PAINTS
PRIMERS
SEALERS
STAINS
VARNISHES
SUPERVARNISHES
MILDEWCIDES
ACRYLICS
ALKYDS
LATEX
PENETRATING STAINS
WIPING STAINS
SHELLACS
ENAMELS
LACQUERS
ANTIQUE FINISHES
GILDING
WAXES
FRENCH POLISHES
FILLERS
PAINT REMOVERS
WALLPAPERS
and many other fine finishes
and surface coatings

Richard V. Nunn

HEARST BOOKS

NEW YORK

Copyright © 1984 by The Hearst Corporation.

ISBN 0-87851-088-5

Library of Congress 84-082099

10 9 8 7 6 5 4 3 2 1

PRINTED IN THE UNITED STATES OF AMERICA

CONTENTS

INTRODUCTION

The do-it-yourselfer often is intimidated when he strolls into a store to buy paint for his house, or a stain for a refinishing project. The massive displays of buckets, bottles, cans and boxes meld into a hodgepodge. And all the containers have strange-sounding names or weird chemical formulas.

If the shopper is lucky, a knowledgeable sales person will be on hand to guide him through the maze. If he's not so lucky, the buyer may go home without the proper finish, and too often is disappointed with the results.

This book can change how you shop for all kinds of surface coatings. And how you apply them. The pages are filled with basic information that will help you buy the right paint and sealant for your various finishing and refinishing projects. You'll save time and money with the information in this book. You'll find data on how different finishes perform, how they are applied, why special preparation techniques are necessary to get the best coverage and lasting benefits.

We're often asked, "What is the best paint on the market today?" It's a good question, but nobody knows the answer. If we did know the answer, it would change tomorrow. What we do know is this:

Paint lines are formulated by any manufacturer (and there are approximately 1000 paint makers in the United States) to be "good," "better," or "best." Frequently an established line of paint is reformulated to meet market conditions, or to cut costs.

If a chain of paint stores, for example, wants to make more profit on a particular line, the quality of the paint may be reduced slightly to assure a better profit margin. The chain must weigh this against the lasting reputation of its paint. This is how companies stay competitive. The difference in a formula may be so subtle that it would take a paint chemist to detect it.

As a general guide you can expect *quality* paints and finishes from most *brand-name* manufacturers— although the quality may vary a bit from time to time.

The "good," "better," and "best" quality labels are usually an accurate guide to quality. You can't expect the same performance from the "good" paint as the "best" paint. The paint from a single vat is not poured into buckets with different labels, contrary to popular belief.

Today, paints and other finishes are a far cut above what they were just a decade ago. Manufacturers have upgraded their products to make painting easy, fast and relatively inexpensive. Certain coatings also have been developed to solve special problems. For example, today you can buy paint that can be applied over *damp* exterior and interior surfaces. And you can buy paint with a life expectancy of ten years or more.

There also have been many improvements in the tools of the trade. Chances are your grandfather never even heard of a paint roller, a pad painter or an aerosol can.

Inside a paint store you'll find a rainbow of colors, beautiful decorative accents, clear and special protective finishes for just about anything you want to seal, protect or decorate. With the help of the information in this book, you'll also find *ideas* in the paint store, ideas that will make your specific project turn out exactly the way you want it to turn out.

Exterior Painting

■ ALMOST ANYONE can paint a house. The paint and paint equipment manufacturers have spent millions in research and development to assure it. In fact, manufacturers are constantly marketing new formulas and gadgets to capture a larger share of the paint dollar in the marketplace. It's a kind of space race of the paint bucket. Fortunately, you are the direct beneficiary of the R&D, whether you spread the paint yourself or pay a pro to apply it.

But don't buy a drop of paint or a brush to spread it until you read this chapter on exterior painting. You may save a lot of time and trouble.

It has been calculated that, of the total time invested in a paint job, 90 percent should be devoted to preparing the surface and 10 percent in spreading the paint. This figure is about right, depending on the condition of the surface to be painted. But what many do-it-yourselfers don't know—or won't recognize—is that the 90 percent figure represents hours upon hours of hard work. The paint container label states succinctly: "Prepare surfaces thoroughly." Washing, scraping, wirebrushing, nailing, sanding, and priming are not so simply done. So, what usually develops is a midsummer's nightmare of painting that started out to be two or three weekends of pleasant outdoor work. If you've done it, you know.

This chapter can minimize the hard work by guiding you down a path that leads from planning to preparing and finally painting.

Which paint for what surface? It's sometimes tough to tell in a paint showroom with a mass display of buckets from floor to ceiling. How to find your way around the maze is the subject of Exterior Painting.

CHAPTER 1

Planning For the Right Image

■ BY CHOOSING the right color combinations you can actually make your home look larger, smaller, wider, shorter, taller. You can, through color combinations, highlight special features of the house, bring out a smart architectural design hidden beneath the wrong color, and even save money on your heating and cooling bills. The right paint and color can even hide a multitude of architectural, material and carpentry sins. This is what is called *"paint behavior,"* i.e., how you can expect paint to perform once it has been applied to the surface.

The good news about planning a paint job is that you don't actually have to try out different colors on your house. And you don't have to hold up tiny paint chips in a store and try to visualize how your house will look with such-and-such a color combination. Instead you can completely color-coordinate on paper on a scale that is practical, meaningful and helpful.

As brief background, many homes built since World War II are somewhat lacking in architectural unity. Builders often used a bit of drop siding here, a wall of masonry over there, and fancy wrought-iron railings in the middle.

The use of so many different materials tends to create a hodgepodge of design that doesn't tie itself together in a package.

You can unify this hodgepodge with paint. The colors work magic by pulling different materials into a pleasing unit.

The material potpourri may not be your problem. Instead, your house may be clean-cut and unified—like a smart New England style saltbox. Here, the problem could be strictly one of the wrong color combination. The accents and the body color of the house don't agree or properly highlight the simplicity of the design that the architect or builder intended. Color restyling is needed.

What some paint store or paint department employees won't (or can't) explain are color combinations that can change the way a house looks. The knowledge of basic colors and how the colors blend together is why.

There are just three primary colors:
1. Yellow
2. Red
3. Blue

There are just three secondary colors. They are formed by mixing the three primary colors:

1. Purple
2. Orange
3. Green

There are colors called "tertiaries." These colors are in 12 basic hues. The hues are created by mixing the primary and the secondary colors.

Chances are these different hues will be presented in a paint store on a color wheel or with color card swatches. Knowing the basics will help you in the store. The hues, of course, can be changed by adding color to a base paint. Theoretically the number of paint colors is unlimited. Actually most paint stores offer up to 1000. With so many available you should be able to find just the right combination.

Below are the basic, *complementary* colors. Use them to work out different combinations:
1. Red/Green
2. Red-Orange/Blue-Green
3. Orange/Blue
4. Yellow-Orange/Blue-Purple
5. Yellow/Purple
6. Yellow-Green/Red-Purple

The basics above can be further split for additional complementary colors.
1. Orange/Yellow/Blue
2. Yellow-Orange/Yellow-Green/Purple
3. Yellow/Green/Red-Purple
4. Yellow-Green/Blue-Green/Red
5. Green/Blue/Red
6. Blue-Green/Blue-Purple/Red-Orange
7. Blue/Purple/Orange
8. Blue-Purple/Red-Purple/Yellow-Orange
9. Purple/Red/Yellow
10. Red-Purple/Red-Orange/Yellow-Green
11. Red/Orange/Green
12. Red-Orange/Yellow-Orange/Blue

You can spin the color wheel still another way: two combinations of colors. The combinations may sound a bit weird, but they match:
1. Yellow-Orange and Blue-Purple go with Red-Orange and Blue-Green
2. Yellow and Purple go with Orange and Blue
3. Yellow-Green and Red-Purple go with Yellow-Orange and Blue-Purple
4. Green and Red go with Yellow and Purple
5. Blue-Green and Red-Orange go with Yellow-Green and Red-Purple
6. Orange and Blue go with Green and Red

Colors also have a definite "size." The large colors are Yellow and Red. The small colors are Green, Blue and Black.

Light colors in a room, for example, will make the room look larger: Yellow and Red and, depending on the hue, Green. By painting the ceiling in a large room a dark color and the walls a light color, the ceiling will drop making the room appear to be smaller. The same applies to the exterior of a house.

Changing the Size of a House

A house painted a light color will appear to be larger than a house painted a dark color. If the house has a dark roof and is painted a light color, the house will appear large but lower on the foundation. If a house with a light roof is painted a dark color, the house will look small but tall. If the house appears to be too high for its width, paint the body of the house approximately the same color as the roof; the house will come into scale. Or, if the roof is low (as on a ranch-style house) and you want to raise the roof, paint the body of the house a contrasting color, i.e., a black roof/white body.

Paint also has reflective qualities. If you reside in a hot, sunny climate, the exterior colors should be light to reflect the heat and save on cooling bills. If you live in a cold climate, the exterior colors should be dark to absorb the heat and save

Stains, varnishes, and furniture refinishing products in a typical paint department are usually separated as to usage: exterior, interior, fine finishes. The thinners and solvents are nearby.

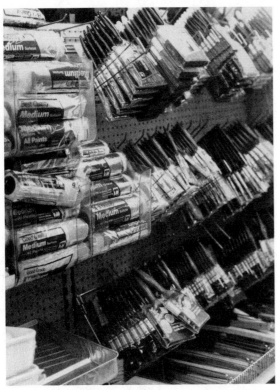

Brushes, rollers, and roller covers in stores are often labeled as to type of paint and surface. You can trust the label. Do not buy pure bristle brushes for water-thinned paint is the No. 1 rule to follow.

Tools and materials needed: Camera, film, graph or tracing paper, photo enlargements, colored pencils, straight-edge ruler, masking tape, soft lead tracing pencil.

The first technique is to sketch the elevation of the house on graph paper and then, with colored pencils, work out a combination of colors within the white space created by the penciled outline. This technique works okay, but unless you are good at sketching the drawing may be lacking in the detail necessary for color harmony. If you do try this method, we suggest using graph paper with small squares, freehanding the sketch first, then transferring the sketch to another sheet of graph paper using a ruler or straightedge for outlining shapes.

The photo technique is easier for most planners although it is more expensive than the graph-paper sketch.

First, take a black-and-white snapshot of the front of the house and another shot of the most prominent side of the house. It's not a bad idea to photograph all four elevations for the best color coordination. Have the snapshots enlarged to 8x10 or 12x15 inches. Ask the photo print shop for "non-glossy" or "matt" prints.

on heating bills. Depending on how well the house is sealed (insulated, calked, weather-stripped), light/dark colors can save on fuel costs.

Reflective qualities of paint colors for comparison purposes include these:

White reflects 80 percent
Ivory or off-white reflects 71 percent
Apricot-beige 66 percent
Lemon-yellow 65 percent
Light buff 56 percent
Salmon 53 percent
Pale green 51 percent
Medium gray 43 percent
Pale blue 41 percent
Deep rose 12 percent
Dark green 9 percent

Experiment with Colored Pencils

For a few dollars you can experiment with different color combinations, such as the basic ones listed above. This cost is not prohibitive when you consider the cost of paint and the labor you spend applying it. There are two techniques. Both have been used by color coordinators for years with a great deal of success.

What You'll Need to Paint Your House

These are the basic tools and materials that you probably will need to paint your house. Much of the equipment will be re-usable for other painting jobs and for general home-improvement and maintenance projects.

- Primers
- Finish paint/stain/trim paint
- Brushes, rollers, pads, sprayers
- Ladders
- Scrapers/putty knives
- Calking/calking gun
- Dropcloths
- Masking tape (1-½-inch width)
- Glazing compound
- Utility knife
- Mixing buckets and paddles
- Garden hose/scrub brush
- Repair tools (hammer, saw, trowels, cold and/or brick chisel, tape measure)
- Repair materials (nails, screws, boards)
- Solvents
- Paint strainers
- Bucket hooks
- Safety glasses
- Gloves
- Sandpaper/sanding block/steel wool

Color-design your home first on paper. Take a photo of it and have the photo enlarged. Then tape the photo to a smooth flat surface, as shown. Supplies you need are colored pencils, a stiff ruler, and a dozen sheets or so of thin tracing paper.

Overlay the taped-down photo with tracing paper, and then free-hand the outline or shape of the house with a soft lead pencil. Put in the windows, doors, shutters, chimney, and any next-to-house plantings.

Lay the prints one at a time on a flat surface and tape them into a more-or-less square position. Use masking tape; it's easier to peel off than cellophane tape.

Cover the print with an overlay of tracing paper. Tape the tracing paper in place so it won't slip. Now lightly, with a soft lead pencil, trace the outline of the house, adding any special details such as porches, bay windows, a chimney, shutters and so on. You don't have to draw the horizontal laps on the drop siding (or any siding) or the mortar joints in masonry. Just get a fairly comprehensive image of the structure. Do four or five tracings of the same elevation. You will use them all.

With colored pencils and the color coordination information in this chapter, fill in the blank white spots bordered by the tracing pencil. Be bold with accent colors such as a red/orange door next to a gray body paint or a new color overlay on mismatched brick or stone surfaces. The magic of the colors will surprise you.

As you work through each color scheme, keep in mind the following tips:

It is easier to paint the house the same color or approximately the same color than to change colors—either light or dark. The new, but similar, color blends in with the old, so brushmarks and other small imperfections are not so noticeable. Also, the new paint will seem to last longer. This is not so. When the new paint film wears thin the base or color underneath it is the same color, and you simply aren't aware of the difference. The surface *does* need paint, however.

The easiest color to paint over with any other color is white, although some colors such as the reds, greens, blues and dark grays often don't hide the white color with one coat. Unless you are an expert, you will see the white peeking through.

The hardest colors to paint over with light colors are the reds, greens, blues, dark or intense yellows, and dark grays. Two and sometimes three coats are needed to properly hide these colors. As the darker colors start to wear and fade (which is normal), you probably will see the lighter base color show through. The only way you can hide the base color is with another topcoat of the same color.

If your house is heavily landscaped, i.e., lots of trees, bushes and shrubs, consider using paint colors that are about the same color value or

With a straight-edge, square the free-hand lines outlining the house. Then, with colored pencils, shade in the colors that you are considering. Example: make the structure of the house gray, the trim white, the shutters white, and the entrance door a vivid yellow, orange, or red. The text in this section will help you determine satisfactory color combinations.

depth as the landscaping. That is, don't use a bright, pastel green with landscaping that is dark green in color.

Avoid horizontal and vertical trim lines if you want the house to look larger. Fascia and trim boards at corners and along the foundation set a definite boundary around the house. Horizontal trim will make the house look lower; vertical trim will make the house look higher. If you have an eyesore chimney at one end of the house, paint it the same color as the house, which will tend to hide it. If the chimney is a feature, however, accent it with a trim color or even leave it natural. The same rule applies to windows and doors. If you want to hide sizes or defects, paint the windows and doors the same color as the body of the house; don't trim either with a different color of paint and don't highlight either with shutters.

The roof of a house represents a surprising 30 to 50 percent of the color of most houses. The color of the roof may be difficult and/or very expensive to change to be compatible with the color of the rest of the house. Below are several basic colors that will be compatible with standard roofing shingles:

Medium to dark green shingles with some flecks

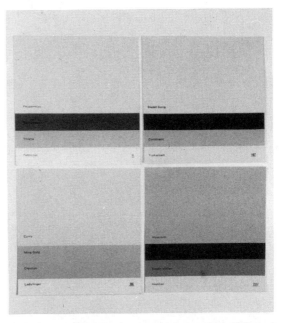

These are color chips from a paint store. The different shadings denote different hues of the base color. The color on the chips can be matched fairly accurately, but the color may not be a *perfect* match. Keep in mind that any paint *always* dries just a tad darker than the color you see in the bucket.

of white: White, gray, light to dark green, the darker or more intense yellows, off-white, brown tones, greenish-blue.

Medium gray to black shingles with limited flecks of white: White, gray to charcoal, light to dark green, off-white, red, greenish-blues.

Brownish-red shingles with limited flecks of white: White, shades of yellow, brown, shades of light to medium green, beige.

Blue to white shingles: Shades of blue, gray and charcoal, shades of yellow, shades of green.

White shingles with flecks of black: Almost any color except a matching white.

When you've worked out the color scheme you want, take it to a paint store for matching. Some stores sell only "stock" colors in exterior paint: red, green, white, yellow, blue and so on. The store may not be able to match the colors you want. However, perfect matching may not be necessary. You can use the approximate stock colors and have the trim colors mixed. Or, you can find a paint store that will correctly match the paint you want. You may have to go shopping, but first try the advertising pages in the telephone directory. You probably will have the best

---

Dropcloths: Plastic or Cloth?

For exterior work we recommend that you use a cloth dropcloth, rather than a plastic one. The reasons include these:
- Cloth stays put; plastic slides if it isn't taped in place or otherwise held firmly.
- Bushes and shrubs that have to be covered nestle down under cloth; branches poke through plastic materials unless it's at least 4 mils thick.
- Cloth absorbs paint spills and splatters. Plastic protects surfaces below, but if a lot of paint is spilled it can trickle over the edges and onto those surfaces. A spill on concrete is difficult to remove.
- Cloth may be used many times; plastic may not be reusable.

Kitchen plastic is an excellent covering for outside lamps, railings, door/window hardware and other items you want to protect. Tape it in place.

---

luck with stores that specialize in paint products only. Expect to pay slightly higher prices for specially mixed paint. The cost, however, will not be prohibitive to get the colors you need for color harmony.

CHAPTER 2

When To Repaint Your House

■ THIS IS A QUESTION that opens the door to lots of other questions. Here's a pat answer: You should repaint your house about every eight years, assuming that the paint wear is normal without blisters, peeling or other problems. This time frame can vary a year or so; the house may be painted every seven or nine years. It is always best to paint the surface before it deteriorates or starts to do so. If the paint is guaranteed to wear for 10, 12 or more years by the manufacturer, stick with the guarantee. You may have to show proof of time of purchase, so keep any sales receipts or other proof.

Here are several guidelines to help you make a paint-or-not-to-paint decision.

• *Show-through.* The house needs paint when the primer or base coat of paint begins to show through the top coat(s) of paint. Look closely. You will see this condition. Also look for the grain of the wood siding showing through the paint film. The "high" grain may be down to bare wood.

• *Brush and/or roller tracks.* As a paint film wears down, you often can see pronounced brush marks or paint roller tracks on the coated surface. What has happened is that the paint was lapped by the brush or roller when it was applied, causing a double coat of paint. The double-coat, of course, is twice the amount of paint and, therefore, wears longer than surfaces that were not double-coated. Besides laps, you may see brush streaks. The streaks are caused by the pigment in the paint aligning with the bristles of the brush as the paint was applied. The effect looks "ridgy" or ropelike. You probably can see actual bristle marks. If the house was spray painted, you may see both laps and thin spots. The siding, when you stand away from it, may look spotted.

• *Paint fading.* This is a normal condition. The elements—especially the sun—cause paint to fade or turn a lighter color. You'll notice this on the south and west sides of the house more than on the east and north sides. Fading usually is more noticeable on darker colors. As the paint wears and becomes thinner, the colors tend to lighten. Red is especially sensitive to fading.

• *Paint failure.* Paint failure actually is an incorrect term, even though it frequently is used to describe certain problems. Paint *seldom* fails. What fails is the surface to which the paint is applied—the substratum. The result is peeling, blistering or flaking. Almost always moisture is to blame. These problems are discussed later in this section. The problems must be resolved, however, before new paint is applied.

Frequently a problem involves not paint failure, but plain old dirt. If you have recently painted your house—within five years or so—and the house looks as if it needs to be painted again, the problem may be dirt in the form of soot, chemical deposits or mildew. What the house needs is a bath, not a paint job. How to give your house a bath is described in this section under "Preparation."

A Word About Ladders

Step and extension ladders are sold by "Type," which basically denotes strength. You'll find the Type listed on the rail of the ladder in the store. As to strength, each Type will hold about five times its listed weight rating.

Type I, household ladders: 200 pounds.
Type II, commercial ladders: 225 pounds.
Type I, industrial ladders: 250 pounds.

We recommend the Type II commercial ladder both in the stepladder and extension styles. This grade offers plenty of strength and a fairly reasonable cost (although the cost of all ladders is high). It is strong enough to support you and all the material that you are likely to carry up the rungs.

What size?

The size, or the length of the extension ladder you need, depends on the longest distance from the ground to the eaves of your house. Below is a selection chart:

Eave Height	Length	Working Length
To 9 feet	16 feet	13 feet
9–13 feet	20 feet	17 feet
13 to 17 feet	24 feet	21 feet
21 to 25 feet	32 feet*	29 feet
25 to 29 feet	36 feet*	33 feet
29 to 32 feet	40 feet*	37 feet

* Buy Type I, industrial grade for strength

Metal or Wood?

It's a toss-up as to whether metal or wood ladders are best buys. The metal ones are lighter in weight than wooden ladders. Wooden ladders don't have the shock potential of metal ladders if the ladder touches an exposed overhead electric wire.

If you buy a wooden ladder, do not paint it. The paint will hide any ladder defects such as cracks and splits. If you want to seal the wood, use a wood preservative or clear repellent.

Before each use, walk the ladder by laying the extensions down flat on the ground and then stepping on each rung. If you find a broken or weak rung—either metal or wood—immediately junk the ladder. Do not repair it.

Basic ladder safety

Always overlap an extension ladder by three rungs. If you're working on a roof, make sure the top of the ladder extends over the eaves by three rungs.

Ascend and descend a ladder using both hands. If materials are involved, have a helper hold the materials until you are firmly set on the ladder.

Always keep your hips between the rails of the ladder. Do not over-reach. Instead, move the ladder.

Extension ladders should be set with the base of the ladder about one-fourth its length from the vertical surface. Example: a 20-ft. ladder should be pulled out from the vertical about 5 feet.

Make sure ladder hooks are firmly locked to the rungs of the ladder before climbing.

Keep all wooden ladders stored under cover. Water rots wood.

Always lean a stepladder when possible. If you open it, make sure the legs are fully spread and the paint bucket or tool shelf is locked in position.

Work from an extension or stepladder that is the right size. Never stand on the next-to-the top or top rung of either ladder.

Scaffolding. Do not use it without professional help.

CHAPTER 3

Choosing the Right Paint

■ PAINT HAS three basic ingredients:

• *Pigment.* Pigment provides "body" and color to the paint.

• *Vehicle.* The vehicle may be oil or water. The vehicle suspends the particles of pigment so the pigment may be applied to the surface.

• *Thinner.* A thinner provides the proper consistency to the pigment and the vehicle.

Paint also may contain certain dryers and other additives such as mildewcide.

For exterior use, paint falls into two general classifications: trim paint and structure or body paint.

Trim paint usually includes special resins and dries to a gloss or semi-gloss finish. The formula makes the paint surfaces (mainly around doors and windows) easier to wash. Also, trim paint withstands the exposure to the elements better and lasts longer. Then why not use trim paint throughout instead of structure paint? Cost, high gloss, limited colors, and difficulty of application are four good reasons.

Structure or body paint (body: the siding on the house) also is specially formulated. Structure paint is a tad more elastic than its interior cousins so the paint film can stretch and shrink with temperature changes. Another feature lets the paint conform better to rough surfaces such as unsanded plywood. As a comparison, structure paint is like plastic food wrap. It stretches, shrinks and conforms to the surfaces.

Is there a "best" paint buy for my house?

There are really no ironclad answers to these questions. But there are opinions that you can consider valid. First, you must assume this: The surface over which the coating will be applied is in good condition to accept the paint. That is, the surface is not dirty, wet or etched with a paint problem such as blisters, peels, alligators, or wrinkles. The best paint money can buy is only as good as the surface to which it is applied.

A quality latex paint probably is the best all-around paint buy. Latex paint certainly is the most popular paint. There are many reasons why, and the reasons are discussed below under the separate paint headings.

What brand name paint is the best buy? There's no way of knowing at any given moment. There are more than 1000 paint manufacturers in the United States. Many of them are regional in distribution. Others manufacture private-label paints for large retailers. Some make paint and sell it under several different brand names. The paint formulas in this hodgepodge are continually changing to meet different marketing conditions. For example, one West Coast retailer ordered the paint formula changed so the paint could be advertised with a 12-year guarantee. The change was to meet the competitor's guarantee of 10 years. That guarantee someday will go to 18 or 20 years, we predict.

You can't stray too far if you buy a quality brand-name paint, although you may be paying several dollars more per gallon for it. If you can, always buy a guaranteed paint. If the *paint* fails you are protected. You may not receive the full price of a new gallon of paint, but you can almost always get a prorated settlement. Brand name manufacturers tend not to quibble over complaints. They settle fast.

Time was when the only outside paint available to consumers and professionals alike was a lead-and-oil finish. The lead used then is now outlawed, except for very small amounts in some mixtures. The oil (linseed) is still used as a vehicle in some paints. Although lead-and-oil was an excellent paint, the products offered today are just as good and usually superior. That's why some paint manufacturers can offer a 10- to 12-year guarantee or warranty against paint failure.

Are Primers Needed?

"Yes" and "no" is the answer. If you are painting a bare surface, a primer definitely is recommended. If you are painting a sealed surface, but the sealed surface is spotted with bare wood or there are different layers (uneven) on the surface, a primer is recommended. If the surface is extremely dry or porous, it ought to be primed before topcoats are applied. Or, if the surface will be incompatible with the topcoats of paint, definitely prime it.

In a word, primer gives *tooth* to the surface so the surface will accept the top coats of paint. And, as noted before, a paint job is only as good as the surface to which the paint is applied.

Pigments in primers generally are less expensive than those used in finish paint. Lots of thinner is used in the mixture so the primer dries fast. Topcoats usually can be applied over a primer in just a couple of hours—sometimes in even less time.

Your temptation may be to thin a finish paint and use it as a primer. It can be done, but the coating isn't as good as the real thing. The pigment in the finish paint is thinned too much.

Therefore, the pigmented coating is skimpy on the surface and can't always provide the necessary tooth for the topcoats. Also, thinning finish paint is poor economy. The primers are less expensive than finish paint.

Applying primers to a surface is easy. However, the temptation is to slop them on in the belief that the topcoat will hide any imperfections or missed spots. Primer should be applied with more care than the finish coats. The primer must be spread out evenly. All of the surface should be covered. Use plenty of primer; don't skimp.

To apply the primer, a brush, a roller or spray gun may be used. We recommend a combination, if you have a choice: a spray gun to apply the primer and a light brush to work the primer into cracks and crevices. Use calking compound and glazing compound after the primer is applied, unless the primer manufacturer specifies otherwise.

Latex Primers

With the exception of bare wood, latex primers may be used over any surface. Latex is especially recommended for masonry surfaces and other porous surfaces such as plaster and gypsum wallboard. Its big advantage on masonry surfaces (brick, block, placed concrete and soft stone) is in sealing out the alkalies that are always present in masonry materials. Once sealed with latex primer, the surface will accept any type finish. If your job calls for sealing bare wood, use an alkyd primer. Then, if you want, you can finish the surface with a latex topcoat.

Latex primers have many of the same features as latex finish paint. The primer has no objectionable odor. It dries quickly (in just an hour or two). Usually, you can apply a topcoat to the primer within four hours. You, the paint tools, and any slopover can be cleaned with soap and water.

Acrylic Primers

The acrylics are part of the latex family of water-based paints. Therefore, application is identical to latex, with perhaps one exception. Acrylic primers and finish paints dry faster than latex primers and finish paints.

Alkyd Primers

The alkyds are oil-based products. Therefore, alkyd as a primer is the best buy to seal bare wood surfaces. When it's dry (12 to 18 hours and sometimes longer) the surface may be topcoated with any other finish paint—even latex, which is contrary to popular belief.

Alkyd primer is not the product to use over gypsum wallboard, although you probably would never find wallboard used outside. The reasons are discussed in the interior paint selection section.

For masonry surfaces, we don't recommend alkyd, although the product can be used on such surfaces. If for some reason you want to use alkyd on masonry, be sure to read the manufacturer's label on the bucket before you buy it.

Alkyd is generally free of a bad odor, but it does have a smell. Clean-up is easy, and the same solvents used to thin the paint must be used to clean tools, splatters, and wayward brush marks.

Oil Primers

The choice should be an alkyd, which is oil-based. However, you can buy an exterior oil-based primer if the surface is steel. This primer has two additives: Portland cement and zinc.

Since some gutters are galvanized steel, the primer with the additives is the product to use.

Quick Guide to Exterior Primers

Primer type	Best suited for . . .	Special application tips
Latex*	Most surfaces except bare wood. Ideal for masonry including stucco. Special formulations for aluminum siding.	Don't thin finish paint and use as a primer. When applying, don't skimp; cover the surface thoroughly. Don't overbrush or overroll.
Alkyd*	Most surfaces, but best for new and/or bare wood.	Don't thin for primer. Try for a uniform application without brush or roller laps. Work from a dry surface to a wet edge. Don't skimp.
Acrylic*	Same as latex.	Dries faster than latex, if this is a buying/application consideration.
Oil	Good for wood. The Portland cement formula is excellent for steel surfaces.	The finish is very slow drying. Apply as evenly as possible.
Filler	Porous surfaces such as masonry. Latex, alkyd, acrylic and oil may be used as a topcoat.	Use a stiff brush.
Preservatives	Bare wood. *Most* surfaces can't be top-coated with a finish paint for several months.	Use a brush or roller. Or apply the finish by dipping the material to be coated in the bucket.
Repellent	Wood. The surface can't be top-coated with regular finish for several years.	A brush is the best applicator, although a roller may be used. Test this finish on scrap before you make a decision to apply it to the structure of your home.
Zinc chromate	Iron and steel.	Thoroughly clean the material to be coated. On new metal, such as rain gutters, wash first with vinegar and water. Rinse with clean water.
Zinc oxide	Galvanized iron and steel.	Same as zinc chromate. Two coats of finish may work best.
Long oil	Badly rusted and scaled iron and steel.	Clean off all loose corrosion, but don't sand, scrape, or brush down to the bare metal.
Aluminum	Metals, although may be used on wood and wood that has been coated with creosote.	Clean the surface thoroughly before applying the paint. Stir the paint often to keep the pigments in suspension in the vehicle.

* Alkyd and oil paint, spar varnish and polyurethane may be used to finish copper metal. A primer is not necessary. Use zinc oxide as a primer on oxidized aluminum metal. Brass metal does not need a primer. For brass, use a clear lacquer or polyurethane as a finish. Keep in mind that copper, aluminum, and brass never need a top finish as such. Polish often restores the original finish.

Estimating Exterior Paint Needs

There are a couple of ways you can determine the amount of exterior finish you need to buy for your house. The most accurate is by measuring the house; the second best is guesstimate, which won't be far off the mark. Both methods are outlined below:

Most paint manufacturers put paint coverage figures on the bucket label. The figure will be in square feet. Example: "Coverage 400 square feet." What this means is that the paint in the container is *estimated* to cover 400 square feet. What the label doesn't say is that the coverage figure is for the paint applied by a professional under optimum conditions on superoptimum surfaces. Chances are your "optimums" will be somewhat lower. Therefore, we recommend that you lower *every* manufacturer's coverage figure 25 square feet. That is, if the label says 400 square feet of coverage, you figure 375 square feet. You will almost always need the extra paint for the best job.

Keep in mind that if you use store stock colors, i.e., not specially-mixed paint, you often can return any paint overage provided the buckets are in a saleable condition. Keep your cash register receipts.

It's important that you know, as best you can estimate, the amount of paint needed before shopping for it. Unfortunately, there are a few paint retailers who will try to oversell paint requirements. There are a few others who will try to undersell paint requirements. The oversellers want to move more paint product, and hope you won't bring back the overage. The undersellers want you to come back to the store in hope that they can interest you in other items on the way to the paint department. If your estimate matches their estimate fairly closely (a gallon or so one way or the other) you can be sure that you are buying the proper amount of paint.

A *measurement* is the best way to determine paint requirements.

1. Measure the width and the height of each side of the house. Include doors and windows, unless the structure is walled in glass.

2. Multiply the two figures. Example: the south side of your house is 20 feet wide by 20 feet high. Multiplied, the area is 20x20, or 400 sq. feet. Consider all surfaces square or rectangle.

3. Add the bottom lines of all four measurements. The answer you get is the area of the house.

4. Divide the coverage of the paint per gallon (minus 25 sq. ft.) into the area. The figure will be the number of gallons of paint you will need to cover the area properly.

If the surface you are painting is especially dry, you will need about 10 percent more paint. If the surface is masonry such as block, brick or stucco, carefully read the coverage estimates on the label. You can use up to 50 percent more paint for these surfaces because they are porous.

Figure about 1 gallon of trim paint for every 4 gallons of structure (body) paint.

If your house has very narrow drop or lap siding, add 10 percent to the total estimate for structure paint. If your house has shingle or shake siding, add 20 percent to the total estimate.

What about gable ends? Consider them square or rectangular. The difference in the amount of paint needed is small.

To guesstimate your paint needs, figure one gallon of structure paint for each room in the house. Example: your home has seven rooms. You will need seven gallons of paint, plus 1 gallon of trim paint for every 4 gallons of structure paint. The same percentages apply (see above) for masonry, narrow lap or drop siding, shingle/shake siding.

Red lead primers that were once used to coat metal have been outlawed, since they contain lead.

Wood Preservative

Wood preservatives are a kind of primer for bare wood, although they are not primers in the true definition.

Basically, preservatives are used to deter wood rot, insects and fungi. They *must* be applied to wood surfaces that *have not* been sealed in any other way with paint, stain, or other waterproof coatings. Preservatives are formulated with copper-naphthenate, creosote, penta-chlorophenol, and phenyl-mercury-oleate. Many preservatives are clear liquids which also dry clear. Others leave a blackish or greenish cast on the surface. Most preservatives may be painted over, but there usually is a conditioning period of about six months before paint (or other finishes) may be applied. Check the label.

If the preservative/primer is creosote, you may be in for finishing trouble. Creosote is a black, tar-like preservative. Before the creosote may be finished with a topcoat, the creosote has to be primed. If it isn't, the creosote will bleed through the finish coats. A primer frequently used to seal creosote is aluminum paint. At least two coats of aluminum are recommended; three coats are better.

What's the difference between pure *raw* and pure *boiled* linseed oil? The boiled linseed oil dries faster than the raw linseed oil. This is basically the only difference between the two. Expect a 2- to 4-day drying time with raw and a 12- to 18-hour drying time with boiled linseed oil.

Both are sealers, but creosote can be used only on wood. And, if used on wood, the wood can't be painted or finished until the creosote is sealed. The water repellent is clear and may be used over almost any material, including leather. It must be applied to unfinished surfaces to do the best job.

Repellent coatings are second cousins to preservatives, and can be used to prime wood. Silicone is part of the base formula, so you can't paint over the surface until the silicone has worn down—or out.

Repellents, which are clear liquids, are intended to seal wood against water. Apply them to decks, wooden patios, fences, planters, and so on. They may be used on siding, of course, so the natural wood can show.

If your home is sided with redwood, cypress or cedar, don't be too quick to seal it with a repellent. These woods rot very, very slowly, so don't need to be coated with anything.

We strongly recommend that you apply the repellent you are considering to a sample scrap of wood. Then make a decision as to whether you want to apply the repellent to your whole house.

Fillers

Concrete and cinder block fillers are primers for these materials. Fillers do what the name implies: fill in the open or porous surfaces of masonry. Although fillers may be applied with a roller, we suggest a brush because the bristles of a brush work the filler down into the voids. After the filler has been applied, it may be topcoated with almost any finish: latex, alkyd, oil.

CHAPTER 4

Smart Shopping in the Paint Store

■ THE QUALITY YOU GET is the quality you pay for. We recommend that you buy a guaranteed product if you can find one.

When you walk into a paint store or paint department, you may be faced with a three- or five-level buying decision:

"Our Good Paint"
"Our Better Paint"
"Our Best Paint"
"Premium Paint"
"Professional Paint"

A fair interpretation of these labels is:

Our Good Paint: Poor to fair hiding power, poor to fair durability—probably two to three years, limited stock color selection, slow drying time.

Our Better Paint: Fair hiding power, fair to good durability—probably three to four years, wider range of stock colors, better resistance to fade, dried surface stays clean longer, better surface flexibility, spreads easily (although the *Good* grade probably spreads as good as any of the grades).

Our Best Paint: Good hiding power, good to excellent durability—usually five to seven years, wide range of stock colors, fade resistant, good scrubability (can be washed), uniform sheen, excellent surface flexibility.

Premium Paint: Overall, about the same as *Our Best Paint,* but with a little more hiding power and more durability—from seven to nine years. Premium usually is guaranteed. A wide range of colors.

Professional Paint: Usually *Our Good Paint* and/or *Our Better Paint* quality. The pros are out to make a profit. If you don't specify the grade of paint, the pro will apply the lesser grades. Therefore, *Professional Paint* may be an advertising gimmick to imply quality, but the quality may not be there.

One-coat Paints

One-coat paints are formulated with pigments that have exceptional hiding power and a vehicle that permits the pigment to be applied to the surface in a thicker film without sagging and dripping. You will pay a premium price for this paint. Its one-coat claims are true enough, but the claims are conditional. The paint is one-coat *if the surface to which the paint is applied is in top condition.* The paint is one-coat *if the paint on the*

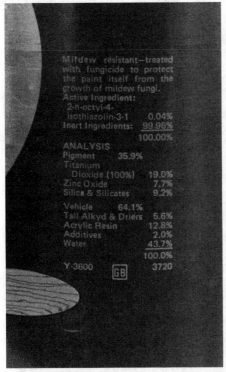

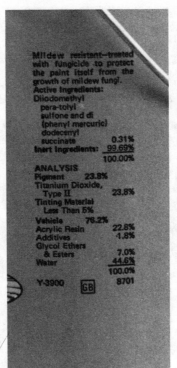

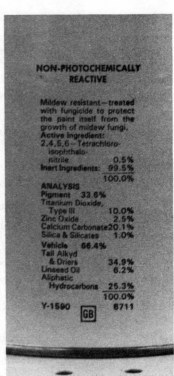

Compare the analysis on the paint bucket labels, and pay special attention to the titanium dioxide precentage in the mixture. As a general rule, the more titanium dioxide, the better hiding power the paint has. Note that the paint—all exterior grade—has been treated with a mildewcide. If you reside in an area where mildew is a special problem, more mildewcide can be added by the retailer to the paint. Some paint manufacturers are now offering a 10 or 12-year guarantee on their products. Buy this guarantee.

surface is almost the same color as the new finish and the old coat is in super condition. Otherwise, the paint will not cover the surface properly in one coat. And the paint will not cover an unpainted surface in one coat.

A one-coat paint job applied by a spray gun is likely to turn out better than a one-coat paint job applied with a brush or roller. With a spray gun you can fill in the thin spots better. A brush or roller tends to drag the paint along the surface in alternating thick-and-thin layers.

Paint selection is a matter of numbers. For example, you may be able to buy an inexpensive paint for $10 per gallon. It will hold up for three years. You can buy a better grade of paint for $15 per gallon. It will hold up for five years. Or you can buy a premium paint for $20 that will last ten years. The inexpensive spread—$10 per gallon—

will have to be repurchased and reapplied every three years. So, assuming the price remains the same, you have an investment of $30 over a nine-year span—plus the labor of applying the paint every three years. By buying the expensive spread—$20 per gallon—you pay $10 less for one additional year before repainting—plus the labor. The same figures can be applied to the medium-priced paint. You will have to paint twice (instead of three times), but you will still pay the same ($30) for the paint. What you're saving is your labor, plus $10 per gallon. Therefore, premium paint is really a bargain.

Latex Finish Paint

If any paint can be called mistake-proof, it is latex. You can apply it in the hot sunshine, in the shade, when it's cool, when it's damp. You can start and stop painting without lapping the material. Latex can be applied to almost any surface but bare wood without special skill or equipment. You can roll it on, brush it on, and/or spray it on.

Latex is formulated so it is not affected by the alkalies of masonry materials. It is fade-, blister-, fume- and mildew-resistant. It is flexible on the surface, durable, stays bright and is nonstaining from chalk wash.

Quick Guide to Exterior Finishes

Name of Finish	Basically used on . . .	Application tools
Latex	All surfaces except bare wood. Especially formulated for aluminum siding; excellent coating for brick, block, stucco and other masonry. Usually can be applied over oil paints, if oil paints are firmly bonded to the surface being topcoated.	Brush, roller, polybrush, pad painters, spray gun.
Acrylic	A type of latex paint, but faster drying. See detail above for latex.	Same as latex.
Alkyd	All surfaces but unprimed masonry and metal. Tops for chalking paint overcoat. Solvent-thinned.	Brush, roller, polybrush, spray.
Oil	Most surfaces. Slow-drying; solvent thinned. Works best on bone-dry surfaces. Can be used on metal.	Brush, roller, spray.
Trim	Formulated for trim: doors, windows, shutters, etc. Available in latex, alkyd, acrylic, and oil. Latex is often color-matched to structure paint.	Brush and roller.
Masonry	Latex is excellent. Also Portland cement mixtures, alkyd, epoxy, and mixtures with bonding formulas.	Brush and roller.
Porch/deck/steps	Latex, acrylic, alkyd, oil, rubber, polyurethane and other finishes specially specified for floor use.	Brush, roller, or floor brush/squeegy combination.
Stain	Wood shingles, shakes, panel siding, decks and outdoor furniture. Two types: semitransparent and pigmented. Use semitransparent to see wood; pigmented to hide most wood grain.	Brush, shake pad painter.
Preservative	Protect raw wood. Can't be topcoated for a period of time. Read labels.	Brush, dipping.
Repellents	Protect and seal raw wood. Can't be top-coated immediately. Limited to some applications. Read labels.	Brush, roller, dipping.
Primers	For new and old wood, metals. Use primer matched to topcoat of finish when possible. Use metal primer on metal. See primer chart, this section.	Brush, roller.

As mentioned earlier, latex paint is thinned with water. Therefore water can be used to clean up equipment, spills and splatters. Being water-thinned, the material is bad-odor-free (it has a slight smell, but is not offensive); you can buy it in a wide range of stock and mixed colors.

Latex paint has some disadvantages. It may not have quite the covering or hiding power of alkyd paint. Also, latex paint may be difficult to apply over a painted surface that is still chalking badly; it may not adhere tightly to such a surface. If chalking is a problem (see definition of chalk-ing, this chapter), alkyd may be the best paint buy.

"Latex System" is a label you may see and hear in a paint store. A latex system is a family of latex paints that includes primers, structure and trim paint. The advantage of the system is that the different paints are absolutely compatible, i.e., work together the same way. The paint is color-matched; that is, the trim paint will match the structure paint perfectly. Also, the paint is batch-numbered. If you buy the same batch numbers, the color will be consistent. The batch

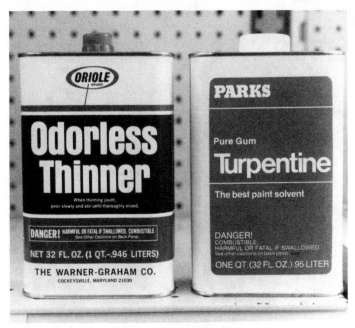

Oderless thinner/mineral spirits smells better and costs less than its counterpart: turpentine. However, turpentine does a faster thinning job. Those are basically the only differences between the two.

Denatured alcohol is for shellac. Lacquer thinner is for lacquer. Do not intermix the two. The alcohol can be used as a stove fuel as well as a thinner; lacquer thinner also can be used as a dried lacquer solvent (see Interior Paints and Finishes) and as a cleaner.

numbers usually are stamped on the bottom of the buckets, or on the lids of the buckets.

Acrylic Finish Paint

The behavior of acrylic finish paint is much the same as latex. The material is water-thinned, easy to apply over the same surfaces as latex—including metal that has been primed, and masonry—and easy to clean up with water.

Acrylic finishes tend to dry faster than latex finishes, so topcoating is even faster, if this is a consideration. The finish is available in flat and semi-gloss (satin), and some manufacturers offer a 50-color selection. Like some latex products, acrylics are touted as a one-coat finish with such features as non-yellowing pigments and no chalk washdown. However, keep in mind that the surface to which the finish is applied has to be in mint condition and the right color for the one coat to cover. Before you buy, check the label on the bucket.

Alkyd Finish Paints

Many of the features of latex and acrylic paints can be tagged to alkyd finishes. The paint has superior hiding power. It may be used over almost any surface including metal and masonry, but the metal and masonry must be primed first.

Alkyd is solvent-thinned, and solvents have an odor. Also, equipment and spills must be cleaned with the solvent, which adds some expense and labor. Alkyd dries slower than its latex and acrylic cousins, but this disadvantage often is unimportant in exterior work. Alkyd is a quality product for wood, and is highly recommended for chalking surfaces. There are plenty of stock colors from which to choose and the price of the product is comparable to other finish paints.

Oil-finish Paints

The tendency is to bum-rap this finish because the other finishes are better. However, like any

If you want the grain of the wood siding to show but still be tinted, use a semi-transparent stain. If you want just some of the wood grain to show but produce a more dense color, use a solid color stain. (See Stains, Finishes Section.) Some exterior stain—like paint—is warranteed or guaranteed. However, stain usually is warranteed only for three to four years while paint is warranteed or guaranteed up to 12 years.

Plywood exterior siding often is plugged with wooden or synthetic patches. It's difficult to tell which. Because of these patches, you should use a pigmented stain, not a clear one. Or use a paint finish. Otherwise, the patches will show through the finish producing an eyesore.

other product you get what you pay for and oil is less expensive so it can't be expected to provide some of the superfeatures.

Oil-finish paint can be expected to last about three to four years. The paint is very durable, if not long-lasting, i.e., it will stand up to the elements and hard use. Oil paint is solvent-thinned with mineral spirits or turpentine. Therefore the mixture has a strong unpleasant smell. It is slow-drying (up to 48 hours or longer). This can be a disadvantage for exterior work: Insects can crawl through the freshly-painted surface and mar it; rain can damage the surface if the paint has not set up when the rain begins to fall.

Shingle and Shake Finishes

If you want to paint shingles and shakes a solid color, you can use latex, acrylic, alkyd, and/or oil finishes. However, if you want a transparent finish on shingles or shakes, buy a shingle stain or wood preservative.

The stains are formulated with a small amount of pigment suspended in a penetrating vehicle. The wood preservatives are clear—no pigment. But they are formulated with special chemicals that deter mold, mildew and rot.

A pigmented stain is recommended for plywood siding. There is a specific reason for this. Plywood blemishes are often "plugged" with synthetic patches that will not absorb stain. The stain lies on top of the patch and seeps into the wood surrounding it. The effect is a patchwork of color. With a pigmented stain, some of the wood qualities show through, and the patches are less noticeable. In fact, the patches usually blend with the surrounding wood surfaces.

As mentioned earlier, redwood, cedar and cypress really don't need any type of coating for protection. If you want to protect them, we recommend a clear wood preservative so the wood underneath can weather and age naturally. The aging process, however, will be slower with a preservative coating.

Shingle and shake bleaches basically give the wood an aged appearance. The wood turns a silver-gray color.

Water repellents sometimes are used for shingles and shakes to preserve the natural look. Once applied, the repellents cannot be topcoated with another type of finish for up to three years or more. Before you make a buying/applying decision, test the repellent you're considering on a piece of scrap wood that matches the house's siding. You may not like the results.

When working with a stain, be sure to keep

Often overlooked, aluminum paint makes an excellent finish for metal on exterior and interior surfaces—as well as on wood and as a primer over wood that has been treated with creosote. The pigment in aluminum tends to sink to the bottom of the bucket, so stir the mixture frequently as it's being used.

stirring the mixture as it is applied. The pigment in exterior stain—from transparent to almost opaque—tends to settle in the bottom of the bucket.

As to wearability, most quality opaque stains can be compared to a quality pigmented finish. The latex stains can be expected to wear longer and stay colorful longer than either alkyd or oil stains. If the material you are staining is subjected to lots of dampness, we recommend a latex stain over an alkyd or oil, which tend to blister.

If you are finishing or refinishing asbestos-cement shingles, you must use a paint recommended only for asbestos-cement. Usually, an additive is added to latex paint for asbestos-cement. See "Special Finishes," this section.

Varnish Finishes

There are basically two types: urethane varnish and spar varnish. Neither has great durability—often less than three years before recoating is needed. Of the two, urethane is the longest-lasting. And a moisture-cured urethane varnish tends to be the most resistant to the elements.

Spar varnish, when dry, remains highly flexible. In fact, when spar varnish is dry, it even feels soft to the touch. The name "spar" comes from the marine field. Spar varnish was first used on the spars (and other parts) of sailing ships. Spar varnish is strictly an exterior product; it wears well outside, but expect to renew it about every two years.

Another varnish, alkyd-based, also is suitable for exterior use. Its durability is about equal to spar varnish. But like spar varnish, alkyd has to be renewed about every 18 to 24 months. Under optimum conditions, it may last up to 30 months.

Porch and Floor Finishes

The oil-based finishes, used for years, are durable but slow drying. The synthetics dry faster, and generally are a better buy because they are multipurpose in a wider range of color choices.

For exterior use, the synthetics include latex, alkyd, acrylic, urethane, epoxy and rubber base. Make sure the bucket label indicates that the finish is formulated for porches, decks and floors. The formula assures you that the finish will withstand the elements and heavy foot traffic.

For concrete floors we recommend a rubber-base finish, latex, epoxy or urethane. If the concrete floor is new, it must be washed thoroughly with a 10-15 percent muriatic acid/water mixture. This provides the best bonding surface for the finish. If the concrete floor is old, it should be thoroughly cleaned before painting. Make sure all peeling paint is removed, along with wax, grease and paint splatters.

Rubber-based finish is somewhat limited in color selection. However, the formula is excellent for concrete floors since it is waterproof and very durable. Expect to pay more for the rubber-base formula; you'll also need special solvents for it. Check the label on the bucket of the product you decide to buy. Different formulas can take different solvents. You can topcoat rubber-base finish, contrary to popular belief, with latex, alkyd and low-gloss oil paint. But the rubber-base must be tightly bonded to the concrete and the surface must be free from grease, oil, dirt, dust and other debris. If you choose an alkyd, the concrete must be primed first. Use a masonry filler primer for this (see primers above).

Over wood decks you can use latex, alkyd, urethane and epoxy paints in a semi-gloss and, sometimes, a flat. Peeling paint is the problem over porch floors, decks and steps that are open underneath. The moisture from the ground and the crawl space penetrates the wood, and off goes the paint film. You can lessen the moisture problem—but not entirely eliminate it—by covering the ground beneath the porch, deck and step surfaces with plastic film. We recommend a 4-mil thickness. Lap the joints about six inches and weight the plastic with bricks or stones. If the plastic will go next to the house foundation or lattice work around the porch foundation or lattice work around the porch perimeter, lap the plastic up the vertical surface about six inches. Staple it in place, or use daubs of asphalt roofing compound to hold it. This seals the earth and, as a bonus, deters plant growth.

Trim Paint

This finish is similar to a varnish and/or porch and deck paint. It is used on the trim and molding around doorways and windows and shutters.

Regular structure paint also may be used for the trim, but it is not as durable and washable as the trim paint—a big consideration.

Trim paint is available in oil, alkyd, and latex gloss and semi-gloss. In comparison, latex is slightly less glossy than alkyd. Latex tends to be more resistant to the alkalies in masonry—a feature when the trim is next to a masonry surface. Also, as mentioned above, latex dries faster than alkyd. Oil, compared to latex and alkyd, ranks high, and it's slow drying and may not be as durable in the long haul. You can use oil over a primed metal surface—such as gutters—and the formulation will give plenty of service.

Masonry Finishes

For brick, block, poured concrete, stucco and other masonry surfaces, we recommend latex; alkyds that have been formulated especially for exterior masonry; cement paint; and rubber-based paints. Rubber-based finish is usually more costly than the other paints, but it's considered best by many for cinder block. It fills well and forms a moisture-tight surface that is smooth.

Like any other surface, masonry must be in good repair before the finish is applied. All crumbling mortar joints should be cleaned and repointed with masonry cement you can buy in bags at most home-center outlets. The procedure is to remove all crumbling mortar with a cold or brick chisel. Then clean the joint with a wire brush, wet it with water, and fill it with the mortar mix. With a joint-strike tool, the new mortar is pressed into a concave configuration. Let the mortar dry a week to 10 days before it is painted.

If the masonry surface is in only fair condition and is chalking heavily, you should first cover the bad surfaces with block filler. Follow directions on the bucket label.

Metal Finishes

There are undercoaters such as aluminum, and you can buy primer/finishes for metal surfaces such as gutters, downspouts, porch railings, galvanized steel, flashing, and so on. Metal paints are oil-based (such as alkyd and the standard oils), and many are available in several colors.

Even though these finishes may be applied directly to the rusted metal, it is recommended that you clean the metal first, especially if flakes of rust have formed. The result is a smoother-looking application. The job will look even better if a topcoat is applied.

Aluminum paint gives a shiny surface to the

metal. The paint—powdered aluminum particles with an alkyd resin or oil vehicle—makes an excellent sealer for woods treated with creosote, as well as almost any metallic surface. Do not use aluminum paint on wooden roof shingles; it will cause rot. Aluminum paint is excellent for corrugated metal roofs and siding, and as a primer for metal railings, lampposts and flashing.

Marine Finishes

Some stores sell marine paints. However, you are most likely to find these finishes stocked by stores that sell marine supplies (such as boats). Spar varnish may be considered a marine finish, although it is widely stocked by home centers and paint stores.

Marine paint in general has more resin in it than most exterior finishes. Types include alkyd, acrylic, epoxy and urethane. Prices for these finishes are higher than other exterior finishes, so their use may be confined to outdoor furniture, trim and metal.

Finishing Fiberglass

Fiberglass panels used outdoors to form patio roofs, siding and decorative accents often can be refinished with a marine type paint rather than an exterior latex, alkyd or oil. Many boats today are formed with fiberglass, so the same finish used on the hulls may be used on the panels in your backyard. Your best bet is to buy a small amount of the finish first and try it on part of a panel that won't show. If compatible with the fiberglass (which it probably will be), you can proceed with the project.

Painting plastic other than fiberglass is not recommended. There are so many different plastic formulas that you would have to have the plastic chemically analyzed to determine what finish it may take. The plastic, of course, can be coated with a latex or acrylic, but the result probably will be streaky and short-lived regardless of the care you use in applying the material.

Screen Paint

The best screen paint is trim paint that has been thinned about 25 percent with turpentine or mineral spirits. However, you can buy regular screen enamel, which is essentially the same thinned oil or alkyd trim paint.

CHAPTER 5

Special Finishes for Special Surfaces

■ IDEALLY, CHOOSING A FINISH for an exterior surface is little more than making a selection between latex, alkyd or oil. Realistically, there are other types of surfaces that take special finishes and special know-how to handle. You probably will find most of these finishes in a store, but the finishes may be on a corner shelf or out of view. Specify exactly what you want.

Finish for Wood Roofs

Use a water-repellent preservative; do not paint the wood roof. A paint finish will hold the moisture in the roof and cause the roof to rot. Also, the moisture will peel and/or blister the paint shortly after the finish has been applied.

If you want to change the color of the roof, use a semitransparent or solid exterior wood stain. Apply the stain directly to the roof with a brush and roller combination. A preservative or water-repellent undercoater is not needed.

Finish for Metal Roofs

Follow the procedures for any exterior metal finishing, as noted above and below. The iron, steel, galvanized steel, or copper roof should have a quality metal primer applied after the surface has been thoroughly cleaned and prepared. When the primer is dry you can topcoat the surface with a softer finish such as alkyd or latex exterior finish paint. Two topcoats will outlast one topcoat.

Terne metal roofs are primed with a special iron-oxide primer. You can use any topcoat over the primer such as alkyd and/or latex.

Finish for Asphalt Roofs

These roofs include asphalt shingles, roll roofing and built-up roofing. Generally, a latex exterior house paint may be used. Do not use a solvent-thinned paint. The solvents in the finish may dissolve the asphalt in the roofing, causing bleed-through of color.

You can use asphalt bituminous roof coating, such as colored aluminum roof coating. There is a limited range of colors from which to choose. If you use latex finish, read the label on the bucket. The finish has to be flexible enough to expand and contract with the shingles. Otherwise, the finish will cause the shingles to curl. It usually takes at least two coats and often three coats to properly cover asphalt shingles.

Mildew Problems

Mildew is a dark fungus that can form on almost any surface of a house. It generally appears in spots, and if you look closely it does indeed look like a fungus growth. Mildew thrives in dampness and warmth.

To remove the mildew before painting, scrub the surfaces with a mixture of one quart household bleach, one-third cup of laundry detergent (powdered), two-thirds cup of cleaner containing trisodium phosphate, and three quarts of warm water. Use plenty of elbow action when applying the mildew solution and don't skimp. When the mildew has been removed, rinse the area thoroughly with clean water. The jet stream from a garden hose does a good job.

The surface should be painted just as soon as it dries. Use a paint with a mildew additive already mixed into the formula. In some sections of the country (especially the South) paint departments may add more mildewcide to the mixture. Check the paint retailer on this before you make a purchase.

Soot Problems

If you live in a highly industrialized area, the chances are good that the exterior of your house is covered with airborne chemicals and soot.

Before you apply a new finish, you should give your house a bath, as detailed below. Use a cleaner with trisodium phosphate. Rinse the surface thoroughly with a jet from a garden hose.

Salt Problems

If you live on the seacoast or about 25 miles from it, the airborne salt particles can cause metal surfaces to rust fast and finished wood surfaces to deteriorate. You can't hold back the ocean, but you can help the paint situation.

First, scrub all surfaces to be finished with clear hot water. Use plenty of water and plenty of elbow grease to remove the salt crystals. Then with a garden hose, thoroughly rinse the surface and let it dry. You may have to wirebrush metal surfaces to remove the corrosion.

When the surfaces are clean, immediately apply a primer. If the topcoat will be water-thinned finish, use a water-thinned primer; if solvent-thinned, use a solvent-thinned primer. Use a metal primer on metal surfaces.

6

Planning for Paint When You Build

■ IF YOU ARE BUILDING a new house or adding a room to your existing home, there is much you can do (or the contractor can do) to help eliminate future paint problems.

Walls and ceilings should be insulated with a vapor barrier where specified (outside walls and ceiling joists or roof rafters). Insulation is "R-Valued" or rated as to heat resistance. The R factor of insulation (with an aluminum foil or draft paper moisture vapor) is charted for various sections of the country. Almost any retailer that sells insulation will give you the recommendations for the insulation needed in your area.

Crawl spaces should be covered with 4-mil-thick polyethylene (plastic) film or 55-pound asphalt-impregnated building felt or roll roofing that weighs at least 55 pounds per 100 square feet. The plastic should be lapped at joints about six inches; the building felt or roll roofing should be lapped about three inches. At vertical surfaces, plastic, felt and roofing should be turned up about six inches. Use asphalt roofing cement to stick the plastic and roofing. Or use staples or roofing nails to hold the material in place.

Basement floor. If the floor will be a concrete slab placed on the bare ground, use a vapor barrier (usually polyethylene) made for this purpose. Home-center stores may sell the vapor barrier; if not, try a hard-material's dealer such as ready-mix concrete company.

Paint is protected in new construction by planning the construction with the proper moisture vapor barriers, flashing, building paper, etc. These components help control water and moisture.

PROJECTED EAVES FLASHING

SET OUT GUTTER

INSULATION VAPOR BARRIER

SCREENED SOFFET VENT

BUILDING PAPER

INSULATION

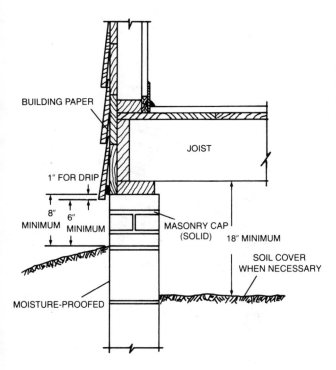

BUILDING PAPER

JOIST

1" FOR DRIP

8"
MINIMUM

6"
MINIMUM

MASONRY CAP
(SOLID)

18" MINIMUM

SOIL COVER
WHEN NECESSARY

MOISTURE-PROOFED

Siding and floor joists are protected from moisture that causes paint problems through construction techniques. The components are placed away from the moisture sources.

Foundation walls. You'll be money ahead if block foundation walls are damp-proofed at the time they are constructed. There are two methods: mortar parging, and applying an asphalt coating to the outside surface (below grade) of the wall. We also recommend that a tile drainage system be installed at the footing of the wall at the time of construction. The tile will funnel away ground water from the foundation and floor. It's very costly to go back and dig around the foundation for the tile installation after the wall is up and backfilled.

Ventilation. Moisture is the main cause of paint failure. Ventilation is the main problem-solver. For example, some wag has figured out that approximately 30 gallons of moisture vapor goes out through the walls and ceilings of an average three-bedroom house per day. If proper ventilation has not been provided for this moisture vapor, pop goes the paint. The paint is not to blame. The moisture vapor simply goes through the siding or other building material and peels or flakes the paint on the other side.

In attics and under flat roofs, the eaves should be ventilated on a basis of net area of the openings equal to 1/250th of the area of the ceiling below the roof.

For gable roofs, louvers should be installed in the siding near the roof ridge at each gable end of the house. The rule of thumb is the total net area of the openings should be 1/300th of the area of the ceiling below. If a ¾-inch slot is left below the eaves, the ventilating area can be reduced to 1/900th of the ceiling area.

For hip roofs, figure a ¾-inch slot below the eaves and a ventilator near the peak of the roof. The net area of the inset should be 1/900th; the outlet should be 1/1,600th of the area of the ceiling below.

In practical terms, measure the width and the length of the ceiling in the new house or addition. Then multiply the two figures. The total will be the ceiling area. Take this figure to a building-material dealer. He will tell you the number, size and position of the vents you need for the project.

Crawl spaces also need ventilation. Don't seal them tight. The rule is 2 square feet of ventilation for each 100 linear feet of exterior wall, plus ⅓ sq. ft. of space for every 100 sq. ft. of crawl space. Plan the foundation for cross-ventilation, if possible. Mesh used in the ventilators should be ¼ to ½-inch. Leave the ventilators open at all times—even in the cold wintertime.

Framing and finishing tips include these: Keep

Gable, soffit, and crawl space ventilation is essential to reduce moisture vapor levels inside the house so the moisture vapor doesn't go through the walls and peel the paint on the siding. Both vents shown here—gable and rectangular—are stock items at hardware and home center stores. The rectangular vents may be used in soffits and crawl spaces.

TRIANGULAR GABLE VENT

joists and other framing lumber at least 18 inches from the ground in crawl spaces and unexcavated areas. Wood sills that are supported by concrete and masonry walls should be eight inches above ground. Keep siding and trim six inches from the ground, along with wood stairsteps.

Porches, decks and other structures with supporting beams and other framing members should be kept 12 to 18 inches above grade. Keep flower boxes, shutters, and other attached components about one inch from siding to promote proper drainage.

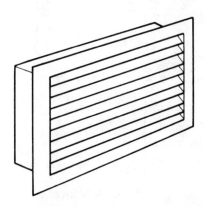

RECTANGULAR SOFFIT/CRAWL SPACE VENT

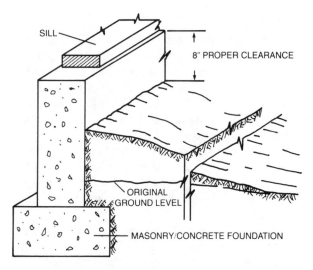

By simply sloping the original grade away from the foundation, you can stop moisture from peeling the paint on a siding of a house.

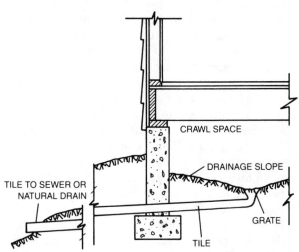

Crawl spaces should be sloped for drainage, and if ground water is a real problem, the space should be tiled to drain water away from the house.

CHAPTER 7

Solving Special Paint Problems

■ A QUALITY EXTERIOR paint properly applied to a properly prepared surface seldom—if ever—fails. The paint, of course, has to be compatible with the surface. If paint problems develop, the cause almost surely is moisture. The moisture can take two forms: moisture vapor escaping from the house through the siding and trim. Or water (rain and melting snow) creeping in back of siding and trim and releasing itself through the siding and trim. Moisture-vapor problems stem from the lack of proper ventilation. Water problems usually can be traced to poor or inadequate rain-carrying systems (gutters and downspouts) and improper sealants (calking compound, fillers, etc.).

Peeling paint. Chances are you will find this condition on the exterior walls of your house for the kitchen, bathrooms, and laundry area. These rooms produce the most moisture vapor, and the vapor, unless vented with an exhaust fan or open window, will penetrate the gypsum wallboard or plaster, insulation, sheathing and siding. Pop goes the paint.

Two other moisture conditions can cause peeling paint: siding or trim exposed for long periods to wetness such as rain or snow; a finish coat (topcoat) of paint applied over a wet surface—especially a solvent-thinned paint.

The solutions are to properly ventilate the areas producing the moisture; install siding vents in the siding; calk open joints in the siding and trim; repair and/or replace rain-carrying systems so open water is routed away from the siding and trim.

Alligatoring paint. Next to moisture, this is the biggest paint problem. It is caused, almost always, by: applying the top coat of paint over a still-wet primer; thinning the paint with too much oil; not stirring the paint so the oil and pigment are properly mixed.

The solution is to remove all finish to the bare wood or surface. Prime the surface, letting the primer dry thoroughly. When you topcoat the primer, make sure the finish paint is *thoroughly* mixed with no vehicle floating on top of the pigment.

Checking paint. You often have to look closely at the siding to discover this condition. You're most likely to find it at the ends of the siding and where the siding joins at corners. The checks will be small—just hairline cracks in the paint film.

Terms Used by the Professionals

ABRASION RESISTANCE. The resistance of paint film to withstand washing, scrubbing, foot traffic.

ACRYLIC. A synthetic resin often used as a latex.

ADHESION. The ''sticking'' quality of paint. Chemicals in the mixture make the paint adhere to the surface.

ALCOHOL. The denatured (ethyl) type is used to thin or ''cut'' shellac.

ALKYD. A synthetic solid or semi-solid substance that is used in the formulation of paints, varnishes and lacquers.

ALLIGATORING. Dried paint that has cracked to resemble the hide of an alligator. The cause is usually due to a hard finish over a soft primer. Or the top-coat of paint has been applied too heavily over the surface so proper drying has been prevented. Alligatoring also can be caused when paint dries in a poorly ventilated area or when applied over wet or unseasoned wood.

ALUMINUM PAINT. Aluminum flakes (usually) mixed with a vehicle such as varnish. Excellent as a primer over creosote; may be used on metal as a primer and topcoat.

BINDER. A paint component that binds the pigments together.

BLEED. The migration of a paint, stain, dye or other finish into the topcoat of another finish. Example: wood pitch and sap seeping or bleeding through to discolor or stain the finish. Big bleeding offenders include wallpaper paste, water stains, sap stains, asphalt, creosote, paint stains, and some paint colors such as reds, blues, greens and yellows.

BLISTERING. A paint failure caused usually by moisture vapor penetrating the paint film from the underside of the film, as through a wall. The condition also can be caused by heat and applying a finish over a damp or wet surface.

BODY. The thickness of the finish. In stores, the term may be ''consistency'' or ''viscosity.'' Example: Latex paint has more body than shellac.

BOXING. Mixing finishes by pouring the finish from one bucket to another.

BREATHER. A paint formula that lets moisture vapor behind the paint film pass through without causing the paint film to peel and blister. Many latex paints (interior and exterior) have this feature.

CALKING. A putty-like material, usually in cardboard cartridges, that is used to fill holes and cracks in various materials such as wood, plaster, masonry. Quality calking retains its flexibility so that it expands and contracts with temperature changes.

CEMENT-BASED PAINT. Basically, the paint formula is Portland cement, lime and pigment. You can buy it in ready-mixed buckets or in powder form. The powder form usually is mixed with water.

CHALKING. A powder residue on paint film caused by weathering. A mild chalking condition is normal and desirable; it has self-cleaning features.

CHECKING OR CRACKING. Tiny breaks in the paint film, sometimes down to the bare wood surface, that usually are caused by moisture. Very hard and brittle paint film also will crack or check.

CHIPPING. Paint that separates from the surface. The problem can be bad paint adhesion or a poor quality paint that dries to a very brittle film.

COLD WATER PAINT. Another name for this material is calcimine or casein. The binder or vehicle is casein or glue. It is water-based.

COVERAGE. The area a specific amount of paint will cover. The coverage figure will be found on the label on the paint or finish container and will be expressed in square feet.

CRAZING. Tiny hairline cracks in paint film. The condition often is caused by unequal contraction of the paint components as the paint dries.

CURE. The time it takes for the paint or finish to become hard enough to be resistant to elements, washing, and so forth.

DRYING. The hardening of paint film. If the label says ''dust free,'' the paint/finish will take the specified time to resist dust particles in the paint/finish. If the label says ''tack-free,'' the paint/finish will take the specified time so you can touch the surface with a finger without the paint/finish adhering to your finger. If the label says ''hard dry,'' the paint film in the specified time will be thoroughly dry.

EGGSHELL. The dull luster of dried paint or other finish. The sheen is neither glossy nor flat. It is similar to that of an eggshell.

ENAMEL. This word takes in a potpourri of paints and finishes. However, the term can be broadly applied to a paint/finish with a varnish vehicle. When dry, an enamel can have a glossy, semi-glossy, or flat surface.

FILM. The thickness of the paint/finish on a surface.

FLAT PAINT. Paint that dries to a non-gloss finish. Both interior and exterior paints are included in this classification. So are stains.

FLEXIBLE. Paint films that expand and contract with temperature changes.

FLOOR AND DECK ENAMEL. Sometimes labeled, ''Porch and Deck Enamel.'' This paint is specially formulated to withstand the elements and foot traffic usually experienced on horizontal exterior surfaces.

FLOW. This actually means ''leveling,'' i.e., the rate or degree the liquid levels itself on a surface.

GLOSS. The shine or luster of paint when it dries.

GLOSS RETENTION. A paint film that holds the gloss or shine for a long (or specified) period of time. Example: porch and deck enamel; some lacquers; varnish.

HIDING POWER. The ability of paint to cover wood grain and applied colors without show-through. Paint with good hiding power (or ''hide'') completely covers the surface to which it is applied. ''One-coat'' paints often are advertised to have great hiding powers; this, however, depends on the surface being covered and the application of the one-coat paint over the surface.

HOT SPOTS. The chemicals in plaster that ''burn'' through paint film applied over the plaster. The spots often can be controlled with a pigmented sealer.

LAP MARKS. Double-coating a surface will cause lap marks. This occurs when strokes of a brush, roller, or spray gun overlap. The laps may not show on freshly-painted surfaces. With wear (weather, scrubbing, time), the laps may show, especially on exterior surfaces.

LATEX. An industry label that refers to a synthetic rubber formulated for use in water-emulsion paints. ''Water-based'' paint usually is latex.

LEVEL. Paint that forms a smooth film without brush, roller or spray marks.

LOW ODOR. Paints that don't smell. Thinners that have only a faint smell.

MILDEW. A fungus that looks like dirt on a painted surface. You can buy paints to help deter mildew. All mildew on surfaces to be painted must be removed. The cause of mildew is basically moisture.

MINERAL SPIRITS. A thinning solvent usually manufactured from petroleum.

NAP. The length of the material used on roller covers.

ORANGE PEEL. A tiny, rough-looking surface on dried paint that resembles the skin of an orange. The condition almost always is associated with sprayed paint and other finishes such as lacquer. The finish dries too quickly or fails to level properly, creating the orange-peel look.

PEELING. Paint that peels off the surface. Main cause is moisture vapor penetrating the subsurface from behind. Or peeling can be caused by painting over a damp or greasy surface.

PIGMENT. The powdered material in paint that adds color and consistency to paint.

PRE-PRIMED. Building material that has been coated with a finish at the time of manufacture.

PRIMER. The first or sealer coat of paint/finish.

PUTTY. A mixture of whiting and linseed oil or white lead. This product seldom is used today. Glazing compound has replaced putty, although the term ''putty'' often is used in reference to glazing around window mullions. White lead, formerly used in putty, has been outlawed.

REMOVER. A chemical formula that softens paint and varnish film so it may be removed from various surfaces with scrapers or scrubbing (washing).

RESIN. A binder for paints.

RUN. A sag or ''curtain'' in the paint film that usually is caused by too much paint/finish applied to the surface. An uneven flow of paint/finish. Enamels and varnishes tend to run more than other finishes.

SEALER. Paint or almost any finish that is applied to a surface to seal the pores.

SELF-SEALER. A finish (paint usually) that serves as its own sealer as well as topcoat.

SILICONE. A synthetic resin used in water repellent finishes. Such finishes are usually clear.

SKIN. A thin layer of dried paint over fresh paint. Example: dried crust over the paint in a bucket.

SKIPS. Small, hard-to-see areas where no paint has been applied.

SPAR VARNISH. A finish formulated for exterior surfaces only. Spar varnish remains flexible after it dries.

SPOT PRIME. To apply primer, sealer or paint to small bare surfaces in an otherwise primed or painted area.

STIPPLE. To create a pattern in fresh finish with a stippling brush or stipple roller before the finish is dry. Similar to texture painting.

SOLVENT. A liquid in which paint/finish can be dissolved. Example: water dissolves water-based paint; turpentine or mineral spirits dissolves oil-based paint; alcohol dissolves shellac.

TACK. The ''stickiness'' of paint/finish.

TEXTURE PAINT. A thick paint with the consistency of whipped cream that can be applied and worked to create a design.

THINNER. A liquid to reduce or regulate the consistency of paint and finishes. Turpentine is a type of thinner.

TITANIUM DIOXIDE. A white pigment in paint that increases the paint's hiding ability. It also increases the brightness of white paint. In general, the more titanium dioxide the more hiding power of the paint.

TURPENTINE. A paint thinner made from pine-tree resins.

VARNISH. A sealing liquid that may or may not contain a pigment. Many porch and deck enamels are varnish based.

VARNISH STAIN. A stain added to varnish.

VEHICLE. The liquid component of paint, enamel and lacquer.

VISCOSITY. The thickness of a liquid product. Motor oil for your car, for example, has viscosity: No. 10 is lighter in viscosity than No. 40. Paints also have viscosity ratings.

WATER REPELLENT. A finish that sheds water, but is not necessarily impervious to water.

WET EDGE. Paint film that stays wet on the surface long enough that more paint may be brushed, rolled or sprayed into it without tearing the film.

Peeling paint is the Number 1 paint problem, but the paint is rarely to blame. Moisture causes paint peeling. This piece of garage door trim, left uncalked along its edges, harbored water in back of the wood. The moisture then soaked through the wood and popped the paint off the trim surface. A new coat of paint will not stick to the surface for any length of time until the moisture source is eliminated. This is true of any wooden house component: siding, trim, fascia, windows, doors.

the bare wood, let the primer dry, and apply the topcoat.

Chalking paint. You rub your fingers across the surface of siding or trim and the paint comes off on your skin like chalk from a blackboard. This is a *normal* condition. Some finishes are formulated to chalk. When it rains, or you wash your house with a hose, the chalking is removed to reveal a clean surface. Chalking can be a problem if the surface above a masonry surface is finished with a chalking paint. The rain washes the chalk dust down on the masonry and streaks it.

The solution on mildly chalking surfaces is to wash the surface with the jet from a garden hose and a scrub brush. Rinse thoroughly, let the surface dry, and then apply a new topcoat.

If the surface is chalking badly, mix a quart of household bleach with a tablespoon of regular household detergent in a two-gallon bucket. Then fill the bucket with warm water. Scrub the

This condition is usually caused by the normal expansion and contraction of materials over a period of time.

The solution is to scrape and wire brush the surface until it's down to bare wood. Prime the bare wood, let the primer dry, and then topcoat the surface. This is a condition where latex paints work wonders. The latex film flexes with the expansion and contraction of the materials. Consider latex if checking is a problem.

Blistering paint. This can be a moisture-vapor problem. However, the problem most likely is a topcoat of paint that has been applied over a wet surface or a wet primer.

The solution is to remove the old paint, prime

Alligatoring paint ranks high on the list of paint problems. Alligatoring can be caused by moisture behind the paint, but most likely the problem will be a finish coat of paint applied over a wet primer. Or, there is too much oil in the paint, either caused by not properly stirring the paint or by adding too much thinner to it.

chalking surfaces with the mixture, and then rinse the surface with water from a garden hose.

Alkyd flat finish, as mentioned above, is a good paint for chalking surfaces.

Bleeding paint. The cause is sap and pitch penetrating from the wood and bleeding through the finish paint. Or bleeding can be caused by crayon marks, grease, rust and even a strong color paint (red, for example) under the topcoat.

The solution is to clean the area with a scraper or wire brush. Then apply a sealer to the knots oozing pitch and sap, and to any color bleeding. The grease, crayon, rust, etc., will come off in the cleaning process. There are various sealers and primers available, as detailed above.

Stained paint. This is an awful problem because it generally is caused by rusting nails. You can, of course, pull out the rusting nails and replace them with hot-dipped galvanized nails, or aluminum nails, which should have been used in the first place. Staining also can be caused by rusting gutters and downspouts (repair and paint or replace them) and metal trim pieces on eaves and siding.

The solution is to cover each rusting nailhead with a metal primer. To speed this job, you can use metal primer in an aerosol can and spot spray individual nailheads. Or you can use a sealing, pigmented shellac. We recommend that you then prime the surfaces, after they have been cleaned, and apply the finish coat over the primer. The idea is to seal both the nailhead and the stain.

Other metal-causing stains should be cleaned and primed with metal paint. Then the surface should be topcoated with a finish paint.

Rotting wood. The cause is moisture. You may not even see the rot under the paint. You can probe for it, however, with the blade of a pocket knife. If the blade slides into the wood with very little or no effort, you can bet the wood is rotten.

The solution, simply, is to find out where the water is coming from and stop it. Generally, the problem of rot will be found at the eaves of the house around the overhang, fascia board, and soffit boards. The cause is poor gutter drainage. Or the roof may be leaking at the eaves. As you investigate, you probably will find the roof sheathing rotted at the eaves. This wood must be replaced entirely. Fascia boards are easy to replace; soffits are fairly easy to replace; roof sheathing is difficult to replace.

Another trouble area is around wooden porch columns at the cap and base. If you detect rot in these areas, the columns should be replaced before the roof caves in. Poor drainage almost always is the source of the problem. Check the roof, gutters and downspouts for damage. Since a lot of weight is involved in changing the columns (weight from the roof), we recommend that you consult a pro before you start replacement work.

8

How to
Apply Paint

■ GETTING THE PAINT from the bucket to the siding and trim is the easiest part of painting. The tools for the job include brushes, rollers, polybrushes, shake painters, pad painters and spray guns. A combination of two tools generally works best. Below is a selection.

Bristle brushes. There are two types: natural bristle (often hoghair) and nylon (or another man-made bristle). Natural-bristle brushes are more costly than their man-made cousins. Always match the brush to the job and to the paint that you will be spreading.

Natural-bristle brushes must always be used to apply a solvent-thinned paint. DO NOT USE NATURAL-BRISTLE BRUSHES IN WATER-THINNED PAINT. Water-thinned paint causes pure or natural-bristle brushes to become soggy and mop-like. Use only synthetic-bristle brushes in water-thinned paints. Nylon brushes should not be used in varnish, enamel or shellac. The solvent in these finishes can damage the bristles.

There are six basic types of brushes used for exterior (and interior) painting. You will need at least two types—perhaps three.

Wall brushes range in size from three to six inches wide. The standard buy is a four-inch brush. If you can handle the weight, we recommend a six-inch brush because it will carry more paint from the bucket to the surface of the siding. However, if the siding is narrow, you should match the width of the brush to the width of the siding. If the siding is narrow—about three inches between laps—buy a four-inch brush and cover part of two rows at one time. A three-inch wall brush is really too small for siding jobs unless it's used for a trim or cutting brush.

Sash/trim brushes. The ends of sash brushes can be cut straight across or at an angle. It is really a matter or preference, but an angled sash brush probably is best for painting the mullions in windows. The straight-cut bristle brush makes an excellent flat trim brush. Sash and trim brushes are generally available in 1-½- to 3-inch widths. Our choice would be the 1-½-inch angled brush for windows.

If you have never handled a round trim brush, we recommend it highly for trimming windows. The round shape may sound inefficient, but the bristles break at the right angle so you can get tight at mullion junctions without smearing the

Quality paint brushes should look and "feel" full of bristles. Spread the bristles and check the plug in the ferrule. The smaller the plug, the more bristles; the more bristles, the more paint the brush will hold. Pure or natural bristle brushes have flags on the tips of the bristles—like a split hair. This, in effect, increases the number of bristles.

paint on the glass. The handle is pencil-like so you sort of "draw" the paint on the surface rather than brush it on the surface.

Quality trim brushes have a pencil or kaiser type handle that is small enough to fit comfortably between your thumb and index finger. Avoid square or beavertail handles (used on wall brushes) on trim brushes. They may not be as efficient.

Masonry brushes. Wall brushes may be used for painting masonry, but the rough surface of the masonry (block and brick especially) wear the bristles to the nub very quickly. Regular masonry brushes have coarser bristles in widths up to nine inches. Buy the big size. The larger the brush the more bristles. The more bristles, the more the brush will hold. Since masonry surfaces soak in paint like a blotter soaks in ink, the more finish you get on the surface the faster the paint job. Also, we recommend that you buy the less expensive masonry brushes. Since the surfaces usually are not critical as to brushmarks, fine

bristles are not really necessary. If a fine finish is called for, apply the bulk of the paint with a masonry brush and smooth the paint film with a more expensive wall brush.

Varnish/enamel brushes. These brushes range from 2 to 3 inches in size; the 2-½-incher is recommended for most general work. If there's lots of surface to cover, you can use a 3-inch trim brush in varnish/enamel. The smaller size lets you put the brush into tight quarters, which can be a buying consideration. The best rule is to match the brush to the job.

Artist brushes. You can buy them with lead-pencil-size tips up to one inch wide. They're tops for touch-up work and surfaces that take delicate, pinpoint accuracy. Example: stripes.

Mits. Sheepskin mits are not brushes but they serve as brushes when applying paint to squares and rounds such as the spindles and rails of a

This brush looks full of bristle. But by bending it back the ferrule plug is quickly and easily exposed. Usually, the lack of bristle signifies a poor quality paint brush. Man-made bristles have an "exploded" tip. The ends of the bristles look crushed. This process softens the bristles so the brush produces a smooth surface on its final pass over the finish. Otherwise, the bristles would create a whiskbroom effect across the paint film.

Angled and round sash brushes are designed to paint mullions in window frames. The handles are pencil-like so the brush can be controlled easier. The angled brush can be used for small trim jobs; the round brush can be used to paint spindles in railings and other small round objects.

porch railing. In stores, the mits usually are tagged as "painter's mits" and they look like a big, baseball-glove type mitten. Expect to get just a couple of uses out of the mit; they're extremely difficult to clean after use; dried paint in the fibers causes streaking.

Throwaway brushes. Real cheapies, these brushes are intended for one use only. Actually the cost of cleaning them is more than the cost of the brush. They are ideal for shellac and lacquer touch-ups, two-part epoxy finishes, some varnishes, and shellac where the surface isn't critical and the finish film doesn't have to be perfect.

Plastic foam brushes. Recent newcomers to the paint market are these "polybrushes" made with a foam-like applicator and a plastic handle. They can be used with most finishes except shellac or lacquer. At first glance in the showroom, polybrushes look very inefficient. Just the opposite is true. With them, the finish flows onto surfaces very smoothly, and, if you use enough finish, the result looks almost spray-painted. We put them in the throwaway category, although they may be

cleaned and used more than once. But buy expecting a one-time usage. The price is right.

How to Buy Paint Brushes

Quality almost always determines the price of paint brushes. But, as explained above, you may not always need quality for the job at hand. Paint brushes have three parts: the handle, ferrule, and bristles. The bristles are secured to the handle via the ferrule, which may be metal or a plastic material. The metal ferrule is the better buy since it is easier to keep clean. Also, look at the way the ferrule is fastened to the handle. Rivets, small nails, or screws are the best fasteners. On less expensive brushes, the ferrule is often friction-fitted to the handle. After a few uses, the ferrule and bristles separate from the handle—sometimes to the bottom of the paint can.

In the store, remove the plastic covering from the bristles. Many brush manufacturers package brushes so you can do this. Then firmly strike the ferrule against the palm of your hand. If the brush is a cheapie, the ferrule probably will slip and wiggle considerably, and a lot of the bristles will fall on the floor. In a quality brush, the ferrule will be tight to the handle when you tap it. A few loose bristles may fall out of the ferrule, but this is normal.

With one hand, spread open the bristles of the brush. They split about in the center of the fer-

Most paint brushes and roller covers are labeled by the manufacturer as to size, type of bristle, and type of finish the brush/roller is to spread. Since this is a natural (pure) bristle brush, it may be used in oil- and solvent-thinned finishes such as enamel, varnish, stain, lacquer.

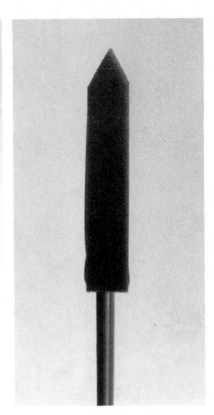

Polyurethane paint brushes don't look like brushes, but they do a topnotch job spreading finish. One side of the chiseled edge is slightly wider than the other. The wide side applies more finish to flat surfaces faster; the narrow side is for small trim jobs. The polybrushes are extremely lightweight and fairly easy to clean. However, you should consider them "throw-away" brushes; initial cost of the brush is less than the solvent to clean it.

rule. In the ferrule you will notice a plug which may be wooden or a rubberlike material. The plug separates the bristles, which are usually glued to the ferrule, and provides support to the bristles. The plug helps keep the bristles from fanning out when you apply pressure to the side of the brush. The important feature is this: the larger the plug, the smaller the amount of bristles. Large plugs will cause the bristles to load with paint. The result will be lots of drips, and paint running down your hand and arm.

Another trick is to hold the handle of the brush in one hand and bend the bristles sharply back with the other hand. Then let go of the bristles. They should spring back to their original shape immediately. The bristles of an inexpensive brush will tend to stay where you bend them and move back slowly.

When you grasp the bristles of a brush in your hand and squeeze them, the brush should feel full of bristle, not compact.

Buying aids provided by manufacturers of brushes are labels on the brush packages. The labels will read (example): "For Latex Paint;" "For Oil Paint;" "Pure Bristle," and so on. If the brush is not so labeled, check the handle of the brush. Often the type of bristle is stamped on the handle.

Pad painters have a fiber-bristle applicator backed by a foam cushion pad that keeps the applicator "level" on irregular and rough surfaces such as shingles and shakes. Other style pads may be used on smooth surfaces. Quality pad painters have a threaded handle for an extension pole so you can reach soffits and other high places without a step or extension ladder. Poles are 5- to 6- ft.

Daily clean-up of brushes and roller covers during a multiple-day job is not necessary. Wrap the brush or roller cover in aluminum foil and stick the package into the freezer compartment of a refrigerator. Thaw-out the equipment before next use—about 30 minutes. The solvents left in the brush/roller will not create an odor or cause any food damage in the freezer. You can leave the tools in the freezer up to 6 weeks or so. Then, they must be cleaned.

How to Buy Paint Rollers

A 7- or 9-inch roller can apply lots of paint fast to almost any surface and do a professional-looking job. If there is any difference between a roller and brush, it is in control. You probably have more control over a brush than a roller. With speed you lose control. Take your choice.

For all-around use, a 9-inch roller usually is your best buy. Depending on the exposure of exterior siding, a 7-inch roller may be better. If you're painting panels and can handle it, an 18-inch roller is faster than a spray gun.

Rollers have three basic parts: the roller cover, the roller frame over which the cover is slipped, and the handle, which usually is threaded to take an extension pole.

The best frame is a birdcage type—a series of wires spaced around parallel wheels. This frame is easier to clean than a solid type. Also, fast-drying finishes won't stick to a wire frame as tightly as to a solid frame.

Specialty rollers include the offset-donut and the cone roller, both used for trim. Both work so-so; you may prefer a brush for better control. A trim roller is similar to a regular roller except it is about 3 to 5 inches wide. Again, you may prefer a brush.

Completing the hardware is a roller tray. You can buy either plastic or metal trays; both are efficient, although the plastic material may be a bit easier to clean. We recommend a tray with metal mesh in the bottom to give bite to the roller cover so it fills properly with paint. The tray also should have ladder hooks built into one end of it.

Most roller covers, like paint brushes, are labeled by manufacturers as to what paints and surfaces they're suited for. Examples: "For Latex Paint"; "For Smooth Surfaces"; "For Masonry Surfaces"; "For Oil Paint"; "For Walls & Ceilings." If the covers are not labeled, use a short nap roller for smooth surfaces; a medium-nap roller for semi-rough surfaces; a long-nap roller for rough surfaces. The covers are manufactured from mohair, Dynel, polyurethane foam, lamb's wool and acetate. These materials are bonded to a roller sleeve and it's important that you buy a sleeve that will be resistant to the water or solvent in the paint. Usually the cover is matched to the type paint, as detailed below. Even so, you usually can, by inspection, determine whether or not the roller sleeve is treated, or is just plain cardboard.

Lamb's-wool covers should be used only with oil- or solvent-thinned finishes.

Mohair covers are intended for high-gloss enamel and varnish finishes. Note the nap; it will be extremely fine.

Dynel covers are best suited for water-thinned finishes.

Acetate and polyurethane foam covers can be used with all finishes—water- or solvent-thinned.

Stippling covers produce a special design on the surface as you roll out the paint. The covers look like embossed floor carpeting and leave a definite pattern. Although used mainly for interior painting, stippling covers can be used to apply exterior finishes if you want a design. You must, however, take extreme care with this cover. The finish should be rolled on so the roller doesn't overlap each stroke. With the pattern, created by the roller cover, alignment is important.

Pad painters were once specified only for applying finish to shingles and shakes. The original models consisted of fiber pads on a flat metal

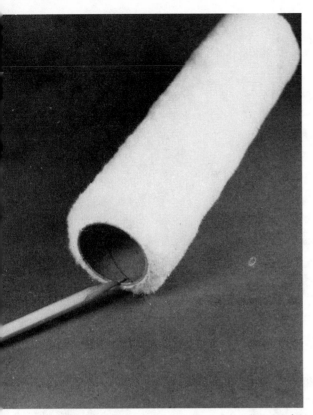

Roller covers—like paint brushes—usually are labeled as to size, type of roller nap, and type of finish the roller is designed to spread. Make sure the base of the roller cover—that part to which the nap is fastened—is treated to withstand both water- and solvent-thinned finishes. If the base is untreated cardboard, it will become soggy and rip. You can tell by looking closely whether or not the base has been treated.

A nonskid grid helps you to load rollers. Hardware cloth is shown, but you can buy a commercial unit.

Use sash flats for window mullions and trim. Other special-purpose pads and daubers will speed the job.

Match the roller to the area to be covered. A small one coats a railing much faster than the standard size.

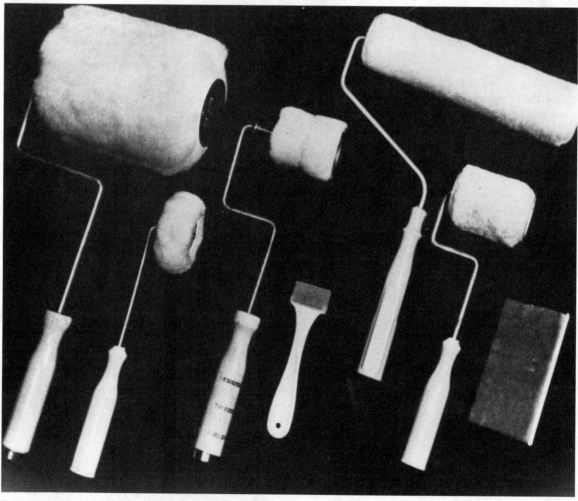

Rollers and painting pads are special-purpose tools. For best results, don't skimp on your equipment.

To clean a roller, hold it by the handle and spin it in a strong blast of water from a garden hose.

To store a roller overnight, just wrap it in foil or a polyethylene bag and put it in the refrigerator.

frame into which a handle was inserted. Today, pad painters are available with covers of fiber, urethane foam, carpeting and a potpourri of other materials. And, they're specified for all types of surfaces, not just shingles and shakes. Pad painters work best on screening, since the frame can be held flat against the material so it doesn't clog the holes in the fine mesh.

Also available on the applicator scene is a display shelf full of pad-type trim painters, special texture pads, and special finish pads.

How to Buy Spray Painters

Great improvements have been made in the past few years in spray-painting equipment for the consumer. Prices are reasonable and the mechanics are easy to understand, making clean-up easier, faster and better. With attachments (on some models) the equipment can be used to calk, nail, sand, chisel, sandblast, staple, glue, etch and inflate—as well as spray paint.

There are advantages to spraying paint: The job goes quickly and you save time; the paint film is more uniform; there are no lap marks. However, with modern paints, lap marks are really not a major problem with brushes and roller equipment.

And there are some disadvantages to spraying paint. The surfaces being sprayed have to be in excellent condition; handling the spray equipment takes practice before you can master it fully; overspray from the gun can be whipped by winds onto surfaces you don't want painted, such as the neighbor's brand-new $20,000 car. Clean-up has to be exact. You can't leave any paint residue—even if it is highly diluted—in the working parts of the equipment. If you do, the residue can clog the parts and the equipment won't work.

Paint preparation also can be a disadvantage if the paint is to be sprayed. Often the paint has to be specially thinned for spraying. Very often the paint has to be strained through a mesh cloth or screening in order to remove chunks of pigment and dried paint from the mixture.

If at all possible, we recommend that you test a sprayer in a store before you buy it. Many stores have demonstration areas for testing. And, sometimes, stores hold clinics on spray painting. The lower priced sprayers—those you see advertised highly—are "airless." This equipment "flips" the paint onto surfaces. Other type sprayers include a pressure-fed, external mixing system for rubber and latex thinned finishes, and internal-mixing spray guns, some of which are the airless types. An air compressor is needed with some sprayers, and this equipment can be costly.

Aerosol spray cans. The spray pressure, of course, is contained in the can. There is a wide range of finishes available. Use spray cans for small paint jobs such as touch-ups and to cover rusting nailheads, Never try to use a spray can to cover a large surface.

CHAPTER 9

The Surface Comes First

■ NO PAINT OR FINISH, regardless of quality or formula, will provide durability and service if the surface to which the finish is applied is not sound and properly prepared. Surface preparation is indeed about 90 percent of any paint job.

There are dozens of tools and techniques to help you prepare the surface. Most of the tools are legitimate; some are gimmicks. But even with the proper tools, you can expect to spend many hours scraping and sanding if the surfaces to be painted are in bad condition. Below we've outlined the super cleaning tools and how they work. Most hardware and home-center stores stock them; some of them can be rented from rent-all outlets.

Give your house a bath before you use any surface preparation tools. The bath will remove dust, dirt, mud and other debris from the surface, and give you an estimate, as you wash, of the condition of the surface. You'll see peeling, checking, rot, staining, and so forth as you go. If your house is in good condition, a washing still will clean the surfaces to accept the paint. You win either way.

For the bathing job, you will need a garden hose; a nozzle that can be adjusted to a jet stream of water; a carwash brush on a long metal handle; a two-gallon galvanized bucket; a GI scrubbrush; and a supply of trisodium phosphate.

Work from the bottom of the siding to the top of the siding—NOT from top to bottom. This way the dirty water runs over a clean surface with very little streaking. If you work from the top down, the water streaks the dirty surface below and you may not be able to wash away the streaks. Professional washers always work from bottom to top.

First wet the area with the hose. Then wash it with a fairly strong mixture of detergent. Dip the carwash brush in the mixture and apply it to the surface. Don't skimp. Work across the siding in small areas. When one small area is finished, rinse it thoroughly with a jet stream from the garden hose and continue on.

Note as you wash any trouble spots, any signs of deterioration. If the house is in good repair, wait 10 days for the siding to dry completely and then start the painting job.

If you find paint and structure problems, here is a list of tools and methods you may need:

Sandblasting. If severe peeling paint is the

problem, you first should determine what's causing the peeling problem and repair it. Look for unventilated kitchens, bathrooms, laundry rooms; check gutters and downspouts for proper pitch and repair; calk the molding and trim over windows, doors, and between dissimilar materials (brick and wood, for example), and fill these cracks.

You can remove peeling paint with scrapers, but the easiest and fastest way is by sandblasting the old finish. Professional sandblasting is fairly expensive, but the process is not prohibitive when you consider the labor and equipment involved. Also consider the end result: a surface that's absolutely ready to paint.

You can rent sandblasting equipment in some areas. It is not difficult to use. Some hardware stores and home centers have these tools available; also look for outlets in the Yellow Pages.

Cold scrapers. If the surfaces are not too large, a quality cold scraper specially manufactured for removing paint is the tool to use. Buy a double-cut metal file with the scraper; you'll need the file to sharpen the scraper blades as you work. The pull-type scrapers remove a lot of old paint fast. In fact, a couple of pulls usually peels the paint down to the bare wood. Almost all home-center

One of the fastest and least expensive ways to remove peeling paint and other paint film problems is with a wire brush—here in a portable electric drill. Another good way is with a simple pull scraper with a sharp blade. Hot scrapers, paint and varnish removers, and abrasives also can be used, but they are best suited for small finish removal jobs.

This is a type of wire brush, only with wide bristles that sort of "flap" off damaged paint finish. The brush is teamed with a power drill; it is tops for removing finish on metal as well as wood that is patterned—such as trim boards and moldings.

Flexibility is the key to exterior calking. It must be able to expand and contract with the structure—here the movement of concrete. It takes approximately seven tubes of calking to seal an average 3-bedroom house.

Calking cartridges, if not properly opened, can "explode" under pressure from the calking gun. The right way to open cartridges is to cut the plastic nozzle at a 45-degree angle. The nozzle is tapered so you can cut it at the width you want the calking to be. With a long nail or pick, break the plastic seal between the nozzle and the cartridge, as shown. Some calking is available in bulk and "rope" form. Silicone, butyl, and vinyl-adhesive calking are the best buys for almost all exterior applications.

and hardware stores sell pull scrapers. The price is inexpensive, even for a quality tool with extra blades.

Hot scrapers. In very small areas, a hot scraper can be used to remove paint finish. The scraper contains a heating element (like a toaster) that operates on horsepower. You press the hot plate of the scraper on the paint surface. The heat softens the paint. You then scrape off the softened paint. Hot scrapers as you would guess are slow to operate; therefore, they're not for large surfaces. At the time this was written the cost of a quality hot scraper was about $25–$30 at hardware stores and home centers.

Do not use a propane torch! Although the torch will do a great job of softening the paint so you can scrape it off, the flames may ignite insulation and structural materials behind the siding. In fact, you may not even know these materials are on fire because the siding hides them from view.

Wire brushes. Often overlooked for cleaning away peeling paint are hand and power-driven wire brushes. They make excellent cleaning tools. On small areas a couple of swipes with a hand brush cleans the surface to the bare wood. You can even save yourself lots of muscle power by using a rotary wire brush in a portable electric drill. The job goes quickly and the surfaces come clean, ready to paint. Use wire brushes on wood, masonry and metal. The cost is nominal for any type brush. They are also available at hardware stores and home centers.

Sanders. Portable electric orbital and/or straight-line sanders are recommended for paint removal, but you'll find it a slow job. To speed the job, a sander and a scraper make good teammates. For small areas, sandpaper stretched over a rubber-type sanding block removes finish and feathers the edges of old paint properly for spot-priming. We do not recommend disc or belt sanders for paint removal. Disc sanders tend to make swirls in wood and masonry surfaces. The paint will not hide the damage. Belt sanders take off lots of finish fast. Often the abrasive is down into the wood or masonry before you know it. These gouges can't be hidden by a coat of paint. Steel wool is excellent for shining rusting surfaces; it is a poor tool to remove the finish, however. Use an abrasive block to remove humps from masonry surfaces. It looks like a brick with a handle attached to one face.

For most sanding jobs, flint paper (open coat) is recommended to remove the old finish. It is inexpensive. Use aluminum oxide abrasive for the final smoothing touches.

Paint and varnish remover. It works in small areas, but the muss and fuss aren't really worth it. Scrapers and wire brushes do the same job better and usually a lot faster.

Materials for filling voids. The best and easiest to apply are calking compounds. Spend enough money and buy the good stuff. The silicones and the butyl rubber compounds (to name two of many) are guaranteed up to 50 years. The oil-based calks usually are not guaranteed. The oil dries out of the compound fast—usually in a couple of years—so you have to clean and recalk.

Fill large holes first with oakum or fiberglass insulation as a base for calk. Then apply the compound over this base. Don't use newspaper or steel wool as a base. Newspaper rots; steel wool rusts and will streak painted surfaces.

A general comparison of calking compounds:

Silicone. Long-lasting—up to 50 years' guarantee on some products. Very expensive. Tops for cracks around outdoor outlets, lighting fixtures, over doors and windows, between dissimilar materials. The calk does not take paint finishes well. Therefore the manufacturers have tinted or colored it in standard outside colors.

Vinyl-adhesive. An excellent interior and exterior calking compound. Made in colors. Highly flexible with an adhesive quality. Will last for years and years; sometimes guaranteed to lifespan.

Butyl. Tops for joints in metal and masonry. Stays flexible for years and is often guaranteed by the manufacturer. Less costly than silicone, but about the same price as vinyl-adhesive. Be sure to read the package label; the calk may be restricted in when it can be used.

Acrylic latex. A good, all-around calk, but it lacks the durability of silicone, vinyl-adhesive and butyl. It is fast-drying and may be used for both indoor and outdoor applications.

Oil-based. It will bond to most surfaces, but the oil dries out of the bulk and the calk falls out of the cracks it was forced into. However, it is very inexpensive if this is a consideration. But plan on early replacement.

Crack and hole fillers. Most of them are not recommended for exterior use. The materials harden. The expansion and contraction of the crack or hole in which the filler was placed causes the filler to break and fall out. Be sure to read the label on the package before you buy.

Mortar. If your house is brick or block, chances are some of the mortar joints are crumbling and will have to be repaired before you apply paint.

You can buy a ready-to-mix mortar formula for this job; it comes in 80-pound bags (sometimes smaller) and you just add water. If you want to mix your own mortar from scratch, use one part mortar to two parts mortar sand. Add water to blend the two into a fairly stiff mixture—about the consistency of whipped cream. The old mortar must be removed from the joint; the joint must be clean and wetted; the new mortar must be pressed firmly into the joint. For this, you will need a mixing bucket, pointing trowel, and a joint strike. Hardware and home-center stores sell all three.

Bonding cement is a form of mortar, and it is used to build-up cracked and broken concrete. The material comes in 10-pound bags. The cost is high. The cement formula contains an epoxy or latex base so the mixture can be feathered out to a very fine edge with a trowel. It's adhesive qualities are excellent.

Interior Painting

10

Interior Paints: Colors and Textures

■ MANY STORES OFFER a thousand and more tones, hues, textures, patterns and surface glosses in interior paints.

The inventory of a well-stocked paint outlet boggles the mind. For example, if you're seeking a little peace and quiet, try the acoustical paint. If you want to paint a blackboard on the kitchen wall, here's the paint to do it. Of if you want to match the color of your sofa, you can do it perfectly. You can buy a finish that will go over plaster, gypsum wallboard, masonry, metal, tile, wood, glass and even some plastics. Almost any finish you can imagine, you can buy.

The first thing you'll notice about interior paints is that they are usually priced lower than their exterior counterparts. This is because the paint formula is slightly different; it doesn't require the weather-resisting chemicals found in exterior paints and finishes. Quality interior paints, however, still carry a fairly heavy price tag because you are buying durability in the formulas, even if it is interior durability. You can expect to get years of service from a quality interior paint: at least 12. Chances are you'll want a new color before the paint wears out.

Like exterior paint, interior paint is basically only as good as the surface to which it is applied. Spread a quality interior paint over grease, dust, dirt or a peeling surface, and the paint film won't stand up. Expect to spend about 90 percent of the paint project preparing the room for paint.

Good Painting Results from Good Planning

Interior paints offer three features: protection, beauty and function. The proper paint protects against moisture damage. Decoration with paints (and finishes) gives you and your family enjoyment. The function of paint (besides protection) can change the size of a room, lessen eye strain, improve interior lighting, and hide defects such as broken and cracked plaster walls.

Protection

The right paint deters moisture, but all paints are not right. For example, it is not recommended that you use latex paint over metal such as iron or steel. Latex paint utilizes water as a vehicle, and water causes rust. Also, oil paint is not the product to use over plaster walls. The plaster contains chemicals that will cause an oil paint to peel. Spar varnish is not recommended for interior surfaces because it isn't hard enough to withstand many household chemicals. Glossy oil paint shouldn't be used to coat wallpaper; a flat alkyd is better.

Choosing the right paint for the right protection or surface isn't as difficult as it may appear. The charts and details of this section are tailored to help you make that decision. But you first must determine what type of surface is to be painted, plan how it is to be painted, and then buy the right products.

Beauty

Painting a room does not necessarily decorate your home. In fact, paint is only a single component of many involved in decorating. A master decorating plan includes not only paint, but furniture, draperies, wallpaper, carpeting and rugs, hardware, pictures and paintings. And the color used for a specific room should tie in with the colors and furnishings of *other* rooms in the house. Planning for decoration is important. Painting is like eating popcorn: once you start, you can't quit. Therefore, before you go paint shopping, think through the color combinations that will balance your home.

Today's paints are advertised as one-coat. You'll also read and hear that you can paint a room and have it ready for dinner guests the same day. Perhaps. But don't plan on it. Leave yourself at least a two-day weekend to paint just a single room. Don't plan to paint the entire house in those two days—even though the ads tout it.

Decorating with color is discussed in Section One on Exterior Paints. With color, you can make a room larger, smaller, lower, higher. Paint can hide an ugly architectural or structural problem; it can deaden sound; it can accent or highlight a special effect.

Paint, for the most part, can be classified into three types of colors which will make the visual alterations that you want. The colors are: Light-to-Dark; Bright; Cool-to-Warm.

Review the color information in the Exterior Paint Section. Then use the information below to help determine color variations.

Light-to-Dark. Black, gray, blue, purple, red and green—in intense form—are considered dark colors. As these colors are lightened into tints, they do indeed become lighter in color, but they are still *intense* colors. Example: A medium shade

of blue is more intense than a medium shade of yellow.

A dark color, therefore, tends to shrink the size of a room, while a light color (bone white) will increase the size of the room. Paint the ceiling of a room a dark, intense color and the walls a light color, and the room will appear to be low. Or paint the entire room a dark, intense color, *then add lots of dramatic lighting* to the room such as track lights at the ceiling and floor lamps, and the room actually will seem larger. You can get the same effect by painting the ceiling and three walls a light color and the fourth wall a dark, intense color.

As a rule of thumb, here is how light-to-dark colors work in an average (12x15-ft.) room:

• All light colors will make the room seem larger and more open.

• Black on a ceiling will lower the ceiling. Black on an open ceiling will hide joists, wires, pipes, bridging, etc., such as in a basement room.

• Paints with highly reflective colors will add space to a room if plenty of light also is added.

Pay attention to batch numbers on paint containers; you want to buy in-sequence numbers so the paint will be the same tone, hue, or color. Batch numbers pertain only to stock paints in store inventory. Custom colors involve a standard tint base liquid.

Custom-mixed colors often are labeled by the store as to color formula. This information is used if you want more paint the same color. When you open the bucket of paint, remove the label and put it in a safe place. Paint drips and splatters down the side of the bucket can cover the label so you don't know the code.

What Colors to Use with Period Furniture

Room decor includes both furniture and paint. Your goal should be to create a striking blend or mixture of both—to create an "era" such as Early American, Victorian, Modern. Here are the traditional colors for various periods:

Modern. Color blends, not contrasts, are used. Example: blue and green. Accents are important, such as bone white walls and ceiling with one or more solid color walls in blue or green. Classic Scandinavian colors are red, blue and yellow.

Early American. Browns, strong reds, muted greens, butternut yellow, pewter.

18th Century. Green, white, brown, Williamsburg blue.

Victorian. Cranberry, ivory, walnut, mahogany, rose.

Formal Contemporary. Formal and related color combinations; strong contrasts of brilliant hues.

Empire. White, gold, black, deep green.

French Provincial. Soft shades of green, blue, rose, and white. Use lots of white.

The vehicle in paint floats to the top of the pigment when the paint sits for a time in the bucket. Example: this yardstick is covered with vehicle from inch marks 5 through 7. Always *thoroughly* stir paint—even if it has just been shaken at the store—so the pigment and vehicle are blended together. Rule of thumb: it takes at least 5 minutes to stir unmixed paint.

Dip brushes in buckets *only* one-third the length of the bristles. Then lightly "slap" out the excess paint in the brush against the inside (and rim) surfaces of the bucket. Dipping the brush deeper only loads the heel of the brush at the ferrule and causes excessive dripping down the handle of the brush, into your hand, and down your forearm.

• A contrasting trim paint will define the perimeter of a room.

• If the floor covering is dark, the walls of a room should be medium to light colors.

• If the floor covering is light, the walls of the room can be medium to dark colors.

• Horizontal lines can lengthen the room; or vertical lines can increase its height.

• Large patterns in wall coverings and draperies tend to make a room look smaller. Small patterns tend to make a room look larger and the walls more distant.

• Moldings—chairrail, crown, cove—painted in a contrasting color can define a room, making the ceiling look lower or higher and the walls seem to be more distant. For example, you can drop a high ceiling by installing crown molding a foot or so below the ceiling line. Then paint the ceiling and walls down to the molding a dark color. The ceiling will appear lower.

Cool-to-Warm. Cool colors are lighter shades of blue and green. Warm colors are various shades of red, yellow and orange. As a rule of thumb, warm colors should be used in north, northwest and northeast rooms, since sunlight doesn't add warmth to these rooms. South, southwest and southeast rooms can handle cool colors and darker colors, since you get plenty of sunlight during daylight hours in these rooms. East and west rooms also are suited to cool colors, such as the blues and greens and pastels.

Bright Colors. These are not "day-glow" finishes, but reds, oranges, yellows and some greens. They can startle your eye. Therefore bright colors are best suited for accents within a room, for use on focal points. The focus can be a fireplace, picture wall, window wall, planter wall, and so on.

Colors have size. The small colors are green, blue and black. The large colors are yellow and red. Therefore, an accent or focal point in a room can be "sized" with bright color.

Bright colors, as with other color—even white—are dominated by light. Example: Paint a room without any windows bone white, with a brilliant red accent wall, and the effect will be lost without light to spark it.

Function

This is the last of the big three reasons for painting and color. Paint may be used for the *function* of creating a moisture vapor barrier between inside and exterior walls. You can use paint for the *function* of hiding defects such as a cracked plaster ceiling or pocked walls.

Cool colors often are used to lessen eye strain. Lighter shades of color are used to increase or improve lighting. A dark, poorly-lighted stairwell, for example, can be made safer with walls painted a light color. Light-reflecting qualities of different paint colors are discussed in the Exterior Painting section.

11

Picking Paints for Interiors

■ WHEN TO PAINT a room really is an arbitrary question. For most rooms the answer is "when I get tired of the color."

As in exterior painting, practical considerations for repainting include show-through of paint and spots under the paint film; brush and roller tracks showing through wear; paint that is fading; paint failure.

Interior paint failure seldom happens, although the paint usually gets the blame. What happens is that the surface to which the paint has been applied fails. Moisture in some form usually is the cause. Until the problem is solved, no paint, regardless of quality, will adhere properly for any length of time. (See Exterior Painting.)

What interior paint should be used on such-and-such a surface? The quick reference chart in this section will help you determine the type. Also, below, is a more detailed listing of paints and finishes for interior surfaces.

Interior paint has three basic components:

1. The pigment. Pigment is a powder that adds color and hiding power to the paint mixture. In addition, the pigment helps give the mixture its consistency (thin-to-thick).

2. The vehicle. The vehicle is the liquid of the paint mixture. It also is called the binder. The vehicle/binder helps disperse the pigment, and helps it adhere to the surface being painted. There are three types:

A. Latex. Latex binders dry by evaporation of the water in the mixture.

B. Two-part systems. The vehicle/binder dries by a chemical action.

C. Oil. Oil dries by oxidation.

3. The thinners. Thinners are what the name implies: thinners thin paint so it may be applied to surfaces easily.

A fourth additive often is used in paint mixtures: drying chemicals. Such chemicals (sometimes called agents) make the paint dry faster. Example: Latex and acrylic paints dry faster than oil paints. Drying agents are partially responsible.

Specific Paints for Specific Surfaces

Gypsum wallboard. Latex primer; latex gloss; latex flat; multi-color; sand; texture; fire-retardant; shellac.

Plaster. Latex primer; latex gloss; latex flat; rubber-base; multi-color; latex sand and texture;

fire-retardant; shellac; some masonry sealers (check labels on bucket).

Concrete. The same as gypsum wallboard and plaster. Also, block fillers can be used along with porch and deck paint, epoxy and urethane. However, check the labels for specifics.

Brick. Glossy latex; alkyd flat; rubber-based; cement; epoxy; porch and deck; multi-color; sand; texture; fire-retardant; polyurethane and epoxy varnish; masonry sealer; block filler. Some of these finishes—polyurethane and epoxy, for example, are specially formulated for brick. Check the labels on the bucket before you buy them.

Glass/ceramic tile. Epoxy; urethane; specially-formulated marine paint; latex sand and texture; epoxy varnish; moisture-treated urethane varnish.

Most metals. Specific metal paint; latex and alkyd paints formulated for metal; epoxy and urethane varnish formulated for metal; acrylic lacquer for steel; oil and alkyd primers; zinc-based and aluminum paints. Some metals (copper, aluminum, for example) take special formulations of standard finishes. The formulations will be so noted on the labels.

Hardboard (Masonite). Glossy and flat oil, latex, and alkyd; epoxy; urethane; porch and deck; marine; latex sand and texture; fire-retardant; alkyd varnish; polyurethane varnish; epoxy varnish; spar varnish, shellac; oil, alkyd, and latex primers; aluminum; wood sealers.

Particleboard (chip and flakeboard). Glossy and flat oil and alkyd; urethane; marine; alkyd and polyurethane varnish; spar varnish; shellac; oil, water, alcohol and varnish stains; bleach; aluminum; wood filler; wood sealer.

Most bare (raw) woods. Glossy and flat oils and alkyds; epoxy; urethane; porch and deck; marine; alkyd, polyurethane, epoxy, and spar varnish; shellac, oil, water, alcohol, latex, varnish stains; aluminum; wood sealer; wood filler.

Quick Guide to Interior Finishes

Name of finish	Basically used on . . .	Application tools
Latex	Walls, ceilings, trim. Almost all surfaces except bare wood. Excellent for interior masonry and plaster.	Brush, roller, polybrush, pad painters, spray.
Acrylic	See latex above. Faster drying than latex. Check label on bucket before buying for specific paint projects.	Same as latex.
Alkyd	All surfaces except unprimed masonry and metal. Solvent-thinned. Do not use on unprimed wallboard.	Brush, roller, polybrush, spray gun.
Rubber-base	Excellent for masonry with a sealer. Makes a good primer for latex, alkyd, oil paints. Don't use high-gloss oil over rubber-base. Check bucket labels.	Brush, roller, squeegee.
Cement	Masonry such as concrete, concrete block, cinder block, brick. May be packaged as a powder which you mix with water. Not a good primer.	Brush
Oil	Most surfaces. Odor; slow drying.	Brush, roller, pad painter, spray.
Epoxy	Kitchen and bathroom walls, trim, glass, tile, metal, masonry. Check bucket labels carefully.	Brush.
Urethane	Bare wood. Over latex, alkyd, oil paint. Check labels on bucket.	Brush.
Texture	Walls and ceilings.	Brush, trowel.
Sand	Walls and ceilings.	Brush, trowel.
Fire-retardant	Walls and ceilings in high-heat areas. In flats only. Check labels on buckets.	Brush, roller.
Multi-color	Most surfaces.	Brush, roller

New Paint Over Old

What type of finish can you apply over a previously painted surface? The question, short of costly chemical analysis of the old paint, really can't be answered. An excellent guess would be latex, oil or alkyd. In general, you can apply most new finishes over old *different* finishes IF the old finish is tightly bonded to the surface and the surface, if glossy, is dulled to accept the new finish.

Contrary to popular belief, alkyd may be applied over oil or latex; latex and alkyd may be applied over each other. Troubles arise if any of the finishes are not bonded to the surface; the surface is not in repair (it is flaking, peeling, crumbling, wet with moisture, greasy, dirty) to receive the new finish; the surface is glossy so the new paint won't stick or adhere properly.

Examples of this include:

Glossy oil and alkyd paint may be applied over flat oil and alkyd paints and primers. Flat latex paint and primers, epoxy paint and varnish, polyurethane paint and varnish; block filler, wood filler, paintable wood sealers, and bleach may be covered with oil, alkyd and latex paints.

Wallpaper may be painted with glossy latex; flat latex and alkyd, and latex and alkyd primers. However, it's usually not a good idea to paint over wallpaper because the vehicle in the paint loosens the wallpaper adhesive, and the paper may peel. Some embossed and flocked papers have distinct patterns that can't be satisfactorily covered with paint. And some vinyl wall coverings can be easily stripped from the wall so you can paint the surface underneath. If you do decide to paint wallpaper, give the surface a coat of oil-based primer and then topcoat the primer.

Types of Interior Finishes

The names of interior paints are similar to the exterior paints. The prime difference between the two is in the chemical formulation. Exterior paints are formulated to withstand the weather; interior paints are not.

Are there some brand-name interior paints that can be recommended over other brand names? We would like to say "yes," but the recommendations today might change tomorrow. Paint formulas are continually changed to meet marketing conditions. A good interior paint you may buy today may be cheapened tomorrow. Or a lower quality paint you buy today may be an improved product tomorrow. You almost always can be assured, however, that a well-known

How to Estimate How Much Interior Paint You Need

To measure the area of a ceiling, multiply the width by the length. Example: the width is 12 ft. and the length is 15 ft. 12×15=180 sq. ft.

Look at the coverage figure on the bucket of paint you plan to buy. It probably will be in the 300 sq. ft. range. Subtract 25 sq. ft. from this coverage figure. Example: 300 sq. ft., minus 25 sq. ft., equals 275 sq. ft. Divide the 180 sq. ft. into the 275 sq. ft. Since the paint you need is less than a gallon, you may be able to get by with 3 quarts of the finish. However, we recommend that you buy the gallon, especially if the paint is to be tinted. Tinting quarts of paint to match is a problem. Also, you probably will need some extra paint for touch-ups later.

Why subtract 25 sq. ft. from the coverage figure on the bucket label? This coverage figure is the manufacturer's estimate and it usually is based on optimum conditions which you may not have. Therefore to be safe and have plenty of paint, subtract 25 sq. ft. from the coverage figure. If you are buying in quarts, for every quart figure add a pint. That is, if you figure one quart of wall paint will do the job, add another pint to the order.

To figure the total area of the walls in a room, measure each wall separately. Example: The width is 20 ft., and the height is 8 ft. 20×8=160 sq. ft. Add together the totals of each wall and divide this total into the coverage figure minus 25 sq. ft. Now from this total, subtract 21 sq. ft. for each door and 15 sq. ft. for each average-sized window. Again, divide the total in the coverage estimate. If the difference is less than 100 sq. ft., buy the full amount. Otherwise, the store will have to mix quarts and pints and this can lead to matching problems.

If the surface you are painting is highly porous you will need at least 25 percent more paint. If the surface is masonry you will need approximately 50 percent more paint. Also in your estimates figure built-ins (cabinets and shelves) if you plan to paint them the same color as the walls.

brand of quality paint is indeed quality. The difference in price reflects the quality of the product, assuming that the *retailer* is reputable.

Latex Primers

These water-based products are odor-free (almost), dry quickly, and tools and equipment are easy to clean in the kitchen sink. Latex primers may be used over plaster, gypsum wallboard, and masonry products such as concrete, cinder block and stucco (some interior walls are stuccoed).

The main purpose of a primer is to seal the surface to be painted and to create a bond between the surface and the top coat of paint.

Therefore, the primer is a must on nonsealed and non-painted surfaces.

Latex primer-sealers (combination) are recommended for use in kitchens and bathrooms where moisture may be a problem. Both these primers may be topcoated with latex finish paint or oil-based paints.

Since the primers go on new surfaces, little preparation is needed. However, the surface must be clean and dry. The primer dries to the touch in about 30 minutes, and it may be topcoated in three to four hours. Coverage depends on the surface that's being painted. You can expect about 300–350 sq. ft. to the gallon. Check the bucket label and follow the estimating formula in this section.

Acrylic Primers

These primers are the same as latex primers. About the only difference between the two is that acrylic primers dry a bit faster.

Alkyd Primers

Alkyd is a solvent-thinned finish, and therefore is the best choice for priming bare wood. Use it also for masonry surfaces. Alkyd is not the product to use over gypsum wallboard. The solvents tend to raise the grain of the paper covering on the gypsum core.

Alkyd primers often are termed undercoaters and are used on trim such as casings and baseboards. The primers (and topcoats) are easy to spread to seal the wood properly. If the trim you are painting is chipped or has peeling or blistered paint, we recommend that you clean the surface and undercoat it—even if it has been sealed. The undercoater will provide an excellent base for any type of topcoat.

Alkyd primers take 8 to 12 hours to dry properly for topcoating. Clean-up is with turpentine, mineral spirits or paint thinner. Expect to get from 300 to 350 sq. ft., of coverage from one gallon, but this depends on the material being primed. A brush is the best application tool; you can use a roller on large surfaces.

Metal Primers

You can buy a potpourri of these coatings for iron, steel and aluminum.

For steel, which is the most common interior metal, an alkyd or oil-type primer with a zinc formulation is recommended. Use the same primer for aluminum—or an epoxy or urethane finish, which serves as both primer and finish coat. You can apply a different top coat over epoxy and urethane finish if you want. If you are painting radiators, which are steel, use a flat paint over the primer.

Primer-Sealer

Basically, this material seals wood and masonry so it may be sanded for top coats of finish. It's an excellent primer for paneling because the formula binds wood fibers together; it makes them hard, and therefore easier to sand. The primer-sealers for masonry are either clear liquids or slightly tinted ones (usually blue) and they can be used on placed concrete, concrete block and cinder block. They help deter moisture seepage, but if the surface has a water problem (open-running water), the sealers are not efficient. The water problem has to be corrected by other means (replacement or repair of rain-carrying systems, for example).

Topcoats including latex, alkyds and oils, may be applied directly over sanding-sealers/primers. Cement type paints may be used over the masonry sealers. But, before you buy the sealer and the finish material, be sure to check the labels. Some formulas may not be compatible.

Most of these sealers/primers dry extremely fast; they are both water and solvent thinned.

Block Fillers

See listing in Exterior Painting section.

Wood Stains/Varnish/Shellac/Bleach

See listing in Fast Wood Finishing section.

Latex Paint

Ideal for almost any surface except bare wood, this water-based paint probably is the nation's most popular interior cover-up. It is odor-free (almost); has good hiding power; dries fast; is durable; tools and equipment are easy to clean with just water. And, the product is fairly inexpensive in a wide range of colors, and color tones and hues.

Almost any other type of paint may be applied over latex, but the latex paint must be bonded tightly to the surface and be in good repair.

Interior latex paints usually come as a "sys- tem," i.e., the trim paints for woodwork are matched to the wall and ceiling finishes.

Drying time for latex is about 30–45 minutes. It may be topcoated in 3 to 4 hours. One gallon of latex will cover from 300 to 350 sq. ft., of sur- face—depending on the surface. Porous surfaces will take more paint than sealed surfaces.

The buckets of most quality latex finishes are batch-numbered. If you're buying stock colors be sure that the batch numbers are the same. The numbers are on the lid or bottom of the contain- ers. Uniform batch numbers mean that the color will be consistent throughout.

Acrylic Paint

This finish is very similar to latex. It is water- thinned and may be applied over the same sur- faces as latex paint. The big difference between the two paints is drying time: acrylic finishes tend to dry a bit faster than latex finishes, if this is a consideration.

The color range for acrylics is also about the same as for latex, and you can expect to get the same coverage with it. See the Exterior Painting section for more details about both paints.

Oil-based Paint

Once the bellwether of paint finishes, oil-based paint has dropped from favor with the latexes, acrylics and alkyd paints taking over. The main reason for this is the odor of oil-based paint, which is solvent-thinned, and the difficult clean- up procedures which must be made with the same solvents used to thin the product. Because of the strong odor, keep the room well ventilated. This can be a problem during the cooler months of the year.

Slow drying time (up to 48 hours) may be an- other factor to consider. However, even with its disadvantages, oil paint, dollar-for-dollar, is a good buy. It is durable, scrubs well and holds its gloss. It would be a likely choice for woodwork and trim pieces within a room.

Alkyd Paint

Alkyd paint is a solvent-thinned product. Syn- thetic resins are used in its formulation. Alkyd is ideal for wood surfaces—especially those that haven't been sealed or painted—and the material may be used on almost any painted surface. However, do not use alkyds on unsealed plaster or masonry components or bare gypsum wall- board.

Finishing Interior Shutters

The best way to paint interior louvered window shutters (and louvered doors) is with a spray outfit or a spray aerosol container. The best paint product is an enamel—semi-gloss or flat. The second best way to paint shutters is with a trim brush. Rollers are not flexible enough for the job.

If the wood has not been sealed, a prime coat should be applied first. The primer will raise the grain of the wood and the surface will be rough. When the primer is dry, sand with medium/fine grit abrasive. Just touch the wood with the abrasive; don't dig into the wood. Then give the surface the topcoat.

Paint all louvers first. Then paint the frames. Be sure to seal all edges to deter moisture and warp.

If the shutters are to be stained, use a trim brush to apply the stain. The first coat on new wood should be a sealer. After the sealer is dry, lightly sand the wood and apply the stain.

For brushing paint or stain, the procedure is:

1. Elevate the shutter on wood blocks or a cou- ple of bricks. Short lengths of 2x4 make excellent blocks—one piece at each end of the unit.

2. Prop open the louvers with a short stick.

3. Paint/stain the louver adjusting rod first.

4. Paint each louver working from adjusting rod toward the ends.

5. Turn over the shutter and follow the same painting procedure.

6. Paint the frames and edges last.

Joint-Tape Separations

Sheets of gypsum wallboard (drywall) are taped at the joints with a wide thin strip of paper called joint tape. The tape is embedded in joint cement; this builds up the joints so they are level with the surrounding surface.

As the house settles, the joint tape sometimes separates from the joint and the wall. The problem usually is most frequent along the wall/ceiling junction particularly at corners.

To repair this joint-tape separation before painting:

1. Very carefully cut away the joint tape, using a sharp utility knife. Leave sharp, clean edges.

2. With a wide scraper or six-inch joint knife (trowel), fill the void between the ceiling and wall with non-shrink spackling compound. Smooth out the compound.

3. When the spackling compound is dry, lightly sand the patch with medium/fine abrasive on a sandpaper block.

If the damage goes three feet or more along the ceiling-wall junction, carefully cut and remove all the joint tape along this section. Then fill the void with non-shrink spackling compound and embed new tape in the void and the spackling. Add a top coat of spackling over the joint tape and smooth the tape and the spackling. Use a joint tape knife for this. When the spackling dries, sand it as described above and prime and paint the wall and ceiling.

Alkyd finishes are extremely durable, although there is a slight odor connected with the solvents. The rooms in which the products are used should be ventilated; the solvents in the finish are flammable and toxic. Be careful.

Although not as fast drying as latex and acrylic finishes, alkyds set well in about five to six hours. Other types of paint may be applied over dried alkyd base coats (primer or finish), but be sure to check the labels on the buckets for specifics. You can expect from 350 to 400 sq. ft. of coverage per gallon (depending on surface) and a quart of product is generally enough to trim an average room. Alkyd paints may be applied with either a brush or roller; use a brush for smaller surfaces.

Rubber-based Paint

See listing in the Exterior Painting Section.

High-gloss Enamels

These finishes are available in pints, quarts, gallons, and in aerosol spray containers. The enamels are formulated (usually) with alkyd oils, and dry to an extremely hard and tough glossy finish. Drying time for high gloss enamels runs from four to eight hours; they may be recoated in 12 to 18 hours. You can brush, roll or spray them on almost any surface; coverage is about 475 sq. ft. per gallon depending on the surface. If you want to apply high-gloss enamel over metal, be sure to prime the metal with a suitable primer.

Epoxy Paint

You can apply epoxy to both walls and wood trim. It is an excellent choice for kitchens, laundry areas and bathrooms where moisture may be a problem. It also may be applied to bare wood, ceramic, tile, glass, fiberglass and concrete floors. Topcoats of oil and alkyd type paints may be applied over epoxy finishes. Although very expensive, epoxy finishes are very durable.

Urethane Paint

Similar to epoxy, urethane finishes may be applied to bare wood, over latex, alkyd, oil and acrylic paint finishes. If the finish is glossy, however, it must be dulled with abrasive before the urethane (or epoxy) is applied.

Special solvents are necessary with both urethane and epoxy finishes; clean-up of equipment requires the special solvents, which are fairly expensive. Be sure to follow the directions on both epoxy and urethane paint labels. There are some restrictions.

Texture Paints

Texture finishes include sand types and heavy-bodied types—both of which are excellent for hiding cracks and blemishes in walls, ceilings and even woodwork and trim.

Sand textures usually are latex paints with a fine sand added to the mixture. The finish produces lots of texture, but with a more-or-less flat appearance. Texture paint, on the other hand, doesn't include sand in its formulation. The paint is extremely heavy and is applied with a brush. Sand textures are applied with a brush or, often, with a flat trowel. Designs in the texture can be made with a brush, trowel, float, comb, stippling roller, and even wads of newspaper pressed into the fresh finish.

Both sand and texture paints come in stock colors; the colors are somewhat limited. Coverage is limited when compared to regular finishes, and the textures shouldn't be thinned.

Multi-colored Paint

Like texture paints, multi-colored paints are formulated to cover cracks, seams and breaks in walls and ceilings. You can use them on primed gypsum wallboard, plaster, masonry and wood to produce a spotty or flecked appearance. If you want to paint over a multi-colored paint, you can use latex, acrylic, alkyd and oil-based finishes. You need at least two coats—maybe three—in order to hide the old paint.

Heat-resistant Paint

This finish—also called fire-retardant paint—is formulated for surfaces that are subjected to heat, i.e., radiators, heat registers, fire-place screens, range hoods. Colors are somewhat limited. In general, heat-resistant paint can be used anywhere latex finishes can be used. However, there are some restrictions, so check the labels before you buy a specific product. One, for example is that heat-resistant paints usually can't be top-coated with another finish.

Colored or Tinted Primers

If you are going to overcoat a bright color (red, green, dark blue, black), it is recommended that you prime the surface to be painted first. The primer can be white, or it can be lightly tinted the same color as the finish coat. We recommend the tint.

Changing Paint Color

Suppose you buy a base paint tinted a special color. You take the paint home and apply it. You don't like the color.

If you want a darker shade of the same color, the retailer can simply add more pigment to the

Quick Guide to Interior Primers

Primer type*	Best suited for . . .	Special application tips
Latex	Walls, ceilings, trim. May be used on all interior masonry. Not recommended for bare wood.	Do not thin finish paint and use it as a primer. Coat surfaces thoroughly; don't skimp. Be careful not to overbrush or overroll. Sand surfaces with medium/fine abrasive on sanding block between primer and topcoats.
Alkyd	Most surfaces. Tops for bare wood. Not recommended for wallboard. Makes good base for other types of paint.	Primer makes an excellent sealer for bare wood, but don't skimp when brushing or rolling. If wallboard has been sealed, alkyd may be used. Let primer dry for at least 12–15 hours before topcoating. May be used on masonry, but check label on bucket.
Acrylic	Same as latex.	Primer dries faster than latex primer. Apply evenly with brush or roller; don't skimp, but don't overcoat.
Oil	Okay for wood, but latex and alkyd are better primers for walls, ceilings and other non-wood surfaces.	Slow drying; some odor. Apply evenly with brush or roller; don't lap or overcoat. Expect some streaking.
Metal—Alkyd Epoxy Urethane Aluminum	Alkyd type is best for steel if it contains zinc. For aluminum, use oil with a zinc base; alkyd metal primer; epoxy; urethane.	Use flat paints on radiators. Epoxy and urethane are self-primers; apply either directly on surface.
Sealers and primer/sealers (sanding sealers)	Clear sealers best for wood and masonry. Sanding sealers usually are white or opaque; use for sealing knots and sap streaks in wood surfaces.	When dry, stain, alkyd paint, oil, varnish may be applied over sealers. Sanding sealers usually can be thinned with alcohol; check label.
Wood fillers	See section on wood finishes.	
Masonry	Plaster, concrete, concrete blocks, cinder blocks. Material may have a blueish cast so you can see where you've applied it.	Read application label on bucket. Masonry sealers can vary widely as to use, application, coverage.

* See "Quick guide to exterior paints"

Different Names But Still the Same

A rose is still a rose, the saying goes, and the same holds true for different names describing paint gloss:

Actual	Also known as
Gloss	High-gloss
	¾ Gloss
Semi-gloss	Eggshell
	Velvet
	Satin
Flat	Dull
	Matte

paint. But if you want a lighter shade of the same color, more base paint added to the tinted paint probably won't lighten the shade appreciably. In short, *it's fairly easy to darken paint and very difficult to lighten it.*

If you are matching paint to a color chip or a piece of fabric or wood from your home, the match *may* be perfect, but realistically it probably will be just a tad lighter or darker.

Paint almost always dries a shade *darker* than the wet paint.

Once mixed by the retailer, paints usually cannot be returned for cash or credit.

If you are especially fussy about picking just the *right* color, we suggest that you buy several pint cans of different colors and apply them as a test to the surfaces you will paint. This is a better way to make a decision than to use small color chips or have gallon-sized buckets custom mixed.

CHAPTER 12

What to Do When You Have Problems

■ UNLIKE EXTERIOR surfaces, interior walls, ceilings and trim remain fairly trouble-free; weather elements are not present.

However, special conditions may cause special problems. Below are several interior paint problems you may find in your home, and ways to solve them.

Peeling/flaking paint. This almost always is a moisture problem. Water—either liquid or moisture vapor—gets behind the painted surface, works its way along the surface, and peels and/or flakes the paint. This is NOT a paint failure as such, although it's easy to blame the paint.

Water in any form is insidious. Peeling paint can be caused by a water leak 10 or 12 feet away; the water runs along pipes, wires and framing members to its outlet point.

The answer to the problem is obvious: Find the leak and correct it. Look for damaged outside rain-carrying systems; uncalked trim above exterior windows and doors; roof leaks; leaking window sash. Inside, look for leaking pipes and pipe fittings.

Moisture vapor probably does more damage than liquid water because it can affect an entire wall or ceiling. Moisture vapor is created through cooking, washing and drying clothing, in bathrooms with tub/shower arrangements. Unless this vapor is vented to the outside, it can pass through walls and ceilings, causing paint to peel and flake.

Dirt and grease. New paint over dirt will feel gritty after the paint dries—like a sand texture. New paint over grease never dries properly.

Before you apply any interior paint to any surface, thoroughly wash the surface with a household detergent and water. The surface should then be rinsed and allowed to dry before the primer/finish is applied. Wash from the bottom of the wall up to the ceiling to prevent streaking. Wash the ceiling last, no matter whether the ceiling is to be painted or just cleaned.

Mildew. Mildew is a fungus that thrives in moist conditions. On painted surfaces, mildew looks like gobs of dirt. Mildew also can be nurtured by lack of ventilation in moisture-producing rooms such as bathrooms, kitchens and laundry areas.

To remove mildew, mix 1 quart of chlorine bleach with 3 quarts of warm (not hot) water. Apply the mixture to the mildewed surfaces and

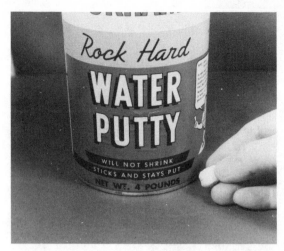

Powdered water putty is the product to buy and use for filling holes and cracks in woodwork and wooden trim components that will be painted. You mix the powder with water to a consistancy of putty, as shown. It should be thick enough so it can be formed in your fingers. On woodwork and trim that will be left natural (not painted), use plastic wood filler for holes and breaks.

There is a difference between spackling compound and glazing compound. The containers on store shelves can be confusing in label colors and names, so double-check before you buy. Spackling compound is formulated for patching gypsum wallboard and plaster. Glazing compound is a putty-like product that is used to glaze window glass around the mullions that hold the glass. Do not use glazing compound to fill holes and cracks in gypsum wallboard or plaster.

scrub the surfaces thoroughly. Then rinse the area with clear water. Wear rubber gloves while you work; the mixture is potent.

You also can buy special mildewcides and removers at stores. Follow the directions on the label. When you repaint, buy a paint with a mildew formula which will help deter the problem. Also, scrub the newly-painted area frequently with a household mildew remover and properly ventilate the areas to reduce the growth of the fungus. In some areas a dehumidifier may solve the problem.

Stains. This problem can be caused by food stains, water stains, or stains from knots and sap in wood trim. Before you paint, wash the area with warm water and household detergent. Rinse. When the surfaces are dry, coat them with a pigmented sealer such as shellac or a primer/sealer that you can buy for this specific purpose. Tip: Apply the sealer with a throw-away brush. The inexpensive brush will be less costly than the solvent to clean it.

Rot. You find this in wood; you also can find it in plaster and gypsum wallboard. It is caused by water, which destroys the wood, plaster and gypsum. To test for rot, push the blade of a knife into the suspected area. If the blade goes into the surface with little resistance, rot probably is the problem.

Wood has to be replaced if it has rotted. In small areas, plaster and gypsum wallboard can be

Painting Baseboards and Casings

Baseboards and casings around doors and windows are the trim pieces in a room. These components are painted last—after walls and ceilings.

To do the job right, first set all nails below the top surface of the trim. Use a nail set for this. Then fill the holes with water putty or a non-shrink spackling compound. Do not use calking or glazing compound.

Sand the trim thoroughly with a medium-to-fine abrasive. If the trim is flat, use abrasive over a sanding block to prevent dips and dings in the wood. For two-coat jobs, sand very lightly between coats, removing all sanding residue.

If for any reason you have to remove the trim pieces and then reset them, pry off the trim with a flat, stiff-bladed puttyknife. With pliers, pull out the finishing nails from the BACK SIDE of the trim pieces—not the front side. Hammering nails through the front side for pulling purposes will split the trim so it can't be reused.

patched or replaced. Spackling compound is used for small areas; all crumbling residue must be cut back and removed before patching. If the area is large, find the joint of the wallboard on both sides. You can probably tell by measuring the studs out from a corner (16-inches on center) or with a magnetic stud-finder. The stud-finder has a needle that wobbles when it passes over a nail-head. When the nailing points at the joints are located, cut out the entire panel of gypsum wallboard and install a new panel cut to size. All of this sounds difficult to do. Actually, replacement is fairly easy involving a minimum of tools: utility knife, hammer, new joint tape, nails, a new panel and joint compound. Buy a wide (at least

6-in.) joint taping knife (trowel) to apply the joint compound.

If crumbling plaster is a problem in a large area, call in a professional to make repairs. New plaster is properly applied in several coats; special tools and equipment are required. In small areas the plaster can be repaired by removing the crumbling material back to hard plaster, and then filling the void with spackling compound or patching plaster.

When working with gypsum wallboard and plaster, be sure to wear safety glasses. The crumbling material, when stripped from the wall or ceiling is sand-like and can cause eye trouble. It's also a good idea to have the room well ventilated.

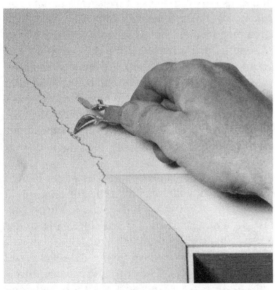

To clean hairline cracks in plaster, use a pointed can opener (church key). The tapered and sharp edges grooves the plaster properly so it may be filled with spackling compound and sanded when the compound has thoroughly dried. Remove all crumbling plaster before patching.

To clean hairline cracks in gypsum wallboard, use a utility knife. The razor-sharp blade cuts through the paper wrapping around the gypsum and produces a clean edge. Undercut the crack deeply enough so the spackling compound patch will stick properly. A non-shrinking spackling compound is recommended for this job.

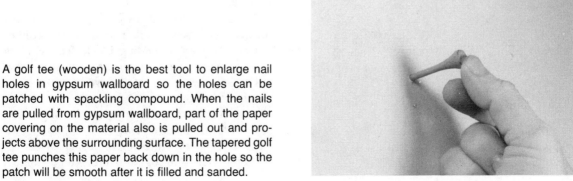

A golf tee (wooden) is the best tool to enlarge nail holes in gypsum wallboard so the holes can be patched with spackling compound. When the nails are pulled from gypsum wallboard, part of the paper covering on the material also is pulled out and projects above the surrounding surface. The tapered golf tee punches this paper back down in the hole so the patch will be smooth after it is filled and sanded.

13

Tools and Equipment for Interior Work

■ WITH PERHAPS the exception of a spray gun, the same paint application equipment—brushes, rollers, trim rollers, pads—is used for interiors as for exteriors.

A spray gun could be used, but furniture and furnishings require too much protection. Professionals sometimes spray the interiors of new homes before fixtures and fittings are installed.

How do you get a professional-looking paint job on interior walls, ceilings, trim and woodwork? The secret is: light.

Light the Room Properly

Do-it-yourselfers, when painting inside the house, usually remove all furnishings possible *including the lights.* Even on sunny days, with light streaming through the windows, there really isn't enough light to illuminate the darker nooks and crannies in the room. Spots are missed or lightly-coated and these blemishes tend to show up after the furnishings and lights have been moved back into the room. The missed spots won't be gross, but they will contribute to the overall appearance of the paint job. Something just doesn't seem right.

Watch a professional painter at work. Part of his equipment will be a light reflector on a tripod with a 250- or 300-watt bulb. The pro knows that just an average paint job will look fine under normal lighting conditions.

Reflectors are sold in many hardware and home center stores. They are inexpensive. Buy a reflector or two for your next paint job, and don't skimp on the light: use 300-watt bulbs.

The Importance of Sandpaper

Do-it-yourselfers when painting a room usually are in too much of a hurry to sandpaper surfaces smooth before painting them. Wash the walls and then spread the paint. It'll probably look okay.

A true professional always lightly sands the surface *before* washing it. The pro uses medium-grit abrasive on a sanding block. The sanding block is wiped across the surface almost haphazardly, but every inch of the walls, ceiling and woodwork is covered.

Abrasive removes the tiny particles of grit and dry finish on the surface. It even smooths down ridges left by brush bristles and roller covers.

If more than one coat of paint is to be applied,

How to Choose Abrasives for Interior or Exterior Work

Type	Grits	Use
Flint	Fine, medium, coarse	To remove old finish; for tacky surfaces; for first-stage sanding
Aluminum oxide	36: extra coarse; 50–60: coarse; 80–100: medium; 120–150: fine; 220–up: extra fine.	For wood, metal, plastic, fiberglass
Emery	Fine, medium-coarse, extra coarse	For polishing metal
Garnet	36: extra coarse; 50–60: coarse; 80–100: medium; 120–150; fine: 220: extra fine	For wood
Silicon carbide	Very fine: 180–240; extra fine: 280–320; super-fine: 400; ultra-fine: 600	For wood, glass, fiberglass, plastic, soft metal, between-coats
Tungsten carbide	Coarse; medium; fine	Hard finishes
Steel wool	No. 3 coarse; No. 2 medium-coarse; No. 1 medium; No. 0 fine; No. 00 very fine; No. 000 extra fine; No. 0000 super-fine	For rust removal, dulling glossy paint finishes
Degreased steel wool	Same as above	For fine furniture refinishing
Pumice	Coarse to fine in powder form	For fine furniture refinishing between coats of finish
Rottenstone	Same as pumice	Same as pumice

Special note: Buy "open coat" abrasives if you are removing gummy finishes. Buy "close-coat" abrasives for non-gummy finishes

the professional also sands between coats and then removes the sanding residue with a brush and damp cloth. The surface is clean, dry and ultra smooth before the paint goes on.

These are the two secrets of a professional job: proper lighting and a light sanding. The extra time and few dollars invested will make a tremendous difference.

Paint Brushes

There are three types for interior work: pure bristle brushes; man-made bristle brushes; man-made plastic or "poly" brushes. In brush selection only one rule applies: Do not use pure bristle brushes in water-based paints. The water will cause the pure bristles to matt and clog; the brush will have all the action of a floor mop.

If you are painting large surfaces (walls and ceilings) with a brush, get one at least 4 inches wide. A 6-inch brush is better. The larger brushes can be loaded with more paint, speeding the job.

For windows, buy an angled sash brush or a round brush. Either type works well, but we favor a round brush because it handles better. The same bristle advice applies: don't use pure bristles in water-based paints.

A trim brush—3 inches—is the tool for wood-work. It's small enough for exacting lines, and it works well for flats, semi-glosses and high-glosses. You also can use it to cut in at ceiling and trim junctions for a roller.

Pure bristle brushes have split or flagged tips on the ends of most bristles. The more flags, the more bristle (in effect) and the smoother or finer the brush stroke. Man-made bristles are "exploded" at the tips (sort of popped out) to give the bristles the flagged feature. The result isn't bad, but it still doesn't produce the smoothness of a quality pure bristle brush.

Quality brushes are chiseled somewhat—both types of bristles. What this means is that the bristles are different lengths, which creates a tapered effect. The bristles lay flat so you can cut a fine line with the tips of them.

Good brushes should be flexible at the tips of the bristles more than at the ferrule or base of the brush. Rule of thumb: the bristles should be 50 percent longer than the width of the brush. (More brush buying tips in the Exterior Painting section.)

Paint Rollers

We recommend a 9-inch wide roller for interior paint jobs. With a 9-incher you can cover lots of area fast; the roller load lasts longer so you

Even with thorough washing after each use, brushes tend to clog with paint. After every-other-use, soak the brush in brush cleaner, as shown. Give expensive roller covers the same treatment. By doing this, you can extend the life of brushes/roller covers for years.

Combs for brushes are sometimes available in stores—but not always. The combs remove loose and dried residue from bristles. An excellent substitute for a standard brush comb is a hair curler comb. The paint particles won't stick to it and the teeth are wide enough to slip through the dense bristle structure. Always "comb out" a brush after it has been soaked in brush cleaner. Then wrap the bristles in foil to keep them properly shaped while the brush is in storage.

aren't constantly dipping into the tray. For most interior work you will need a smooth-nap roller cover (most walls and ceilings are smooth), or a medium nap roller. Long nap rollers are for rough surfaces only. Today most roller covers are marked for the type of finish they are designed to spread: latex, oil, alkyd, all-types. The covers also are marked as to the nap.

Many retailers offer bargain roller covers. Beware of these. The bargain brands often are out-of-round and tend to smear paint because they don't track properly on the roller cage (that part that accepts the roller). Also, the material to which the roller cover nap is attached should be a plastic, not cardboard, so it won't absorb the vehicle from the paint. Inexpensive roller covers often are manufactured with cardboard.

Roller handles should be threaded to accept a roller extension pole for painting ceilings and other high spots. This saves climbing up and down a stepladder for each painting set. Also, the cage of the roller should be a series of wires. The roller cover should slip easily over the cage; don't buy a roller handle where the end caps have to be removed with a screwdriver in order to remove or install the roller cover. They're messy.

Most roller trays are made of stamped aluminum. Most are standard in design with little ridges running along the bottom of the tray. The ridges are designed to help turn the roller cover in the tray so the roller cover can be loaded with paint. The ridges are a good idea, but they don't work as effectively as a screen grid that you can fit into the bottom of the tray. Roller trays also should have a fairly large paint well at the front end and spring-like clips at the back end. The clips spread easily and hold tight on ladder steps. The stiff clips are difficult to adapt.

It is as important to clean a roller tray and grid as it is to clean a roller cover or brush when you're finished with it. If the tray/grid isn't cleaned, bits of dried paint can work up into the fresh paint the next time you use the equipment.

Rollers are not limited to the 9-inch sizes. You can also buy 7, inchers and donut-type trim rollers; tapered or cone-shaped rollers; and narrow 2-inch rollers for trim. We like the trim brushes better because they are easier to handle.

Pad painters with short, bristle-like nap are fairly new on the do-it-yourself painting scene, and they do a good job. Some models have wheels that run along projected trim boards so you don't paint the trim, and the pads may be adjusted accordingly. Some models have fixed pads—no wheels—for wall and ceiling areas.

Roller Nap Selection Guide

	Smooth Wallboard Plaster Hardboard Plywood Floors	Semi-Rough Cement block Cinder block Sand finishes Textured plywood Some bricks	Rough Stucco Brick Acoustical ceilings Some block
Water-thinned paints/finishes—Latex, rubber-base, acrylic	Short-nap synthetic 1/8"-3/8"	Medium-nap synthetic 3/8"-3/4"	Long-nap synthetic 3/4"-1-1/4"
Oil-based and solvent paints/finishes	Short-nap synthetic or mohair	Medium-nap synthetic or lambswool	Long-nap synthetic 3/4"-1-1/4"
Alkyd, enamels, oil	1/8"-3/8"	3/8"-3/4"	
Lacquer finishes	Pure mohair	Medium nap lambswool	Long nap lambswool

NOTE: Plastic bases (to which the nap is attached) are the best buy. Cardboard bases tend to soften and tear.

Like trim brushes as compared to trim rollers, selecting a pad painter boils down to a matter of personal preference. Since the pads are inexpensive, give one a try. As you work with a pad, don't overload it with paint and don't press down too hard on the handle. Stroke the pad over the surface very lightly for best results.

Polybrushes

Polyurethane brushes are more like pad painters than brushes. Polybrushes do an excellent job at trim and small jobs with results that almost resemble a quality pure bristle brush. With a light touch the paint flows onto the surfaces smoothly and levels itself properly.

The drawback to polybrushes is that they are usually one-use products. When cleaned, the poly-pads tend to unravel, producing a ragged tip. However polybrushes are inexpensive, so you can afford to junk one after it's done its job.

Ladders for Interior Painting

Most interior painting projects require a stepladder. Our recommendation is a 6-foot ladder for 8-foot-high ceilings; an 8-foot ladder for 10-foot-high ceilings. Type I, industrial grade ladder with a 250-pound weight rating, is the best buy. (See Section I, Exterior Painting, for ladder buying and safety tips.)

Why use a 6-foot stepladder for 8-foot ceilings? The length provides safety and security and puts you up at eye level for ceiling-wall trimming. A short stepladder tends to be tippy. It is dangerous to stand on the two top rungs of any stepladder.

Aerosol Spray Cans

You have a choice of color and type of finish in these spray cans. However, the products are really designed for small jobs and touch-ups—not for spraying an entire room.

Power Rollers

Power rollers are new on the do-it-yourself paint market. They are akin to power sprayers—but without the overspray.

In operation, paint is force-fed into the roller by a small air compressor. On the handle of the roller is a trigger. When you want more paint, you pull the trigger. The trigger controls the paint flow to the roller cover, which in turn provides an equal or uniform distribution of paint to the surface.

On some models, a one-gallon paint can is set into a cannister and sealed. This puts the paint under pressure so it can be fed through a flexible hose to the roller. Manufacturers say that you can spread a full gallon of paint in 20 minutes. Our tests showed that more time was needed for the best job, but even so the power outfit did put out a lot of paint fast.

Accessories for some units include a handle extension, splatter shield, 3-inch trim roller, trim pad, trim brush, and 3- and 9-inch roller covers in various nap lengths. The unit works off housepower.

For brushes, rollers and pads, we suggest that you buy an extra mixing bucket (two-gallon size), at least two extra roller covers, a couple of paint paddles for stirring and mixing, and a brush

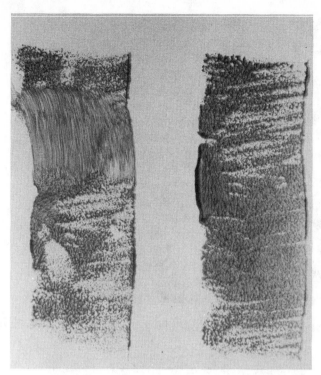

Not enough paint on the roller cover (right) causes inadequate paint coverage. It comes off in globs. An inexpensive roller cover (left) tends to skip on the surface being painted causing "dragging" and smears.

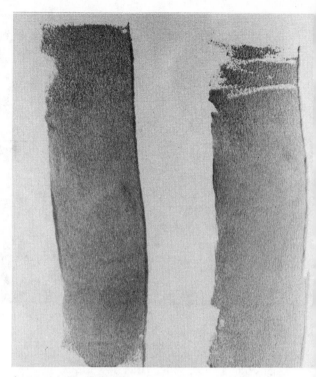

A properly loaded roller cover gives a smooth even coating of paint on the surface. Even so, there is a slight "dimpled" or "stipped" effect with a roller, which is why the roller should work in a "M" or "W" configuration across the surface. Watch paint coverage along the ends of the roller. Paint build-up is especially critical at these points (shown in both examples) and especially so with inexpensive roller covers.

One stroke with a pure-bristle brush is illustrated here. Note the ridges left by the bristles. If the same color topcoat goes over the same color undercoat, the ridges won't be as noticeable. Light sanding between coats will level the ridges. If only one coat is used, the final stroke of the brush—at the tip of the brush—should be a cross-stroke to level the paint and help rid the surface of ridges.

Two coats of paint with a pure-bristle brush (one right on top of the other without drying time) shows the hiding power of the paint along with the smoothness of the stroke. You seldom can get the hiding power with one brush stroke—even though the brush may be loaded with paint. It's best to use two "coats," i.e., a fully-loaded brush stroke on the first swipe and about a half-loaded brush stroke on the second swipe.

Polybrushes track about the same as pure-bristle brushes, as this illustration shows. In fact, the polybrush delivers more paint more smoothly than the bristle brush (left). Double-coated (right) the hiding result is about the same as the single stroke, although the ridges left by the polybrush are less noticeable in the double-coated example.

spinner. The spinner has a hand crank that spins dry brushes locked in a device opposite the crank. The spinner is a good buy to keep quality brushes clean and useful for years and years.

Other interior painting equipment you should consider includes:

Masking tape. Buy the wide rolls, not the narrow ones. Also, buy quality masking tape. The cheap stuff tears easily and you will spend lots of time trying to unstick the end from the roll. The good tape pulls off easily.

Wall scraper. A 3- or 4-inch scraper is plenty good for most conditions. If you have to remove lots of paint, buy a pull-type scraper and extra blades to go with it. Also buy a double-cut file to sharpen the blades.

Gypsum wallboard knife. Patching holes and damage in gypsumboard (and plaster) requires a special tool called a joint knife or trowel. The 10-inch width is recommended, although you may be more comfortable with the 6-inch-width. Don't use a puttyknife to apply joint compound or spackling to a large area. The puttyknife is too narrow for this job and the edges will dig into the patch causing all kinds of smoothing and sanding trouble. A joint knife is fairly inexpensive.

Putty knives. Have two types on hand: one with a flexible blade and one with a stiff blade.

What You'll Need for Interior Painting

Below is a list of the tools and materials that you may need to paint the interior of your home. Much of the equipment and some of the materials will be usable again for other painting and general home improvement and maintenance jobs.

- Primers
- Sealers
- Interior paint/stain/enamel/varnish
- Brushes, rollers, pads
- Trimmers and edgers
- Stepladder
- Scrapers/puttyknives
- Latex painter's calk and calking gun
- Dropcloths
- Masking tape
- Wiping cloths
- Utility knife
- Mixing buckets and paddles
- Repair tools such as a hammer, saw, nailset, pliers
- Abrasives
- Sanding block
- Phillips and standard screwdrivers
- Gloves
- Light reflector and 250-watt bulb

Level and unbroken surfaces should always be smoothed with abrasive on a sanding block. This type sanding block has a rubber base over which self-sticking abrasive is attached. Other types of sanding blocks are solid rubber with slits at each end of the block. The slits are opened by hand to insert the abrasive on sharp steel retaining pegs.

Steel wool—and other abrasives—are marked as to their coarseness. For example, the "#0000" on this package of steel wool means that the product is very fine, as compared to "#0," which is just "fine." Steel wool is best suited for rust removal and dulling paint gloss. Use degreased types for furniture refinishing.

Utility knives. One type has a blade that is retractable in the housing. It is used for scraping paint spatters and brush marks from window glass. Another type has a fixed blade that is triangular-shaped. Use this knife to cut gypsum wallboard tape and to undercut cracks in gypsumboard and plaster.

Can opener. The "church key" type with a pointed end makes an excellent crack cleaner-outer.

Paint shield. This is a length of light-weight metal with a handle that can be butted against trim so paint isn't smeared on the trim by a brush or a roller. It does an excellent job—*after* you learn how to paint with one hand and control the shield with the other.

Extension pole. A must if you are painting a ceiling or high walls with a roller.

Brush comb. If you can find one in a store, buy it for combing loose and dried paint from bristle brushes. If you can't find one, substitute a wide-tooth hair comb or a roller comb (the type your wife uses in her hair).

Sponges. Buy two for washing the walls.

Dropcloths. The cloth ones are excellent and worth the money if you plan to do lots of painting over the years. The plastic ones protect from spatters and the spray from roller covers, but they tend to tear and are very slick underfoot. If you go plastic, be sure to anchor the dropcloths with masking tape. Otherwise, the plastic will be underfoot instead of protecting furnishings.

If you prefer plastic, don't overlook the plastic sheets used as a moisture vapor barrier. You can buy a huge roll for about $10 and the plastic is much thicker than the sheets sold as dropcloths. Another good dropcloth (and it may not cost you a cent) is the plastic used to cover lumber and plywood stacked on pallets. This stuff is really tough, but it's flexible enough to cover odd-shaped objects in a room to be painted. Ask a building materials dealer if he has any throw-aways. Often he'll give them to you.

Wiping cloths. Your old shirt will work just as well as cheesecloth—if you have an old shirt. The best buy in wiping cloths is old toweling that often is washed and bundled by industrial towel and uniform services. The toweling is ragged, but

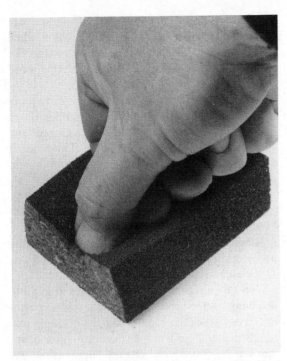

Sponge type abrasive blocks have the abrasive glued or fastened directly on the sponge. The block is very flexible (which standard blocks are not) for smoothing irregular surfaces. Different grits—coarse-to-smooth—are available. The block may be washed in plain water to remove the sanding residue and restore the abrasive to its almost original condition.

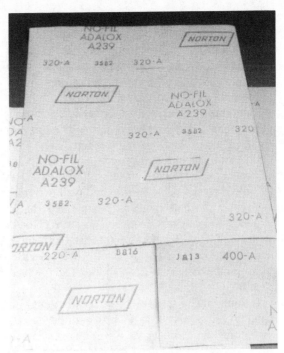

Sandpaper or sheet abrasive is available in many grits, coats, and abrasive types. Almost all abrasive products of this type are marked with types of grits in numbers (see abrasive chart, this Section). As a rule, the larger the number the finer the grit. This sample is marked "320-A." It is "extra fine" grit and the A stands for aluminum oxide.

it's clean and highly absorbent, and it is not cost-prohibitive. You'll find toweling companies listed in the advertising pages of a telephone directory. If you have lots of painting to do, it may be worth the call.

Light reflectors. Buy two. One type has a spring clip that snaps onto ladder steps, dividers in windows, doors, spindles, and other structural components in a room. The other type has a three-legged tripod.

Sanding blocks. Some are split at the ends so the abrasive paper can be inserted. Some have rubber pads at the bottom to which adhesive-coated abrasives are stuck. Either type works well. You need a sanding block to keep the sandpaper flush against the surface that you are sanding. If you use your fingers to apply the pressure to the back of the paper, you can dig into soft plaster and gypsumboard walls and ceilings and even woodwork and trim. Always sand in a circular motion, not back-and-forth in a straight line.

You can use a power sander for interior work, but the sander should be the orbital type. Go easy with it; too much pressure can eat away the surface. Never use a disc or belt sander for any type of interior sanding.

Abrasives (sandpaper). You probably will use more medium-fine and fine-grit abrasives for interior painting jobs than the coarse-grit papers, so buy accordingly. If you have to do lots of sanding over soft and gummy paints, use an open-coat abrasive. If, however, you have to do lots of light sanding over hard and dry-painted surfaces, choose a closed-coat paper.

When sandpaper becomes loaded with residue you often can clean it with a whiskbroom or stiff scrub brush; or tap the paper against a hard surface. If the paper is fully loaded, change the paper so it doesn't damage the surface that you're trying to smooth.

Wire brushes. Okay for removing paint from metal. Don't use them on wood, plaster or gypsum wallboard.

Pole sanders. These are extension handles that are fitted with a pad device over which sandpaper is stretched. Save your money.

Painting mitts. Excellent for spindles and

rounds. But be sure to clean them thoroughly. A counterpart would be an oval paintbrush.

Tack cloth. Really for fine finishes. Washing the walls after sanding will do an excellent job of picking up debris. The brush extension on your vacuum cleaner does a good job also.

Joint tape. This product is made for taping gypsumboard joints. Always use joint tape, not masking tape, when making this repair.

Painter's calking. This product is really a latex or acrylic type calking compound that is excellent for filling cracks between trim and wall or ceiling surfaces. The calk remains flexible, so that it expands and contracts with temperature changes without fall-out. Do not use oil-based calking; it dries out too quickly—especially indoors. (See calking information in the Exterior Painting section.)

If your calking skills are not too sharp and the calking you apply is in humps and ridges, try smoothing the calking with a wet finger, or use a throw-away brush soaked in water. You will get very smooth and even surfaces.

Spackling compound. This is used for filling cracks, holes, and small broken areas in plaster and gypsum wallboard. You can buy it in various qualities.

Glazing compound. Use this product for glazing window glass. Since most glass is glazed on the exterior, you probably won't need glazing compound for interior painting jobs. Do NOT use glazing compound to fill holes, cracks and broken areas in plaster and gypsum wallboard. Do NOT use glazing compound to patch woodwork and trim. Water putty and latex calking are better products for these projects.

Water putty. A good product for patching cracks and holes in woodwork and trim. Water putty is a powder that is mixed to the consistency of putty and pressed into voids with a putty knife. The woodwork and trim must be primed and painted after the water putty repair or the patches will show.

Wood plastic. The material looks like fine sawdust and smells like lacquer thinner. It's a natural wood filler in species' colors (walnut, oak, mahogany, etc.) that bonds with wood and can be sanded, shaped and tooled like wood when dry. A top coating is not necessary over the filler if the filler is matched to the wood. Use wood plastic for patching fine woodwork.

Striping tape. Use it to apply imaginative paint designs to walls and ceilings. It strips off surfaces better than masking tape and makes cleaner and sharper edges than masking tape. The price is about the same as masking tape; narrow widths are easier to work with than the wider ones.

Safety glasses. A bother but an eye-saver, especially when chipping away at plaster, gypsumboard and masonry building units.

Gloves. Buy the rubber ones for washing walls and working with strong chemicals, such as masonry-etching products.

Gypsum patches. Fairly large holes in gypsum wallboard often need back-patches of gypsumboard as part of the repair. Ask the building materials dealer if he has a section of gypsumboard that has been damaged during shipment. Or ask him if you can have a couple of gypsum spacers used in palletizing lumber, molding, and other building products. Most retailers are delighted to get rid of this debris free.

Scaffolding. Don't use it; it's dangerous. Work from a stepladder.

Adhesive. For warped wooden trim pieces and plastic/rubber type moldings, the best adhesive is paneling or subfloor adhesive in a calking-type cartridge. Just a little bit will stick almost any product or material to any other product or material.

Paste. To restick wall coverings (wallpaper, burlap, fabrics, etc.) use a wheat-based adhesive for porous papers and a vinyl paste for vinyl, foil and plastic papers. Straight or common pins make excellent clamps to hold papers to surfaces while the adhesive sets. Just push the pins through the paper and into the wall surface. Remove them when the paste dries. The holes won't be noticeable. The same trick works for torn paper coverings on gypsum wallboard if the paper can be glued back into position for painting.

CHAPTER

14

Surfaces Are the Key to Appearances

■ IN GENERAL you won't run into surface preparation problems inside the house that you may encounter outside. Walls and ceilings should be first sanded, then washed thoroughly before paint is applied. Cracks and holes should be filled with the proper filler and the patches should be sanded smooth with the surrounding surfaces. And don't forget to wipe up the residue when you finish.

Removing old paint. Paint on walls and ceilings usually doesn't have to be removed. Indeed it often is impossible to remove it without causing even more problems. If the surface is in bad condition, your options may be to cover it with textured paint, or install ceiling tile.

Interior paint damage usually is confined to window sills, casings and mullions. The best way to remove the damaged paint film usually is with a pull scraper followed by sanding with a medium-fine grit paper and then a fine-grit paper. A power sander (orbital) does a quick removal/smoothing job, but you must be careful not to oversand through wood veneers, or to sand so unevenly you dish or cup the surface.

Another good paint removal tool is paint and varnish remover—especially if the damaged area is not too large. After you brush on the paint and varnish remover, give the compound plenty of time to soften the paint so it can be easily scraped off. You can retard the chemical action for a better and less expensive job by covering the remover-coated surface with a piece of aluminum foil.

Still another tool for interior paint removal is a hot scraper. It is ideal for small areas, but the cost may be prohibitive unless you have lots of paint that needs removing.

Do not use a propane torch to remove paint.

When using power sanders, hot scrapers and paint and varnish removers, be sure the room is properly ventilated. The residue and chemicals can be dangerous to your health.

Below is a checklist of other procedures that will help create a professional-looking interior paint job:

Removing gloss from trim: Buff the gloss with steel wool, or lightly sand the surface with fine open-coat abrasive. Or you can use "liquid sandpaper" that will dull the gloss. It is sold by many trade names; the dealer will know what you want

Hardware that can't be removed should always be covered with masking tape or a combination of plastic and masking tape. Use a utility knife to cut through the paint seal around hardware such as switch plates. If this seal isn't broken, you can peel off the paper that covers gypsum wallboard panels, causing a paint cover-up problem.

The correct way to mask along baseboard and trim is to first lay a strip of masking tape on the carpeting or floor, as shown. Buy wide masking tape—not the thin, narrow stuff—for most masking jobs. Quality masking tape is the best buy; it doesn't tear and/or rip as easily as the inexpensive products. For masking, strength is necessary.

if you ask for it as "deglosser" or "liquid sandpaper."

Removing old wallpaper: Some wallpaper is strippable. Just peel back an edge of it at the top of the wall next to the ceiling and pull down. If the wallpaper is not strippable and hugs the wall like the price sticker on a Christmas present, rent a wallpaper steamer and remove the paper.

Nail pops: Drive the nail flush with the drywall surface, then hit it one more time with a hammer to dimple the surface. Then patch.

Nails in trim: Countersink these fasteners with a nailset and hammer. Then fill the holes with water putty or wood plastic.

Stains of all types: Remove as much residue as possible with household detergent and water. Then seal the stain with a pigmented shellac or any one of a number of stain sealers available.

Plaster hot-spots: Seal with a pigmented shellac.

Paint on interior masonry: If concrete, try sanding the area with aluminum oxide abrasive or an abrasive block. For candle wax on brick, try applying cold water and scrubbing the area with a wire brush. For soot, use household detergent in water. Or use a commercial cleaner, following the direction on the label. Be careful; commercial cleaners often contain an acid: wear gloves and

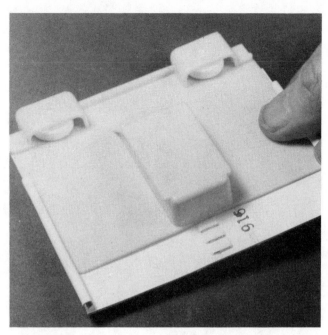

Pad painters may have a fixed paint pad or an adjustable one, as shown. This model has wheels for trim painting, although it may be reversed and adjusted so the wheels don't come into play. This type of pad painter generally is used for "cutting-in" trim next to wall surfaces so a paint roller may be used without smearing the trim with paint.

Dropcloths or paper coverings are then fitted over the first strip of masking tape. A second strip of tape is then affixed to the covering and the first strip which makes a complete unit. It takes a little more time to mask this way, but you can be sure that you won't have brush marks, spills, and splatters on the floor or floor covering when you've finished painting. Also, after the paint is set or dry, remove the masking tape from the surface to which it is applied. If you leave it for several days, the adhesive on the tape can pull paint off the surfaces or leave a mark.

safety glasses. For dirt and dust, wash with household detergent in warm water and rinse. If there is efflorescence, try a wire brush to remove the white stuff, or use a commercial cleaner. For grease or oil, use household detergent, a couple of tablespoons of ammonia, and warm water. Rinse with clean water. Or use mineral spirits, but ventilate the room.

Acoustical plaster ceilings: Don't wash them. Scrubbing can dislodge the tiny acoustical bumps. Paint them instead, using a long nap roller.

Acoustical tile: Wash it gently with mild household detergent and warm water. Rinse. Acoustical tile may be painted. Use a thin coat, and don't block the holes with paint or the acoustical properties of the tile will be lost.

The wheel pad painter in action. The wheels roll along the edge of the trim and the pad can be adjusted so it leaves a clean edge next to, but not on, the edge of the trim molding. Pad painters provide good paint coverage—about that of a polybrush (see photo).

Buy roller trays that have spring clips for ladder steps. Ladder steps often vary in thickness, and the unbendable clips can be a problem. Also, when you buy roller trays, buy a screen-type grid for the bottom of the tray. The grid provides extra traction for the roller cover so the roller cover can pick up the right amount of paint.

Paint trim guards work the opposite of pad trim painters. The metal guards help keep trim paint off wall and ceiling surfaces. The trick is to move the guard along with the brush. After a few practice strokes, the coordination becomes easy.

Floor tile: You can scrub it with detergent to clean it; or you can replace it. Don't paint it.

Concrete floors: Use a degreaser in clean water prior to painting. A detergent bath also helps, following the degreaser/water treatment. Let the area dry thoroughly before applying the finish.

Wood floors. See the section on Wood Finishing.

Wall heat registers (cold and hot): Use the hose attachment for your vacuum cleaner and thoroughly remove all dust and dirt wedged in the fins. If rusted, remove the rust with steel wool/abrasive and give the metal a prime coat of metal paint.

Radiators: Clean with a vacuum attachment. Clean and prime all rusted spots with a metal primer.

Ceiling registers: See *wall heat registers*.

Hardware: Remove what you can; mask the rest.

Recessed lighting fixtures: Mask the flanges; you probably can't remove the metal tube/reflectors. If you want to paint the rims, make sure the metal is cleaned and primed.

Finishing and Refinishing

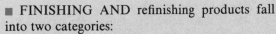

■ FINISHING AND refinishing products fall into two categories:

1. Off-the-store-shelf, ready to apply.
2. Mix-from-scratch, from pigments and vehicle.

Time was when mix-it-yourself finishes were about the only way to get a good finishing or refinishing job. The technique, of course, still adds an aura of professionalism to the final look, and conjures up images of old craftsmen in even older workshops rubbing finish on wood for a lasting sheen. Chances are, those same craftsmen today are using a finish out of cans or bottles they bought from a mass-producer. And chances are that the finish will be better and last longer than those mixed-from-scratch.

The store-boughts today are available in so many wood tones and colors and complete start-to-finish "systems" that tailor-made finishes may be questionable to use at all—especially for first-time finishers and do-it-yourselfers with not much patience. But if you are a supercraftsman and like to experiment, the mix-from-scratch formulas are the way to go.

If you fall into this category, you probably already have a metal lockbox full of wood-finishing formulas and recipes which you guard like diamonds.

Where to Buy Finishes

Wood-finishing products are sold at:
• Home center stores
• Hardware stores
• Paint and wallpaper outlets
• Hobby shops
• Some general merchandise stores such as Sears
• Stores specializing in craftsman supplies

Wood finishes basically include:
• Stains
• Varnishes
• Shellac
• Enamel
• Tung oil (a type of penetrating oil stain)
• Lacquers
• Acrylics

There are, of course, variations and combinations:
• Sealer/stains
• Sanding/sealers
• Brushing stains

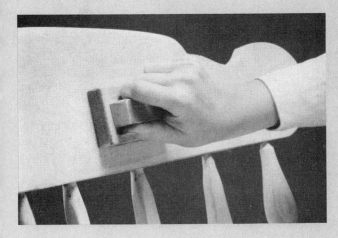

- Wiping stains
- Spraying lacquers
- Spraying enamels
- Brushing lacquers
- Brushing enamels

All of these products stacked on a paint-store shelf can be confusing. But it's really not difficult to sort them out by reducing each product to its common denominator.

There are just four ways to refinish or finish most woods:

1. You can apply a finish to bare wood for a natural finish.

2. You can stain the wood and then top coat it.

3. You can paint the wood (enamel it).

4. You can bleach the wood, stain it and top coat it. Or you can just top coat it for a lighter or darker tone.

In other words:

1. Seal or varnish the wood.

2. Apply a penetrating stain to the wood and varnish it.

3. Enamel the wood. Or antique the wood with a finish over a base enamel.

4. Treat the wood with wood bleach and then varnish it.

The common finish denominator is, then:

Stain
Varnish
Shellac
Lacquer
Enamel

15

Choosing and Using Stains

■ STAINS ONCE WERE a headache to use. On the wood they often became blotchy, cloudy, streaky, lappy, glossy and dull.

Modern stains behave much differently. Most stains flow over the wood smoothly; and won't lap, blotch or gloss.

About 98 percent of the stain you buy falls into one of three categories:

1. Penetrating stains with an oil or latex-based vehicle. They are either brushed or wiped (usually brushed) onto the surface.

2. Water stains that dye the wood fibers.

3. Non-grain-raising (NGR) stains that dry fast, preventing the grain in the wood from swelling.

The penetrating stains, in general, have less pigment than their first cousins, *the pigmented stains,* which have a considerable amount of pigment.

The big difference is this:

Penetrating stains penetrate into the wood. When dry they tend to reveal the grain and structure of the wood so you can readily see it. Pigmented stains also penetrate into the wood, but when dry they tend to hide the wood's grain and structure.

Your buying choice is this: If you have a wonderful piece of wood with outstanding grain pattern that you want to enhance, yet seal from moisture damage, buy a penetrating stain.

If you have a so-so piece of wood that is knotty and sappy, but with some pretty wood grain, and you want to seal the wood and at the same time hide some of the defects, use a pigmented stain.

Most manufacturers recommend that you brush on pigmented and penetrating stains, let them dry, then seal them with a clear finish. But this rule is not cast in bronze. You can wipe on these stains with a lint-free cloth, controlling the color and grain shading as you go.

If the wood is open-grained (lots of pores as in oak, walnut, mahogany), the pigment in the stain will tend to stick in the pores (unless you fill them with wood filler) and accent them. You may or may not like the effect.

Different wood species take stains differently. The softwoods such as pine, pecan and some firs will darken at a rapid rate when stain is applied. Hardwoods, such as walnut, mahogany and teak, resist stain penetration. You may need several applications to produce the color that you want.

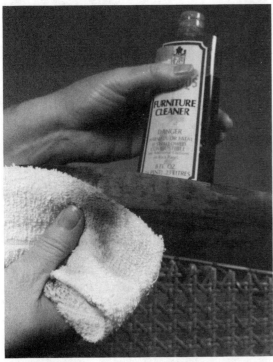

Does it need refinishing? Sometimes a good cleaning with a quality furniture cleaner will add a bright new finish without a lot of work. Always try cleaning at the outset, and then make a decision. Is the piece that you'll refinish or finish worth it? Sometimes the cost of materials and your effort applying them are more valuable than the surface you would restore.

The choice then is lighter stain colors for soft-woods and darker stain colors for hardwoods. Overall you probably will get the best results from staining the softwoods and clear-finishing (varnish or lacquer) the hardwoods. Either way, we recommend that you conduct a stain/finish test on a piece of scrap wood—or in a place on the piece that won't show—before you commit to a stain and varnish.

Water stains are water-based; *pigmented stains* are usually solvent-based. Water stains are really (for the most part) aniline dyes. Therefore, they *dye* the wood just as you would dye a piece of fabric. The aniline dyes come in powder form. They are mixed with boiling water to dissolve them properly. You may not find aniline dyes readily available in many paint stores. You can almost always find them, however, in paint stores that cater to the serious woodworker.

Water stains give you lots to like. First, the stains are available in a wide range of colors. They are inexpensive, which means that you can perform mix-and-match experiments without a big cash outlay. The stains are stable and go over the wood evenly. Drawback: The advertised colors may vary somewhat, i.e., the cherry color may not be your idea of cherry. But you can remix and come up with just what you are after. If you buy water stains that are both water and alcohol soluble, you may get a different color with water than with alcohol.

Non-Grain-Raising stains have a denatured alcohol or methanol vehicle, which speeds the drying process. The vehicle/pigment is applied with a brush in even strokes. Several thin layers of the stain are preferred to one big blob. You can brush one color over another color, which can be an advantage. However, if you get results that are too dark, the only way that you can correct your error is to bleach the wood.

NGR stains are not recommended for soft-woods. They are ideal for hardwoods. The stains may be difficult to find in many paint stores, but you often can buy them where craftsman's supplies are sold.

Varnish stains, as the name implies, are stains mixed with varnish. You can find several wood tones stocked on most retailers' shelves, but there is not a wide selection as with penetrating stains and water stains. The big advantage of varnish stains is that they are extremely easy to apply to wood that has been properly prepared. The varnish stains are brushed onto the surface. They do not penetrate the surface as deeply (if at all) as a penetrating or even pigmented stain. In short,

varnish stains are surface coatings; they sit right there on top.

Varnish stains probably are best suited for finishing projects that are not critical, such as an old hand-me-down chest of drawers that you want to renew but will never become a family heirloom. Varnish stains also are suited to shelving; books and other objects cover most of the finished wood, so the wood doesn't have to glow like a grand piano at Carnegie Hall.

Like all varnishes, varnish stain is applied with a pure-bristle brush. It dries slowly (about two hours to the touch, depending on heat and humidity). Most stores stock this product, which is moderate in cost.

Pigmented sealers can be used as stains. The sealers are sold in clear finishes and wood tones.

Furniture and other wood fix-ups can come in a pre-packaged form, saving you plenty of expense in restoration. For example, nicks in furniture and paneling can be hidden with colored wax paneling "sticks." Special hardware is available to strengthen wobbly chair and table legs, split seats in chairs, loose spindles. New cabinet hardware on old pieces can change the look instantly. The best sanding technique is to sand first with the grain of the wood. Always use a sanding block on flat surfaces—never your fingers. The sanding block prevents dips and cuts in the wood and provides a smooth and level surface. You can buy several different types of sanding blocks—all do essentially the same job. Or, you can make your own sanding block from $1 \times 3 \times 3$ wood.

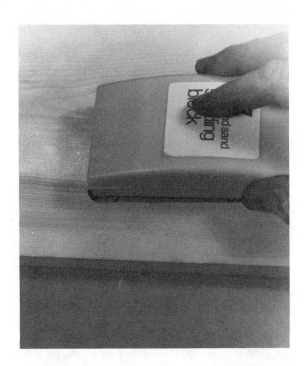

When the wood is smooth after sanding it with the grain, go over the surface once again slightly against the grain at an angle. This will remove any "tooth" that has been flattened into the grain of the wood. Then, before you apply any finish, very, very lightly dampen the wood with water and blot up any excess water. Let the wood dry (about 20 minutes). With a finer grit of sandpaper (also on the sanding block), sand the surface once again with and slightly against the grain of the wood. The water will raise the grain slightly (as would the finish). Therefore, with water, you get the smoothest base possible without the cost of the finish.

They give wood surfaces a hand-rubbed oil look. Pigmented sealers are applied with a lint-free cloth.

Stains you make. Stain is anything that will discolor wood. The range of discolorants is a wide one, including some oldtime recipes. There's chewing tobacco, for example, mixed with alcohol. There is spit and shoepolish; nails allowed to rust in water; cow dung and water; writing ink; graphite and oil; used crankcase (auto) oil; fabric dye. Experienced refinishers have recipe cards filled with home-made treatments. And, of course, each produces "the finest finish ever."

We suggest that you be more practical and stick with pigments mixed with oil, alcohol or water. Homemade varieties can look great when first applied, but the beauty often fades with time.

A Place to Work

Finishing work is a bit different than other types of painting projects. Finishing and refinishing require a special place to work. That place should be as clean and well-lighted as possible. If you make the furnishings portable, the work area can be almost anywhere in your home (spouse permitting)—the spare bedroom, a nook in the kitchen, or a corner of the dining room. Or you may be able to set up a special area in your workshop. But be aware that almost any finishing job you tackle will be subject to drifting sawdust if a workshop is chosen.

When setting up a finishing area:

• Stay away from high and low temperature areas. The best temperature at which to apply most finishes is 70° F. Don't apply finishes if the temperature is below about 50° F. or above about 90° F., or in excessive humidity. Some finishes are temperature-rated; you will find this information on the label.

• Steer clear of forced air ducts. They distribute fine particles of household dust that are attracted to wet finishes.

• Have plenty of ventilation. Solvent-based finishes are often smelly and the prolonged breathing of the vapors may cause injury. Take a breath-break occasionally.

• Have plenty of light. You can't finish what you can't see. Clip-on light reflectors, which you can buy at most hardware stores and home centers, cost very little. They direct lots of light where you need it.

• Be careful with fire. Many solvent-based finishes are highly volatile.

• Build a special worktable for projects. The height should be from about 38 to 42 inches—higher than regular tables. The height lets you stand up straighter while you're working.

• Have a separate table near the main worktable. Sawhorses with a ½- to ⅓-inch thick plywood top make an ideal spot to set aside projects that have—or will be—finished.

Penetrating stains do what the name implies: penetrate the wood and seal it and stain it. Compared with pigmented stains, penetrating stains are thin and watery. The stain is best applied with a brush with the grain of the wood. However, it may be applied with a cloth, but a cloth often does not give the stain enough time to work its way down into the wood fibers. You can wipe off more stain than you apply. Once covered, the wood should be left alone until the stain dries or almost dries. Then you can lightly buff it with a lint-free cloth.

Penetrating stains, when dry, can be either waxed or coated with a clear finish such as this polyurethane varnish. Notice how the clear varnish brings up the grain pattern and makes the wood shine. A wax finish will do somewhat the same, but it does not offer the wood the protection of a clear finish. The difference can be important, especially on such surfaces as tabletops.

Lightly covered with penetrating stain and wiped this piece of birch wood shows how the penetrating stain brings up the highlight of the wood grain. By using a darker stain, or recoating the wood several times with a lighter stain, you can deepen the color to the exact degree that you want. But remember this: it is easy to darken wood with penetrating stain, but it is extremely difficult to lighten it again if you use too much stain. Therefore, use caution when you apply the stain. Better you use several thin coats than one big heavy coat. You can also control color by wiping the surface before the stain dries.

Staining Tips

Most stains are applied with a brush. Some stains are formulated to be applied with a lint-free cloth. The fact is that *all* stains may be applied with either a brush or a lint-free cloth. A combination of both is common.

Although some stains have pigments suspended in the vehicle, it is good practice to stir or shake the products as they are being used. Before you use any stain, test it on a piece of wood that is the same species. If you can't do this, pick an inconspicuous place on the wood and test the stain where it won't show. This experiment will provide you with a color comparison, furnish you with an idea of how much stain you will have to use to create a color, and let you know how long it will take for the stain to properly penetrate and dry.

If you are new to finishing/refinishing with stain, we recommend that you thin the stain slightly with whatever vehicle is used in the product: oil, alcohol or water. The thinned stain will be easier to control for color. The first coats will

Quick Reference Guide to Buying Stains

Stain is used to seal and color wood. There are basically six types of stains:

1. *Pigmented stains* with an oil or latex-type base are recommended for use on woods that have grain defects that you want to hide, but not completely cover. Pigmented stains can be applied with a brush or wiped on with a lint-free cloth.

2. *Penetrating stains* have pigment suspended in the vehicle. Unlike pigmented stains, you don't have to keep stirring the stain to keep the pigment afloat. Penetrating stains leave the wood so you can clearly see grain and other wood markings. Therefore these stains are recommended for fine furniture and top grade woods such as walnut, cherry, maple and birch. Penetrating stains may be applied with a brush or wiped on with a lint-free cloth.

3. *Oil stains.* The penetrating types are dyes in an oil base. The pigments are in suspension. After the stain has been applied, you'll notice an intense color—a highlight—that is not as common as with regular pigmented stains. These stains (Minwax is an example) are extremely easy for a first-time finisher to use and they produce excellent results with little muss or fuss.

If you are finishing a really fine piece of wood, a penetrating oil stain will bring out the beauty of the wood perhaps a bit better than a pigmented stain. CAUTION: penetrating oil stains really penetrate soft woods deeply and very fast. Therefore, you will get a dark finish on the softer grain and a much lighter finish on harder grain. This absorption rate can be detered, however, with a wash coat of sealer before the stain is applied to the wood.

4. *Water stains* are made from aniline dyes in powder form. You mix them with water or alcohol or a little of both. Water stains may be difficult to locate, but they may be ordered from specialty retailers. If you have some experience in wood finishing, water stains are easy to apply and control. There is a wide range of colors in water stains, but the colors may not be consistent or look the way you want them.

5. *NGR stains* are basically non-grain-raising and usually "solvent"-mixed, so drying time is speeded. You can slow the drying time by adding several drops of water. NGR stains are not recommended for softwoods. And these stains may be difficult to locate.

6. *Varnish stains* are just what the name implies: a varnish with a stain in it. This is a surface coating, i.e., it doesn't penetrate very deeply into the wood fibers. Instead, it simply lies on the surface of the material that you are coating. If the wood is properly cleaned, varnish stains are extremely easy to apply and look good for the time and money spent. Varnish stains are ideal for the beginning finisher and for finishing work that isn't too demanding. They are applied with a brush—like varnish—and have a fairly slow drying time. The cost is moderate.

Pigmented stains can be mixed from oil colors and linseed oil. You're most likely to find these tubes of colors at stores specializing in paint products, although some hardware stores and home centers do carry a limited selection of color. The best mixing technique is in a ceramic bowl or saucer you "borrow" from the kitchen. An old case knife makes an excellent paddle.

Stir in the linseed oil until the raw color becomes a paste. Boiled linseed oil is best because it dries faster than raw linseed oil. Pigmented stain is different than penetrating stain. Pigmented stain "lays" on the surface, with just a little penetration into the wood. The grain, therefore, won't be as noticeable.

Pigmented stain can be either brushed or wiped on the surface. We recommend wiping because you are better able to control the color as it pertains to blemishes in the wood grain. If you find the stain too thick, it can be thinned slightly with turpentine or mineral spirits. See the text for details on this.

Steel wool (0000) can be used to apply pigmented stain. With steel wool, you get a "depth" application in the wood that you don't get with a cloth, but you still can control the color as it is applied to the wood. Always work either the cloth or the steel wool in the direction of the wood grain, if possible. Results are better.

The cloth-applied pigmented stain is shown at right; the steel wool-applied pigmented stain is shown at left. Note the difference in the depth of the color. The cloth-applied stain is just a tad lighter. Once this stain is applied and dried, you can finish the wood with a clear finish such as varnish. Or the surface may be waxed and buffed to a dull shine.

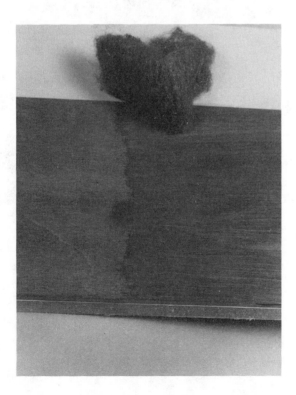

Sealing Wash Coats

To partially seal softwoods before staining them, use a wash coat of shellac. This sealer will prepare the wood for the stain so the stain goes on evenly. A good wash-coat mixture is one part white shellac to seven parts alcohol. The surface, after being sealed, should be sanded *very* lightly to remove the tooth of the wood grain.

Already-mixed pigmented stains (they have to be stirred by you or shaken on the mixing machine at the store) are just the same as the ones that you mix from scratch. The only difference is that you have more color control over the stuff you mix than the pre-mixed—and the fun of mixing, too. The pigment is held in suspension by the vehicle, so be sure you continually stir the mixture as it is applied to the surface.

This stain was brushed on the surface. You can see at the feathered edge of the brush how quickly and how dark the wood takes the brushed pigmented stain. You do, of course, have some control over color and tone with the brush, especially if you work with a fairly dry brush. The stain should be applied very evenly, however.

Applied with a cloth, pigmented stain can be controlled better, although it is more messy than with a brush. The results, however, are about the same as with a brush, but generally a little "lighter." Soft woods absorb stain a lot faster than hardwoods. Grain in soft woods also absorb stain more slowly than surrounding surfaces.

The real control factor, however, is wiping the stain with a cloth after it has been applied with a cloth or a brush. By rubbing with the grain, you can tone the stain to accent grain—or hide it. But you have to work fast before the stain penetrates too deeply or dries on the surface of the wood.

Special Terms of the Finishing Trade

ABRASIVE. Anything, but usually sandpaper or steel wool, that has enough grit to remove wood, metal or finishes from a surface. Even burlap can be considered an abrasive in the finishing process.

ACETONE. A chemical solvent that is used in the formulation of lacquers.

ACETIC ACID. A 6 percent solution of this chemical is excellent for removing ink stains from wood.

AMMONIA. The refinishing pros use it to fume oak. You can use it in a water stain to add penetration to the stain.

ANILINES. They can be vegetable or coal-tar additives that are used to make liquid stains. When on the surface, aniline stain is clear, penetrates deep into the wood, and the colors remain constant. The powders are dissolved in water, alcohol or benzene.

ANTIQUING. A base paint over which a stain or enamel is applied and then wiped off in some manner to produce a contrast between the two finishes. Antiquing, in short, gives an old look to a furniture piece by highlighting moldings and trim pieces.

BEESWAX. A component in furniture wax. It makes a good filler, when melted, for small dents and dings in furniture pieces.

BENZOIN. Used as a resin in glaze.

BLEACHING. Making dark wood lighter with hydrogen peroxide and oxalic acid—and sometimes just common household bleach. You can buy wood bleach in stores. It usually is a two-part system (although not always).

BORAX. A component used in wood strippers and in some water varnishes.

BROWN UMBER. Raw pigment that's mixed with turpentine, mineral spirits, or water to make a stain.

BURNT UMBER. The same as brown umber, but slightly darker in color.

CHECKING. The appearance of broken finish—a checkered look. Cause: usually the expansion and contraction of the wood from moisture, which cracks the finish.

CHINA CLAY. A component in wood filler.

CHLORIDE OF LIME. Used on oak, it turns the wood gray. It promotes a weathered finish.

COPPERAS. This is a chemical in crystal form. It will take the red out of mahogany and produce a blue-grayish tone in oak. The green copperas (sulphate of iron) are probably the best buy, but the wood has to be sealed with white polish (a whiting used in putty) before copperas are used.

DISTRESSING. Banging on the wood with a piece of chain or nails driven into a board to produce a worn look. Such dents and dings are made before the piece is finished.

DRAGON'S BLOOD. A red chemical used for changing the color of a polish. If you can't find it for sale, use an aniline dye, which is about as good as dragon's blood.

DRIER. A chemical that is added to a stain or varnish to speed the drying of the finish.

EMERY PAPER. A type of sandpaper used to polish metals.

EOSIN POWDER. If you can find it, use it in water stain to help enhance the tone. It is red in color.

EPOXY. A synthetic resin. It's tough as nails and is used in finishes and adhesives. Once, epoxy finishes were mixed from two parts at the time of use. Now many epoxy finishes are preblended.

FADING. Fading usually is caused by too much sunlight on the finished piece. Also, some finishes fade faster than others.

FILLER, WOOD. There are many products sold as "fillers." You can buy wood putty or wood plastic, which is used to fill holes. Or you can buy a paste-like filler that is used to fill the pores in open-grained woods such as oak. The purpose of the filler for open-grained woods is to fill the pores before the finish is applied. The filler takes the stain. If not tinted, the filler will produce white "zits" under the finish.

FILM. The thickness of the finish.

FULLER'S EARTH. In varnishing, it removes oiliness. Fuller's earth also can be used on upholstery fabrics to remove oil and grease spots. It is the base of many commercial spot removers.

FRENCH POLISH. Rubbing shellac on wood produces a high-gloss finish when there is enough shellac build-up on the surface. This is called French polishing.

GESSO. A process to make raised designs. Mix plaster of Paris, water, and water-soluble white glue for the design. When dry, the mixture produces a very smooth surface that can be finished.

GLAZING. Another word for antiquing.

GRAIN. The pattern (grain) in wood. Some woods (oak, walnut, hickory, pecan) have open-grain pores, which may or may not be filled before finishing. Other wood species (birch, maple) have close-grained pores that are not filled before finishing. Each species has its own grain characteristics such as "birdseyes" and swirls.

GRAINING. Adding grain to a piece of wood by first giving the wood a base coat of finish, and then highlighting the wood with a darker color finish. The darker finish is then rubbed or wire-brushed to produce a grained look. The process is similar to antiquing.

HARDBOARD. A brownish, flat panelboard made from wood chips and used in the manufacture of furniture pieces. Hardboard often is the backing for simulated wood-grain panels used in cabinets. It finishes well with varnish and enamels, but because of its dark color, stains are limited.

HARDWOOD. Wood from nonconiferous trees. Walnut, maple, birch, mahogany, teak and ebony are hardwoods. However the term ''hardwood'' can be misleading. Some softwoods, such as southern pine and fir, are harder than some hardwoods.

HYDROGEN PEROXIDE. A chemical used to bleach wood.

IMPREG. Wood that has been modified, e.g., thin veneers of wood that are coated with phenolic resin, allowed to thoroughly dry, and then are laminated together. Plywood is the most common example of this process.

JAPAN COLOR. Dry colors you mix with Japan dryer to color wood lacquer. If you mix the colors with turpentine, you get a quick-drying oil stain that is lightly pigmented, depending on the amount of color that you add.

JOINT. The union of two pieces of wood or veneer.

KERF, SAW. The space left by the passage of a sawblade through a piece of wood.

KNOT. A grainlike configuration in wood caused by a tree branch growing out of the main stem. Pin knots in wood are classed as less than ½-inch in diameter. A ''sound'' knot is as hard and solid as the wood that surrounds it.

LAMINATED WOOD. Layers of wood that have been glued together. Plywood is an example. So are butcher blocks.

LAMP BLACK. A black powder that is dissolved in water for coloring wood and metal. It also is used in some finishing waxes.

LINSEED OIL. There are two types: raw and boiled. The only difference in characteristics is that boiled linseed oil dries faster (by about four hours depending on the humidity) than raw linseed oil. Raw linseed oil is often used in French polishing since it kills the white in filler.

LUMBER. Any sawn wood that is at least 1½-inches thick but less than 3½ inches thick. Boards are 1-inch thick or less. Timbers are 5 inches thick; posts are 4 inches thick. If you are buying lumber for a furniture project, for example, you can expect to get a product that is at least 1½ inches thick by your specified measurement in width.

METHYLATED SPIRITS. Alcohol used in the manufacture of French polish and stains.

MILLWORK. Wood that has been cut in a pattern for use in finish work. An example is the trim around doors and windows.

MITER. An angle cut in wood or any other material.

MORTISE. A slot cut in wood. The slot can be cut to receive a hinge, tenon or escutcheon.

NAPHTHA. A solvent. It sometimes is used in varnishing to remove the ridges.

N.G.R. STAIN. The N.G.R. stands for ''non-grain-raising.'' Components of this finish have very fast drying agents that help prevent the grain of the wood from raising or swelling.

NITRIC ACID. You can use this chemical to remove ink stains. It also is sometimes used in the manufacture of finishing stains.

OIL COLORS. Oil colors come in tubes like toothpaste. There is a wide range of them, and by mixing the colors with linseed oil you can create almost any color or hue you want. Oil colors also are used to tint paint. Oil colors don't dry as quickly as Japan colors, but they may be easier to locate.

OPAQUE. A finish that hides the surface of the material to which the finish is applied.

OVERCOAT. A finish applied over an existing finish coat.

OXALIC ACID. A chemical for bleaching wood. You probably can't buy oxalic acid in its pure form because it is a poison. However, you can buy it as an ingredient in a wood bleaching solution.

PADDING. A folded-up strip of cloth that is used to apply finish.

PERMANGANATE OF POTASH. It comes in crystal form and can be used for making stain. The stuff looks purple when you mix it with water. On wood it turns to a very rich brown color.

PLASTER OF PARIS. Use it for molding designs or replacing them on wood carvings. Spackling compound also can be used for this purpose.

PLASTICISER. It is used in some polishes to prevent brittleness of the polish.

POLYURETHANE. A urethane resin that is used by manufacturers in the formula of varnish and enamel.

PORES. The tiny grain openings in open-grained wood.

PUMICE. Pumice is a very fine abrasive powder that is used to dull and smooth finishes between coats.

PYROGALLIC ACID. If you can find it, it can be used in fuming oak. The chemical produces a warm tone on the wood.

REAMALGAMATION. A wood-finishing process. You apply a solvent to a hardened finish, such as applying alcohol to shellac, and the finish becomes slightly fluid. When the finish dries and hardens again, any blemishes such as scratches will be smoothed out. Reamalgamation is a quick, easy and inexpensive way to redo an old finish without much work.

ROTTENSTONE. Rottenstone is an abrasive, like pumice, and is used to smooth and dull finishes between coats. It comes in different grades of fineness. Rottenstone sometimes is termed, ''Tripoli.''

RUSSIAN TALLOW. A filler.

RUBBING. A way to smooth down a coat of finish. Rottenstone and steel wool, for example, are considered ''rubbing'' abrasives.

RUBBING VARNISH. It is specially formulated so it can be rubbed between coats with pumice and oil or water. The result is an extremely hard finish that has a satin look to it.

SANDING-SEALER. The prime part of this combination is a wash liquid of sealer that is applied to wood. It doesn't penetrate very deeply, but enough to raise the grain of the wood so you can sand out the irregular surfaces for smoothness.

SAP. The water in a tree. You'll see it as gum in streaks along the grain of wood, especially pine. Untreated sap bleeds through finishes, so the spots should be sealed before finishing. Shellac makes a good sealer. So do some of the sanding sealers formulated for sap. Check the labels.

SHELLAC. It's manufactured from the resinous secretions of the lac bug. Shellac is a type of finish/sealer that remains "soft" even when it is dry. It can vary in color. White shellac is orange shellac that has been bleached. Orange shellac has a reddish cast to it.

STICK SHELLAC. Shellac in puttylike form. There are colors from which to choose. The stick usually has to be melted so the shellac can be pressed into dings and dents with a flexible putty or case kife. Before heat is applied the sticks are rigid and somewhat brittle.

STAIN. A liquid made with water, oil or alcohol and a pigment that colors wood.

TACK RAG. Used for removing dirt, dust and other residue from surfaces to be finished. You can make a tack rag with any lint-free cloth. Soak the cloth with varnish and a bit of turpentine.

THINNER. Similar to a solvent. A thinner can be water, alcohol, turpentine or mineral spirits. You mix it with any finish that is compatible: water with water-based paint; alcohol with shellac.

TRIM. Moldings.

TONERS. Spray lacquers that are transparent are called toners. They are basically used to shade areas of different colors in the same piece of wood so all the wood has a uniform color.

TUNG OIL. It is an oil crushed from the nut of the tung tree. You'll find it in some varnishes, and it is popular as an oil finish that is rubbed onto the wood surface. Tung oil finishes are hard, water-resistant and alkali-resistant.

UNDERCOAT OR UNDERCOATER. A sealer or prime coat of paint, enamel or varnish. The bottom coat of a multiple-coat finish.

UNDERLAYMENT. The base to which cabinet-grade woods or veneers are attached.

VENEER. Thin pieces of wood (or other materials) that are laminated to a base or underlayment. The top face of plywood, for example, is a veneer. Most furniture-grade pieces today are made from veneers instead of solid wood.

VENETIAN RED. Used for a reddish tone tint in some stains and finishes.

WAX. Used in polishing wood and other materials. The basic types are: beeswax; Japan wax; ozokerite wax; paraffin wax; carnauba wax.

WHITING. Used in the manufacture of putty.

YELLOW OCHRE. A powder (usually) that is used to color wood filler.

---

be light. You simply recoat the surface until you get the color that you want. Uniformity of stain is another bonus you get with thinning the stain.

Most stains take from 8 to 12 hours of drying time before they can be recoated. This is rule-of-thumb; check the label on the stain you are using. If the first coat is too dark, and the stain is still wet, you may be able to lighten the color considerably by wiping the surface with mineral spirits or water (depending on the base). If the stain is dry, the only way to lighten it is to resand the wood. This can be a problem—especially on veneers—so apply the material carefully.

The color samples at the paint store—those little blocks of wood that have been stained and, usually, finished—are not necessarily true colors. Stain colors react differently on different wood species, and, in fact, can react differently on the same wood species. What you are seeing on the samples are *approximations* of colors and tones. Never take them literally.

Don't be discouraged. You can blend stains by

wiping and recoating, and this is the saving factor. You *can* get the color you want.

One warning: You are, for example, staining a piece of case furniture. The doors on the piece are maple; the sides and top are pine. The stain you use on the maple doors will not turn out the same on the pine sides and top. Therefore you will have to change stains to get the color coordination you want.

It was mentioned earlier, but it's worth repeating: Hardwoods do not absorb stain as readily as softwoods. The color you are seeing in the wood comes partly from the stain pigments in the wood. Woods such as walnut show the stain more than other woods, especially in the darker wood tones. In effect, the finish produces a sort of two-tone effect. But don't be disheartened. Take a look at very expensive furniture pieces. You will not find uniformity in color; in fact, the richness of the wood comes through better when the color isn't uniform.

16

Clear Finishes

■ AFTER THE WOOD has been stained, it usually (but not always) is topcoated with a clear finish. The clear finish can be glossy, semi-glossy, satin-looking or flat. The finish itself can be varnish, shellac, lacquer, penetrating resin, wax or oil.

Wax, oil and penetrating resin, in that order, are the easiest to apply. Varnish is more difficult; shellac is easy in one way, but difficult in another; and lacquer is more difficult than varnish or shellac—especially if you are inexperienced.

All of these products are available wherever paints are sold—unlike some of the stains that have to be special-ordered.

The Varnish Finishes

Varnish may be used over stain or over a surface that has been previously finished with another product. Varnish by itself can be very attractive. Apply it to bare sanded wood if you want, but plan on giving the wood several coats for best results.

Varnish is a surface coating. It doesn't penetrate very deeply.

If you haven't tackled many finishing/refinishing projects, varnish probably is the best finish for you to use.

The general categories of varnish are:
1. Clear
2. Pigmented
3. Flat
4. Semi-gloss (a satin sheen when dry)
5. High gloss

Varnish can be used for finishing wood (and sometimes metal) indoors or out. Outside, the best product to use is *polyurethane* varnish or *spar* varnish.

Clear varnish (interior) is sold in pints, quarts, gallons and big containers used for floor refinishing. Varnish is applied with a clean (new, if possible) brush in multiple coats. Several coats build up a film for the best wood protection. Do not apply clear varnish—or any varnish for that matter—by pouring it onto a surface and then leveling it with a brush.

Two coats of varnish are standard. Three coats are recommended. Therefore, read the coverage information on the varnish can so you buy the right amount. One coat of varnish seldom is enough—especially on bare wood. The finish will penetrate the wood slightly, leaving the surface splotchy—dull in some spots, glossy in others.

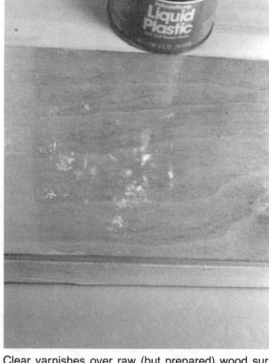

A packaged finishing system such as Formby's uses a finishing sealer which is applied to the wood surface with fine steel wool. Like a pigmented or penetrating stain, this sealer/stain can be controlled by you as to lightness or darkness. You can bring out the wood grain as a highlight—or hide it under the pigment if you want. The packaged systems, in our opinion are excellent for the beginning finisher as well as the more experienced finisher. Expect to pay a slightly higher price for the system, however.

Clear varnishes over raw (but prepared) wood surfaces tend to darken the wood slightly (sometimes yellow it, especially with age) and bring out the highlights of the wood grain. You can buy varnish in several different types of glosses: high, semigloss, satin, flat.

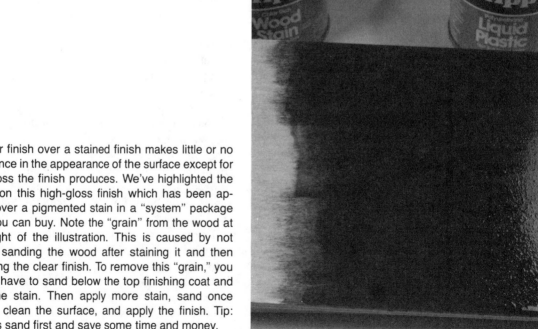

A clear finish over a stained finish makes little or no difference in the appearance of the surface except for the gloss the finish produces. We've highlighted the shine on this high-gloss finish which has been applied over a pigmented stain in a "system" package that you can buy. Note the "grain" from the wood at the right of the illustration. This is caused by not lightly sanding the wood after staining it and then applying the clear finish. To remove this "grain," you would have to sand below the top finishing coat and into the stain. Then apply more stain, sand once again, clean the surface, and apply the finish. Tip: always sand first and save some time and money.

Each coat of varnish dries in about 24 hours (depending on heat and humidity). The 24-hour period applies to all varnishes. Polyurethane dries a bit quicker, but it's best to let it set 24 hours before applying another coat. Actually, we recommend a 48-hour drying time. The extra time allows for any margin of error.

Some varnishes are superior to other types. Here's a list of what you can expect:

Gloss varnish. You get a very high gloss or shine with this product. It darkens the wood slightly, leaving a pale-looking to yellow surface. It offers very good protection to the surface. You apply it with a brush, or it may be sprayed on the surface. Most stores offer varnish in an aerosol spray container. Don't believe the coverage figures on the spray can, however.

Semi-gloss varnish has a duller shine to it; this product also dries to a pale to yellow color. You will need at least two coats of semi-gloss for best results, but a good trick is to use glossy varnish as the first coat, dull the finish with fine steel wool after it dries, and then topcoat with semi-gloss varnish. Although you are applying two coats, you may be able to eliminate the third coat that semi-gloss varnish frequently requires.

Semi-gloss varnish may be applied with a brush or by spraying. The finish must be very lightly sanded between coats. Drying time is 24 hours (48 if you can wait) between coats.

Satin varnish. The word "satin" applies to the finish when it is dry. The finish has a satin-like luster to it—neither high nor low gloss.

Satin varnish, like semi-gloss varnish, affords good surface protection, but not as good as high-gloss varnish.

Flat varnish dries with no shine or luster. It's protection can be rated as only fair. It may be applied with a brush or spray. It must be lightly sanded between coats. It dries in about 24 hours.

Urethane varnishes. These varnishes are available in gloss, semi-gloss, satin and flat. The urethanes offer better protection than regular varnishes, and are excellent finishes for outdoor furniture.

These products tend to darken wood slightly. The finish dries to a pale, slightly off-color yellow—but it is so pale that it is hardly noticeable. The drying time of urethane varnishes varies depending on the manufacturer, so be sure to read the label on the can. Urethanes may be brushed or sprayed.

Vinyl-type varnishes dry very quickly—in 15 to 20 minutes—depending on heat and humidity. They are available only in gloss or semi-gloss.

A wax finish often is very satisfactory over stains. Some waxes you can buy are slightly colored to match the tone of the wood. The wax is applied with a clean lint-free cloth in the direction of the wood grain. Then the wax is buffed to a shine. You probably won't get a lasting high-gloss as with a clear varnish, but the wax will provide a rich, deep look to the wood. See the chart on different wax types, this Section.

Both offer good protection. You will need at least two coats for an adequate cover job; three coats are best. You can apply them with a brush or spray.

What's the Best Type?

You, of course, will have to determine the best type of varnish for a particular use, and this comes from experience in using them all. We rate them this way:

Vinyl is probably the most flexible. It is similar to spar varnish: the finish expands and contracts with the wood, preventing cracking and crazing.

Urethane is a wonderful product for brushing. It also rubs well with finishing papers and compounds. However, the alkyds and phenolics are about equal with the urethanes. It's really a toss-up. The big features of the vinyls, urethanes, alkyds and phenolics is that they dry fast. A fast drying time means less time for dust and other airborne debris to botch the job.

Yellowing? Phenolic varnish tends to yellow more than any of the others with age. The alkyds vary in color; buy a good quality and you probably will wonder where some of the yellow went. The urethanes and vinyls probably will stay clear longer than all the others. In fact, tests we've run show very little, if any, color change over several years.

Some Application Rules

Varnish manufacturers say that varnish should never be stirred because it adds air bubbles to the finish. Air bubbles are difficult to level out with a brush. We'll go along with this recommendation, with this exception: Satin and flat varnishes ought to be stirred before and during application. These varnishes contain a flattening agent that sinks to the bottom of the bucket.

If you are applying varnish to wood that has been stained, or applying varnish directly to bare wood, it's a good idea to thin the varnish with turpentine, using the mixture as a sealer coat. The formula is 1 part (or, perhaps about 1⅓ parts) of turpentine to 4 parts of varnish. A tad more turpentine seems to work best in varnish

Enamels are nothing more than pigmented varnishes. Therefore, the enamels are applied the very same way as the varnishes. Enamels hide all wood grain, of course, so make sure you prefer an enamel finish before it is applied. Once on, it takes paint & varnish remover to get it off.

used over bare wood. What happens here is that the thinned turpentine becomes the sealer coat and you want the sealer to penetrate the wood. A thinned version does indeed penetrate.

Top coats of varnish (not the sealer) usually should be applied right out of the can without thinning. However, if you find that the varnish is difficult to spread and the brush tends to drag through the finish, we recommend that you thin the varnish with just a bit of turpentine. How much is a guess. A couple of tablespoons of turpentine might be about right. If the drag is eliminated, the varnish is thinned enough. If some drag still persists, add another tablespoon or two, and stir again. Stir in the turpentine very slowly and carefully so as not to cause the mixture to bubble. If you can wait an hour or so, we've found, after you've mixed in the thinner, the varnish goes on without bubbles.

If you value the finish at all (and your time and effort involved) we highly recommend that you use a brand new brush for varnish application. A good pure-bristle brush is fairly expensive (about $6.00 as this is written) but we feel it is worth the investment. A used or dirty brush can really gum up the works and botch a good varnish job that you've worked so hard to prepare.

Ideally, apply varnish this way:

1. Have plenty of light on the bench or table where you will work. The light will reveal spots that you have missed altogether or have skimped.

2. Apply varnish, whenever possible, to a surface that is horizontal. This can be most surfaces if you plan the work. For example, you can remove drawers, set them on their backs, and varnish the faces in a horizontal mode. Skirts around tables can be laid horizontal.

3. We suggest that you varnish the corners, edges, curves and gimcracks first, leaving the flat surfaces until last.

Apply the varnish in smooth, even strokes. Do not slap it on surfaces with the flat of the brush, and do not dump a puddle of the finish on a surface and then level it with the brush. On legs and spindles, apply the varnish in a cross-stroke, and then level it with a length-wise stroke, using just the tip of the brush.

4. Different finishers have different ways of applying varnish to large flat surfaces. Some pros brush varnish on the surface in even rows spaced about a brush width (3 inches) apart. Then they brush across the rows at right angles, again leaving a brush width between rows. Then the little squares are filled in and the varnish is leveled with the tip of the varnish brush.

Apply paint and varnish remover with a brush you can afford to throw away when you are finished. Use plenty of paint remover and brush it out as evenly as possible. Don't skimp on the remover, but don't drown the surface of the wood with the chemical either.

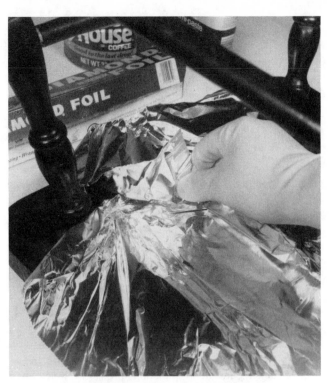

With aluminum cooking foil, cover the paint remover. Just lay the foil over the area. If the surface is vertical, you can crimp the foil lightly to hold it in place. Let the paint remover work for at least 20 minutes; 30 minutes is better. The foil helps prevent the chemicals in the remover from evaporating quickly.

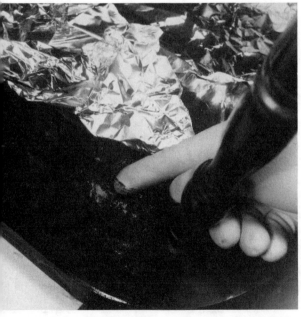

How has the paint remover worked? Check it by rubbing a finger into the finish. When you can press *easily* down to bare wood, the old paint or varnish is ready to be scraped or washed off the surface. When working with paint remover, always wear gloves and safety glasses.

Scrape the paint with a pull scraper with the blade removed, a regular flat scraper, putty knife, or any tool that will snowplow off the softened finish. If when you start to scrape you find that the remover is not coming off the surface easily, stop scraping. Then recoat the area with another coat of remover, cover it with foil, and wait for about 15-20 more minutes.

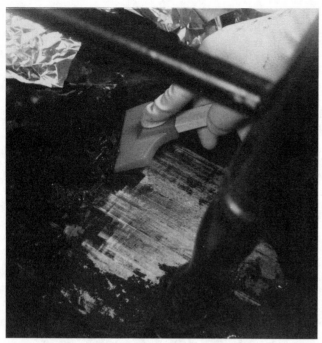

Scrape the surface once again. This time, you should strike bare wood without a problem. Here, we're using a plastic windshield scraper to illustrate that almost any type scraping tool will do a good removal job. The plastic scraper is a good idea on very soft wood surfaces.

Teaming the scraper with a stiff brush dipped in paint and varnish remover sometimes speeds the jobs and gets down into cracks and crevices that a scraper can't go. Stick with a fiber-bristled brush; a steel brush—especially on soft woods—may scratch the bare wood surface too much.

After a few circular swipes with the package system remover, most of the finish has desolved into the steel wool pad, as this illustration shows. We found the remover works fairly slowly, but efficiently; you do have to use a lot of muscle power in rubbing for the best results.

A final "wash" with a steel wool pad completes the job. All the finish (which was varnish) has been removed; there is still some specks of finish in the grain of the wood which can be easily sanded out. This surface, after a light sanding, is now ready to finish.

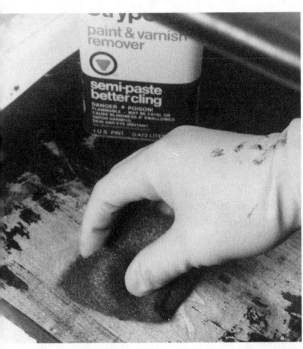

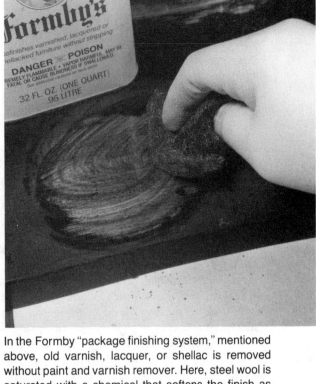

Steel wool (00) teamed with paint remover is another good way to clean away paint and varnish down to the bare wood after the surface has been initially coated and the finish has started to soften. The steel wool will gum up fairly quickly, so use this trick after you scrape off all the residue you can with a scraper or putty knife.

In the Formby "package finishing system," mentioned above, old varnish, lacquer, or shellac is removed without paint and varnish remover. Here, steel wool is saturated with a chemical that softens the finish as the steel wool picks it off the surface. This material is more expensive than most paint and varnish removers, but in our tests it does an excellent job of removal.

The comparison. We spent 30 minutes soaking the left half of this chair bottom with paint remover. Then we spent five minutes (35 total minutes) scraping off the old finish. With the packaged system we spent a total of 5 minutes on the spot you see to take the finish off to the bare wood. Although more paint was removed on the left in 5 minutes, the results were not as good as the 5 minutes we spent on the right. Our opinion is that, time-wise, the packaged system has a slight advantage over regular paint and varnish remover, so far as waiting for the remover to work is concerned.

Seal Both Sides

Wood is subject to moisture, which makes the wood expand or contract. When finishing or refinishing a piece, some beginners finish only the part that shows. The parts that don't show are left untreated.

In finishing and refinishing, all wood surfaces should be sealed. The insides of drawers are one example. The backs of cabinets are another.

Just one coat of a good clear penetrating sealer on these out-of-sight surfaces can help prevent warp, splitting, loose joints and expansion and contraction of the wood because of moisture. You don't have to be especially careful in the way you apply the sealer. Just brush it on the bare surfaces. You should, of course, be careful not to get the sealer on surfaces that will be finished in another way.

Some other finishers start at one end and coat the surface as they go, always working from the dry surface to the wet surface. Whichever way you go, criss-cross or straight across, this rule applies: Brush on the varnish with smooth and even strokes. Then, with the tip of the brush and very little pressure on the bristles, level or spread-out the varnish. Easy does it. Don't press hard on the bristles. Just give the brush enough downward and forward pressure to move it along the surface. Now, "tip-off" the finish, using just the very ends of the bristles and moving in just one direction.

After the tip-off, DO NOT go back over the finish again. Consider the tip-off the last brushing stoke. In performing the tip-off, take a running jump at the surface. What we mean is this: Start the brush in motion and lower it onto the surface while in motion. Follow through on the stroke, and at the end lift the brush off the surface while it still is in motion. In short, don't let the brush touch the surface unless it's in motion.

5. Do not drag the brush over corners. Doing so will cause a "fat" edge—a build-up of varnish on the edge. Instead, brush near the edge and then, as you get to the exact edge, lift the brush off the surface. You'll have to practice this technique, but it is not tough to master.

Between-coats Advice

Most manufacturers recommend that you wait 24 hours between coats. We won't disagree with the manufacturers, and we don't think they will disagree with us if we recommend that you wait from 36 to 48 hours between coats. The longer drying period, in our opinion, lets the varnish harden longer and gives you a better sanding base for the second and third coats.

How much you have to sand the first (and second) coats really depends on how smoothly you applied the varnish. If you have thick and thin spots—and missed spots—you should sand the surface so it is as level as possible. This can be a problem that takes lots of time to solve.

Quick Reference Guide to Clear Finishes

Finish	Dries	Appearance	You Should Know . . .
Epoxy (2-Part)	First coat, 4 hours; second coat, 9 hours	High gloss	Best applied with a brush. Wood filler can be a problem; check container label for recommendations.
Lacquer	Fast—within minutes	Varies from high gloss to dull sheen	Better applied by spray than brush, although brushing lacquers are available. Material is best applied in thin coats evenly. Wait 50 hours (depending on humidity) before rubbing with 0000 steel wool or hard wax.
Polyurethane varnish	Two hours; wait 15 hours to topcoat	Varies from high gloss to dull sheen	Best applied with a pure-bristle brush, spray gun. Can be rolled. Not compatible over a shellac base. Finish is hard; stays clear in use.
Resin oil	12 hours	Satin; handrubbed look	This is a penetrating sealer/stain. It can be brushed on the surface, but application and rubbing with a lint-free cloth is suggested. Give the surface at least three coats.
Shellac	2 hours; wait about 4 hours to topcoat	Varies from high gloss to dull sheen depending on how it is rubbed	Brush. Rub with 0000 steel wool.
Varnish	30 hours	Varies from high gloss to low sheen, or even dull sheen	Brush or spray can is best for application. Or it may be "padded." Make sure surface is squeaky clean before application; try to work in dust-free area if possible.

If the finish is thin, you can remove it from hard-to-get at spots with a wire brush and portable electric drill. The wirebrush treatment also is a good idea on open-grained woods where finish sticks in the wood pours.

If the surface is smooth and level, you need to sand just enough to give it a little tooth and dull the shine slightly. On horizontal or flat surfaces, ALWAYS use a sanding block and ALWAYS make sure that all of the gloss is removed. After the sanding treatment, if you spot some tiny glossy places, buff them lightly with 0000 steel wool to remove the gloss.

Varnish and Dirt

The biggest enemy of any finish is dirt particles which settle in the wet finish and show (or can be felt with the fingers) after the finish is dry. Varnish attracts its share of this dirt and dust. There are several tricks to eliminate dirt and dust—or at least minimize it.
• Work away from any air movement such as heating or cooling ducts.
• Wear lint-free clothing. A dirty shirt and trousers, oddly, tend to be more lint-free than freshly laundered clothing.
• Brush, vacuum and clean the surfaces before finishing. Wait a couple of hours, then go back to the workplace and vacuum once again. Do not brush or otherwise stir up dust.

• Just before you start applying the varnish, go over the surfaces with a tack rag. You can buy tack rags in paint stores. Or, you can make one with lint-free cheesecloth and water, turpentine and varnish. Soak the cheesecloth in water and wring it damp-dry. Then add an ounce or two of turpentine to the cloth and wring it dry again. Then, with a tablespoon, add varnish to the cloth,

Specialty Retailers

When you can't find a special tool, finish, special hardware, wood veneer, and other items in local home center and hardware stores, the firms listed below may have exactly what you want. In addition, most of the craftsman specialty retailers listed below publish catalogs of the items that they inventory. There may be a small charge for this publication, or the cost will be absorbed in your first purchase.

Robert M. Albrecht
18701 Barthenia
Northridge, CA 91324

Constantine & Son
2050 Eastchester Rd.
Bronx, NY 10461

Craftsman Wood Service
1735 West Cortland Ct.
Addison, IL 60101

Exotic Woodshed
65 North York Rd.
Warminster, PA 18974

The Hardwood Connection
420 Oak St.
Dekalb, IL 60115

M&M Hardwood
5344 Vineland Avenue
North Hollywood, CA 91601

Bob Morgan Woodworking Supplies
1123 Bardstown
Louisville, KY 40204

Real Wood Veneers
107 Trumbull St.
Elizabeth, NJ 10009

H. L. Wild
510 East 11th Street
New York, NY 10009

The Woodworkers' Store
21801 Industrial Blvd.
Rogers, MN 55374

For "grooved" round surfaces a twisted string of regular steel wool makes an excellent paint and varnish removing tool and also dulls finishes so second and multiple coats of finishes may be applied. Just pull out a string of wool from the pad and twist it slightly. Then buff the surfaces shoeshine fashion.

Some "grooves" on rounds are too small to take a steel wool string. Here, use a regular piece of string to remove the finish—or dull it. We prefer binder twine string because it is "rough." But cord type string will work just as well, if not as fast. Work shoeshine fashion.

For smoothing, removing old finish, and buffing crevices and narrow "ledges," a strip of sandpaper folded around an ice cream stick makes an excellent tool. The width of the stick fits these areas perfectly and you keep the wood "square." With your fingers, you can sand away these square edges and still not reach the finish.

working the varnish into the fibers. About two tablespoons of varnish probably will be plenty, depending on the size of the cloth. What you want when you're finished is a rag that is tacky or sticky. As you work the tack rag will dry out. Just add a bit more water and turpentine.

• After sanding between coats, always wipe off the residue with a tack rag.

• When the final coat is on the surface and has started to dry, sight across the surface with a light beyond it. You will spot any lint in the light. You

What the Sandpaper Terms Mean

Open coat: The abrasive particles cover about 50 percent of the backing surface.

Closed coat: The abrasive particles cover about 90 percent of the backing surface.

Stiff backing: The paper or cloth backing is stiff, almost inflexible. Use this abrasive on flat surfaces. Bending stiff backings loosens the abrasive particles causing scratches on the materials that you are trying to smooth.

Soft backing: Best for use on irregular surfaces where the abrasive has to conform with curves, grooves and bevels.

can remove it with what the pros call a "pick-stick."

A pickstick is a matchstick (wooden, kitchen type) that has a small ball of rosin stuck to one end. You melt the rosin and let it start to harden. Then you form a bit of the rosin into a ball and press it onto the end of the match. The rosin remains sticky. Simply touch any dirt or lint with the rosin end of the pickstick and lift it off the surface.

Spraying Varnish

You can spray varnish on surfaces with an aersol container, which is sold in paint stores. If you want a fast finish and don't care too much about the results, the spray method is recommended. The problem with spray cans is not the spray or the varnish, but how the spray is applied, which can be somewhat difficult.

You'll get the best results if you run a test pattern. The spray coming out the nozzle of the can will be round in shape. You will have to cross-lap the pattern just slightly as you go over the surface. Know the width of the spray. If you hold the nozzle too far away from the work, the spray width will be quite large and you will lose varnish coverage from spray drift. Position the can about 18 inches from the surface to be varnished. By knowing the width of the spray at this distance, you can fairly well judge the lapping sequence as you go back and forth across the work. Keep lapping of the spray pattern at a minimum or you will have two layers of varnish (or more) where you want just one. Since the finish is relatively clear, it is difficult to see these lap marks. Also, as you spray, keep the nozzle as square to the work as you can. If you rotate the can as you make a pass across the surface, the finish will be thicker in the middle than at the ends.

Start each stroke with the spray can in motion. Sweep across the work with the spray going full force, and then end the stroke with the spray can in motion. If you jerk the spray can over the surface, or stop and start the spray, you will get varnish build-up.

Shellac Finishes

There are many advantages to shellac as a finish. There is probably only one big disadvantage:

On small areas an electric heat gun or an electric hot plate is a good way to soften and remove finishes. Both tools do a good job—about the speed of paint remover generally. With this equipment, however, you eliminate the mess created by liquid removers.

Shellac Shelf Life

Over a period of time while sitting on a workshop shelf, shellac loses some of its qualities. Therefore, using old shellac can cause finishing problems.

If you suspect aging but really aren't too sure, test shellac on a piece of scrap wood. Old shellac takes a long period to dry. It's noticeably more difficult to spread evenly. It may look cloudy on the surface.

Since shellac is an inexpensive finishing product, junk any shellac that has symptoms of old age and start your project with brand new material.

Shellac is a "soft" finish, which means that the surface is easy to damage and quick to support white rings when a glass is set on the surface. The surface may also turn white with age.

All in all, though, shellac is a good finish to use on pieces that are not subjected to hard and abrasive wear.

Shellac is available anywhere paint is sold. It is available in two colors: white and orange. As a

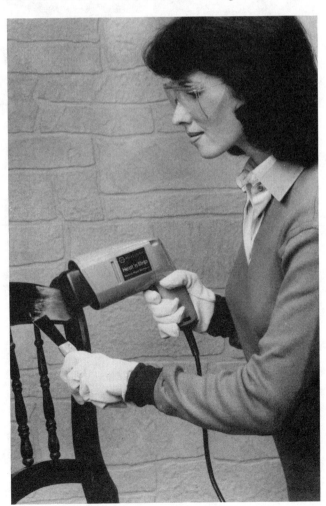

rule of thumb, white shellac is used for light woods; orange shellac is used on the darker woods. The finish, when rubbed and dry, is mellow, rich and deep. The finish takes a polish well; it is an excellent choice for walnut and mahogany.

Shellac is thinned or "cut" with alcohol. You may find shellac labels that read "4-pound cut" or "3-pound cut." Check the shellac thinning chart for a complete explanation.

You can apply shellac over any stain except a stain that has an alcohol base. NGR stains usually have an alcohol base; most other stains do not.

You can use shellac as a wash coat or sealer coat for other finishes, as mentioned above. Thin the shellac when using it as a sealer. White shellac is suggested for sealer coats, although orange shellac may be used.

Applied with a brush, shellac has a fast drying time—about two hours—and may be topcoated in about four hours.

When buying shellac, don't confuse white shellac, which is really colorless, with white *pigmented* shellac, which is a formulated stain and, sometimes, sanding sealer. The labels can be confusing.

Shellac is applied somewhat like varnish, only you can flow more of it onto the surface at the outset before brushing it out level. The technique is to put plenty of shellac on the surface with a quality brush. Then, with the brush, work it level in long, smooth, even strokes. Work from the dry surface to the wet surface. Tip off the shellac with

A multi-formed sanding tool is a good way to remove rust spots on metal surfaces or sanding tight or sharp angles, curves, grooves and other hard-to-get-at wood, metal, and plastic surfaces. You can cut the abrasive yourself or buy it pre-cut for this equipment.

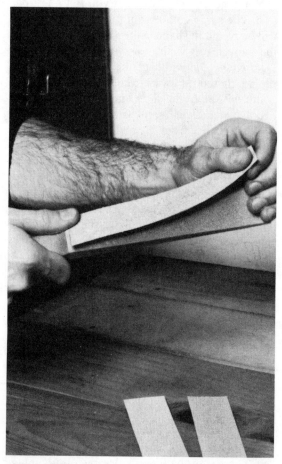

The sanding tool is pushed forward, backward, and sideways at the same time. The flat surface of the sanding tool keeps the paper flat on the surfaces being sanded so there are no digs, dips, and rounded edges. Self-sticking sandpaper was used here. It simply is peeled and stuck to the surface of the sander.

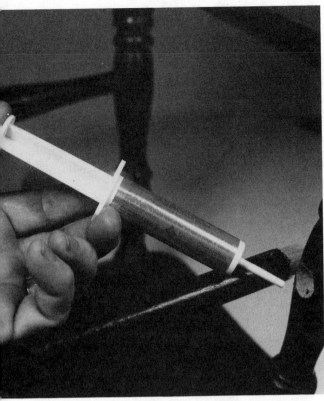

A glue syringe should be part of your furniture repair and maintenance equipment. With the syringe, you can force adhesive in tight quarters without disassembling the furniture piece. The tool is inexpensive to own and there is enough adhesive for several average projects.

the brush—like varnish—making sure the brush is relatively dry. Tipping off will smooth the surface and eliminate brush marks. Whenever possible, work the shellac in the direction of the wood grain.

Shellac shouldn't be applied in high humidity; moisture tends to turn the finish white. Drying time also is increased with high humidity, and shellac should be absolutely dry before you attempt to dull the finish for recoating, or rub the finish to tone it and highlight wood grain. Never attempt to sand or steel-wool shellac when it is partly dry. Half-dry shellac is extremely sticky and the residue from sandpaper and steel wool will contaminate the surface. It is almost impossible to remove this residue without removing the shellac entirely and starting the finishing process all over again.

The final finish over shellac is wax, which protects its soft film. But before the wax is applied, you should stroke the surface with 0000 steel wool, working the abrasive with the wood grain. We recommend that you wait at least 48 hours before the final smoothing and waxing. Sixty hours is better if you can spare the time. This time frame assures you that the coating is as hard as it will ever get, and can be worked without damage. After the wax is applied, buff the surface to a low gloss with a lint-free cloth.

Performance-Grade Abrasives: The Naturals

GARNET
A fairly hard mineral, garnet is considered as one of the best of the natural minerals for abrasives. The grains of garnet on sandpaper tend to remain sharp and cut properly even when the paper looks worn out. Use garnet for sanding and smoothing bare wood, and for sanding between coats of finish such as varnish.

EMERY
This abrasive is used in the manufacture of emery cloth. Its best use—contrary to popular belief—is for *polishing* metals. The mineral really doesn't have a high abrasive or cutting quality (such as garnet).

FLINT
The common natural grit is flint. However, flint isn't too durable; it wears out fast. Inexpensive flint sandpaper—especially open coat—is a good abrasive to buy for removing old finish, especially if the finish is gummy from paint remover. One problem with flint as a finishing product is that flint granules tend to work loose from the backing. You may find grit where you don't want it.

Performance-Grade Abrasives: The Synthetics

ALUMINUM OXIDE
Aluminum oxide abrasive may be used on wood and many other materials such as steel. Aluminum oxide abrasive is considered the toughest and most durable of any of the abrasives listed here. Because of its characteristics, you will pay a higher price for it. But the cost is not prohibitive. The fine grits in aluminum oxide papers are extremely high in cutting quality.

SILICON CARBIDE
You can use this man-made abrasive wet or dry. The grit is extremely hard. Particles of the abrasive break off during use, exposing new and sharp cutting edges. Therefore silicon carbide is a best buy because of its lasting qualities. Expect to pay a bit more for it. Use silicon carbide on hardwoods and metals. It is recommended for sanding between coats. And it is excellent (wetted with oil) for rubbing a lacquer finish to a satinlike shine.

Shellac Reamalgamation

"Reamalgamation" is a mouthful word that applies to shellac (and lacquer) finishes after the finish has been applied and has dried. Reamalgamation lets you hide fairly wide surface scratches in the finish by simply recoating the surface with alcohol (for shellac) or lacquer thinner (for lacquer). The full-strength solvent actually softens the finish so it becomes liquid and spreads smoothly across the surface. Presto: no scratches.

The technique:
• Clean the surface.
• Apply the thinner, using a new brush.
• Spread out the thinner evenly. Work quickly.
• In 30 minutes or so, the surface will turn from a gloss to a dull matte. At this point, lightly rub the surface in one direction—with the grain—with 0000 steel wool.
• Lightly wipe the surface with a clean, lint-free cloth. Then wax and buff shine the finish.

French Polishing with Shellac

Shellac is the basic product used in French polish finishes. This finish is recommended for close-grained woods only. Use it in combination with NGR, or NGR and water stain, for color.

The technique:
• Carefully measure and mix two tablespoons of boiled linseed oil into one pint of 1-pound-cut white shellac.
• Fold over a lint-free cloth so the cloth is about the size of the palm of your hand. We recommend cheesecloth for this, but you can use any soft fabric.
• Wrap the pad in a clean and lint-free square of linen. Cotton will work, but linen is preferred. Both layers of cloth should be about the size of the palm of your hand.
• Press the bottom of the pad into the mixture of linseed oil and shellac. A pie pan makes an excellent container. Don't soak the pad in the mixture, but don't skimp, either. The bottom of the pad should be kept stretched so there are no wrinkles as the finish is applied.
• Spread the mixture onto the entire surface (the wood, of course, has been properly stained and sanded).
• Now with a figure-8 stroke go over the surface with lots of downward pressure on the pad. Use plenty of elbow grease, working the mixture into the wood. Your goal is to work up a bit of heat from the friction of the pad moving across the surface.

• After lots of rubbing in the figure-8 configuration, the mixture will work itself down into the wood. Continue until the entire surface looks glossy, and there are no dark blotches or marks. Let the surface dry for 24 hours.
• Repeat the steps above.
• Let the second coat dry at least three full days. Then repeat the steps above.
• Let the surface dry for one week, but not more than 10 days. Then clean the surface. Coat it with a quality hard wax and buff the wax until the finish has a high sheen.

Working with Lacquer

Lacquers are probably the most difficult of the clear finishes to apply (there are colored lacquers, too, which are equally difficult to apply) because lacquers dry very quickly and leave you little margin for error.

Some lacquers are made for application with a brush; others are sprayed on with regular spray equipment; still others are in an aerosol container.

Basically, lacquer is much more durable than shellac, and sometimes even more durable than varnish. It is applied in a series of thin coats. You can buy different gloss finishes: high gloss, satin, matte, clear, and stain colors.

The big benefit—as well as drawback—of lacquer is its fast drying time. It is a benefit because it dries almost dust-free. It is a drawback because you have to work so fast that mistakes can creep in to spoil the job.

If you have never worked with lacquer, we suggest that you use a spraying lacquer first. As you gain experience, try brushing it.

Other than rosewood and mahogany, lacquer may be used on all woods. These two exceptions have an oil in the wood that tends to bleed through the lacquer coatings. You can use lacquer over any lacquer-based water and NGR stains, and over lacquer-based wood fillers. If the solvent is anything other than lacquer-based, beware. The lacquer solvents can dissolve other solvents.

If you apply lacquer with a brush, use a fairly wide brush that is brand-new. Work in small areas, and add enough thinner to the lacquer so it brushes on smoothly and evenly without drag on the brush. You'll have to work fast. Therefore, work a small area at a time and complete each one before you move on. Make sure the coverage is complete and the finish is as smooth and level as you can make it.

Ratio of Alcohol to Shellac for Thinning

Cut	3-pound base shellac		4-pound base shellac		5-pound base shellac	
	Shellac	Alcohol	Shellac	Alcohol	Shellac	Alcohol
½ pound	1 part	4 parts	1 part	5 parts	1 part	7 parts
1 pound	3 parts	4 parts	1 part	2 parts	1 part	2 parts
2 pound	5 parts	2 parts	4 parts	3 parts	1 part	1 part
2½ pound	5 parts	1 part	2 parts	1 part	3 parts	2 parts
3 pound	—	—	4 parts	1 part	2 parts	1 part

Let the first coat of lacquer dry for about four hours. Then lightly buff the surface with 0000 steel wool. The steel wool should remove any dust particles and bubbles from the finish, but don't rub so hard that you go through the finish. Light even strokes are best. Then give the surface another coat of lacquer, following the same directions as above. Let it dry for four hours, buff again with 0000 steel wool. Then apply the third coat. Lightly buff the surface after four to six hours with 0000 steel wool. Then wax and shine the surface with a soft, lint-free cloth. If, after application of the third coat, you are not satisfied with the depth of the finish, you can buff the surface once again, as before, and apply one—or several—more coats of lacquer.

If you apply the lacquer from a spray can, test the spray pattern of the can so you don't double-coat surfaces with overlap from the spray. Keep the can about 18 inches away from the work and move the can horizontally across the surface evenly without stopping. If you hold the can too close to the surface the lacquer will tend to "orange peel" from the propellent in the can. If you move too slowly across the surface, the finish may sag. The trick is to apply *many* thin coats of lacquer to the surface in order to build up the film evenly. When you're finished with the coating, lightly buff the surface with 0000 steel wool, wax and buff.

When spraying, you may get too much lacquer on the surface and it will start to sag. Your first temptation will be to level the finish by brushing it with a paintbrush. Don't brush it! Instead, let the lacquer dry and even out the sags with steel wool. Then apply additional coats of lacquer until you get the film you want.

Although steel wool is a good abrasive for

Finishing Products That Are Compatible

Finish	Sealer	Stain	Wood filler	Apply with
Enamel	Shellac wash coat	No	Any type	Brush/spray
Lacquer	Shellac wash coat; thinned lacquer; sanding-sealer with a lacquer base	Yes, if lacquer-based; water stain; NGR stain	Okay if lacquer based	Spray/brush
Oil	None needed	Any type but oil-based	Any type	Brush/spray
Penetrating resin	None. But use a shellac wash coat under any stain	Any type but varnish or vinyl-base	None	Brush
Polyurethane varnish	Thin varnish as the sealer. Or use a sanding-sealer if the base is compatible with varnish	Any type	Any type that is compatible	Brush/spray
Shellac	Shellac wash coat	Any type but those with an alcohol base	Any type	Brush/spray
Wax	Use thinned shellac under stain. No sealer needed otherwise	Any type. None necessary with a sealer/stain	Any type	Cheesecloth or lint-free cloth

buffing and/or rubbing lacquer finishes, you may prefer to use FFF powdered pumice and boiled linseed oil. Pumice is extremely fine and doesn't look as if it would cut any finish. Be careful. Pumice cuts very fast—faster than fine steel wool—so work slowly. Your best bet is to make a cheesecloth or felt pad and use the pad to apply linseed oil and pumice. An old salt shaker makes an excellent container to sprinkle the pumice onto the surface. Always use a tack cloth to clean away the residue left by buffing.

CAUTION: Lacquer fumes are toxic. The mist also is flammable. Have plenty of ventilation when you apply lacquer finishes, and keep the finishing process away from any flame. Be especially careful if you spray the lacquer.

If you are applying lacquer to metal, you can buy special rubbing compounds for between-coat and finish-coat application. Metal lacquers and compounds are not always available at paint stores. You generally can find a good selection where automotive finishes are sold.

Finishing Waxes and Stain-sealers

Clear finishes include paste-type hard waxes and stain-sealers, which provide a clear coating even if slightly colored or toned.

On close-grained woods, you can produce an excellent finish with just paste wax. However, the surface of the wood must be well sanded and clean before the wax is applied with a soft, lint-free cloth. Even clear wax will change the color of bare wood slightly. You may want to experiment on a test sample of the same wood before investing your time. You also can buy colored waxes, which work well on dark woods: walnut, mahogany and teak. The wax is a surface treatment. It does not penetrate the wood very deeply and it does not stain the wood as such.

"Hot wax treatment" is simply paste wax that has been heated to the melting point and then applied to the surface with a cloth. We're doubtful whether the "hot" treatment is any more beneficial than just rubbing on the stuff right out of the can.

The stain-sealers (Minwax is an example) are tinkerproof and, in our opinion, are excellent finishes for the beginner as well as the more experienced finisher. It is difficult to make a mistake with this type finish. There is a wide selection of colors.

Stain-sealers do what the name implies: stain the wood and seal it in one operation. The top coat is at least two coats of paste wax, each coat buffed to a high gloss with a soft, lint-free cloth.

Stain-sealers must be stirred while working—although directions may state otherwise—because the finish is pigmented. The pigment is held in suspension by the vehicle, for the most part, but we recommend an occasional stirring to assure that all the pigment is where it belongs. The product may be applied with a brush or a soft, lint-free wiping cloth. A brush seems to work better than the cloth, especially if you have lots of surface to coat.

Like any other finish, try to test stain-sealer on a piece of scrap. The surface, of course, must be properly prepared and thoroughly clean before the stain-sealer is applied.

It is applied with the direction of the grain. Let it set on the surface for about 10 minutes. Then wipe off any excess with a lint-free cloth. If you have the tone you want, let the surface dry for 30 hours and then wax it. If you don't have the tone you want, recoat the surface, let it set about 10 minutes, then wipe off the excess. You can keep repeating this process until the proper tone is reached (three coats is about average) without wood damage. However, if the wood then is not the tone you want, you will have to resand the surface to remove the stain; and even resanding may not get it all off. That's the reason for the scrap-wood test. And the test is especially important if you are staining veneer. Veneer is thin; if it has to be resanded deeply, the veneer may be damaged.

Thinning Reference for Paste Wood Filler					
Light mix		Medium mix		Heavy mix	
Filler	Thinner	Filler	Thinner	Filler	Thinner
8 oz.	1 pt.	8 oz.	10½ oz.	8 oz.	8 oz.
1 pt.	2 pts.	1 pt.	1 pt., 5 oz.	1 pt.	1 pt.
1 qt.	2 qts.	1 qt.	2 pts., 10 oz.	1 qt.	1 qt.

Some stain-sealer systems have colored paste wax to compliment the wood tone of the stain. That is, the wax will be a dark color for application over dark-colored stains; a light color for application over light-colored stains.

Oil Finishes

Traditionally, finishing oils have a linseed oil base. Application is sticky and messy, and it takes many coats to reach the desired rich and glossy finish.

Finishing oils are easy to find (and fairly reasonable in cost); they're labeled: "Tung Oil," or "Danish Oil," or with some root word that suggests Scandinavia—Norway, Sweden, Denmark or Iceland.

The finishing oils are penetrating. They have to be reapplied from time to time—like furniture polish—to maintain their good looks. You can buy them in a semigloss or a high-gloss mixture; they are also available in several stain or wood tone colors. Oil finishes labeled "Danish" usually produce a satin finish.

Oil finishes may be applied with a brush or lint-free cloth. The cloth may work best for you. You shade the finish by wiping it to control its density on the wood.

If you decide on a homemade linseed oil finish, here's a good formula: equal parts of boiled linseed oil, turpentine, and clear varnish. Mix the ingredients and let the mixture set several days before you apply it. Expect to do lots of rubbing. The finish has to go on in layers to produce a deep rich appearance.

CAUTION: Oil finishes may be applied over bare wood that has been properly sanded and prepared, or over wood that has been stained. However, the stain should be water or NGR stain—*NOT a stain that has an oil base.* If the wood is open-grained, it is recommended that you fill it (see chart on fillers, this section). You do not have to seal the wood since oil finishes themselves are sealers.

Oil finishes should be applied in a circular or figure-8 motion with a cloth. You can brush them on, but the cloth forces them into the wood. Use plenty of oil and keep rubbing until it is absorbed. Don't fool yourself here and wipe up the excess thinking that the wood has absorbed all it will absorb. The surface generally will take just a little more, even though your elbow is protesting.

The friction of rubbing (between the cloth and the wood) creates a small amount of heat, which makes the wood absorb more oil faster. If you are using so-called Danish or tung oil, you may not have to rub as hard or as long.

When you're finished, let the surface dry for 24 hours, and then go over it again with another coat of oil. If you are using a linseed oil formula, let the finish dry for one week before recoating it. *Do not* add more formula to the surface until the coating on the surface is thoroughly dry. You may need as many as 15 coatings to reach the desired finish. If you jump the gun and apply another coat over a wet coat, the finish will be sticky. Another factor: If you are working in high humidity, it will take longer for the finish to properly dry. As you can readily see, it may take many weeks or even months to achieve a rich, deep oil finish.

A linseed oil finish is especially good on walnut, teak and other dark woods. It is resistant to heat, but water, alcohol and chemicals can mar the surface. It is not resistant to abrasion. But the final, rich finish may appear to be a mile deep, and well worth the effort.

17

The Enamels

■ ENAMELS ARE basically pigmented varnishes. Because the pigment can hide a lot of sins, you may think that enamel is the product to use. You may also think it is easy to apply. Not so. Enamel can be very difficult to apply. Enamel over a poorly prepared surface can look absolutely horrid. Varnish is the better choice: It is clear and you can make excuses for the wood!

Paint dealers stock oil-base and water-thinned enamels in a wide variety of colors. The advantages of water-thinned enamels over oil-base enamels are easy-clean-up, no odor, no fire hazard. And manufacturers have formulated water-based enamels so they are just as durable—if not more so—than oil-based ones.

The label will indicate whether the enamel is oil-based or water-thinned. A latex or acrylic enamel will be water-thinned; an alkyd or "varnish" or "lacquer" enamel probably will be solvent-thinned.

A variety of glosses are available: high, satin, flat. As a rule, there are more colors in high-gloss enamels than the other finishes. Some dealers will mix enamel to your specifications.

There is a difference in enamel usage. A trim paint is often called an enamel. However, this type enamel is really a paint to be used on exterior or interior trim. Do not use it for furniture pieces—built-ins, cabinets, and so on. Here you want a product specially formulated for finishing and refinishing. It provides a hard, tough surface.

Enamels are applied the same way as varnish. If you are coating bare wood, the enamel can be used over any filler. However, think twice about enameling wood that needs to be filled. Open-grained woods are walnut, mahogany, teak. You may not want to hide these expensive woods under a coat of enamel.

If the surface has been finished, it should be sanded and then sealed with thinned shellac, an enamel undercoater, or a thinned finish enamel. An old finish doesn't have to be removed; it should be dulled, however, so the enamel adheres properly to the surface. And, of course, the surface must be thoroughly clean.

Enamel undercoaters for large surfaces are worth the price. They are less costly than finish enamels, and they prepare the wood or surface you are coating properly. Most undercoaters are white. If you are topcoating with another color, you probably will need two topcoats. You can

On Curved Surfaces

Do It This Way

Do Not Do It This Way

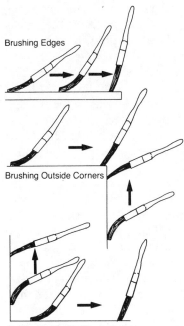

Brushing Edges

Brushing Outside Corners

Brushing Inside Corners

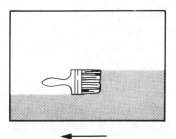

To apply varnish (and enamel) to flat surfaces work with the direction of the grain, being careful not to overlap the finish to any great degree. Brush just in one direction, as the illustration indicates.

To use the "criss-cross" technique in applying varnish or enamel, apply the finish in strips approximately the width of the brush you are using. Also brush in the direction of the grain with this stroke.

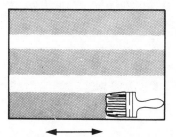

Now apply the finish the opposite direction, filling in the bare spots and creating a "checkerboard" effect. In both techniques, your final brush stroke, with the grain of the wood, should be with just the tip of the brush.

Varnishes (and enamels) are applied as this illustration shows. Brush around chair legs, rungs, and other round and curved surfaces. On flat surfaces, brush just to the edge. At outside corners, go to the edge and stop. Then apply the finish to the right-angled surface up to the edge. On inside corners, go just to the corner in one direction, and then reverse directions as you paint the adjoining surfaces. These techniques prevent finish built-up that results in "fat" edges.

tint the undercoater with a little finish enamel, or the paint dealer may be able to add pigment to the undercoater, then mix it by machine. Let any sealers or undercoaters dry for two to three days before you start topcoating. Humidity may slow drying time.

When applying enamel, keep the surface horizontal if you possibly can do so. For example, you can set a case piece level on two sides, enamel the sides, let the finish dry, and coat the other two sides. By working horizontally, you can avoid sags and runs, the big bugaboos of enameling.

Always apply enamel with a new, high quality brush. Your brush strokes should be smooth and even and, if possible, with the grain of the wood.

We recommend that you apply the enamel in brush-wide strips. Then go back over the surface in cross strips, filling in the gaps. The purpose of this technique is to make sure that the enamel is applied in an even coat. Cross-hatching is the best way to do this; it gives you some control.

After each strip has been applied, tip it off with the tips of the bristles, smoothing it even. When the surface is completely covered, tip off the entire surface with the grain. If you work with the project between you and a light, you can see thin spots, lint, bubbles, and any other problem that may occur. Add more paint, pick off the lint with a rosin picker, and brush out the bubbles. You may see some brush marks. Usually these marks will even out as the enamel dries.

If the enamel seems too thick and drags on the brush, thin it slightly. A *small* amount of thinner will not harm the formula.

Sometimes you will have to work on vertical surfaces. Here is where enamel tends to sag, curtain and run. The trick is to work with a fairly dry brush. Spread the enamel on the surface,

working from a dry surface to a wet surface. Also, keep the brush in motion as you go into the stroke and come out of the stroke.

Tip off the job as you would on a horizontal surface. Then, in about 15 minutes, go back and inspect the work. If you spot any sags or runs, tip them off with the ends of the bristles. You may have to go over the sag area twice. If the enamel sets too long, the brush will drag on the surface and produce brushmarks that won't self-level.

At outside corners, brush to the edge, then pick up any runs down the edge. It may be helpful to know that sometimes brushing in reverse—edge-to-flat—will prevent running. The main idea, however, is to get the runs before they sag down the edge. If you forget, by the time you get to the edges the finish may be so dry you'll have to sand to remove the runs.

At inside corners, brush to within one inch of the edge. Then tip the bristles into the corner and brush out away from the corner. This trick prevents build-up in the corner.

If you come across a spot that has a series of tiny pinholes, coat the spot with enamel and tip it off with the brush—just once. Don't keep going back over it. The holes usually will fill properly as the enamel dries.

Enamel build-up occurs mostly on edges. This build-up is called a "fat" edge. It's amost like a rim around a flat surface. To remove the fat edge, go over and over the surface with a dry brush, using just the tip ends of the bristles. Better yet avoid a fat edge by using the proper brushing technique.

Raised panel doors on cabinet pieces are especially prone to fat edges from enamel and varnish. The trick is to apply the finish first to the panels. Then finish the flat frame of the door. If you get fat edges at the miters in the frame (because sometimes the miters are not tightly fitted), try going over the build-up with a dry brush.

Drying times for enamels depend on the thinners and the humidity. The label on the enamel container will give you approximate drying time; we'd opt for at least two days. You may get by with one coat, but it's doubtful. For a second coat, let the surface dry a week. Then lightly buff the surface with a fine abrasive to remove any gloss. Use a sanding block on all flat surfaces. Clean the surface with a vacuum and tack rag. Apply the second coat of enamel and let it dry a week. Apply a third coat if needed, again after you lightly sand and clean the surface. Then let the finish dry for at least four weeks before you apply paste wax and buff the surface.

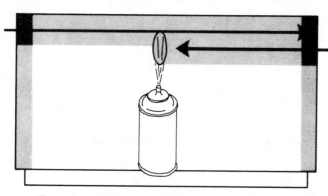

To apply varnish (or enamel or almost any type finish) with a spray can, hold the can at right angles to the surface being finished and keep the can at right angles as you move through the stroke. Also, before you start, determine the spray pattern of the spray can on a test board or sheet of paper. This way, you won't overlap the pattern and spray on too much finish that is bound to sag and run. You must test each container because the patterns almost always are slightly different although the finish is from the same manufacturer.

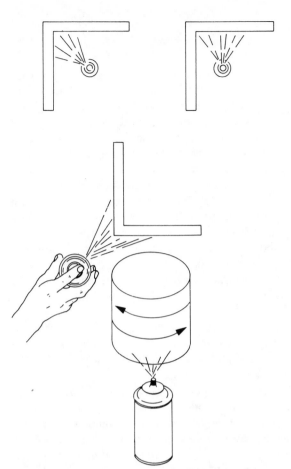

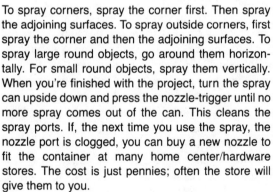

To spray corners, spray the corner first. Then spray the adjoining surfaces. To spray outside corners, first spray the corner and then the adjoining surfaces. To spray large round objects, go around them horizontally. For small round objects, spray them vertically. When you're finished with the project, turn the spray can upside down and press the nozzle-trigger until no more spray comes out of the can. This cleans the spray ports. If, the next time you use the spray, the nozzle port is clogged, you can buy a new nozzle to fit the container at many home center/hardware stores. The cost is just pennies; often the store will give them to you.

For French polishing—and some lacquer finishes—you first hand rub the surface as explained in the text. Then you apply the shellac/oil mixture (or whatever) with a filled pad, as shown, and rub it in with either a circular or figure 8 motion. You must rub for up to 45 minutes or longer in order to get the fine finish. You'll probably have to add more finish to the pad as the rubbing continues.

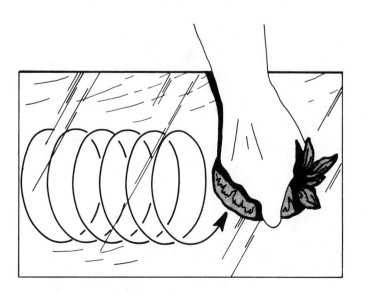

CHAPTER 18

Specialty Finishes

■ ANTIQUING SIMPLY is a glaze wiped over an enamel, varnish or lacquer finish. And it's just about that simple to do. You can make an old, hand-me-down piece of junk furniture look like an antique. And, because the finishes are wiped onto the surface, you don't have to be especially careful with the materials.

Antique finishes are generally sold by paint retailers in kits. That is, you buy a package that contains a base finish, a glaze and a set of instructions. Often included are application tools and wiping cloths. The cost you pay for the system is a bit less than the cost of buying the products separately. Many retailers have samples of what you can expect from each antiquing process.

Your color choice should be determined by the base color and not the glaze. The glaze is the top-coating, and most of it will be wiped off of the surface.

Here's the general procedure for antiquing:

1. Remove all wax, dirt, dust and loose finish from the piece you will antique. At this time make all necessary repairs. You may want to remodel the furniture slightly, doing away with doodads and gimcracks.

2. You may have to fill open-grained wood, if the wood is bare. If there are bubbles in the veneer of the piece, you can cut out the bubbles with a sharp utility knife and then patch the area with spackling compound. Sand it smooth when it dries. Any patches and filler will be covered with the base coat. However, you want the base coat to go over a smooth surface.

3. Apply the base coat with a new, clean brush. It goes on like enamel; make sure you don't have sags and runs. You don't have to be especially careful; you just don't want an uneven surface.

4. Let the base coat dry two days. Humidity can have a role in drying time.

5. Apply the glaze with a clean new brush after you're sure the base is dry. The glaze will streak on the base surface, but don't worry about this. Just brush on the glaze and stop.

6. Let the glaze set for about 10 to 15 minutes. Then, with a cheesecloth pad or a lint-free cloth, wipe off the glaze. Always move the pad in the same direction. This will produce a straight grain pattern.

7. When you're through wiping (the glaze is as sticky as jelly on a kitchen counter) you will no-

Antiquing is, more-than-less, an enameling and stain-ing technique. The base coat is applied to the wood surface after the wood has been properly prepared, as explained in the text. It should be spread out evenly, but you don't have to use the care and patience with the base as you would with varnish or enamel. Antiquing kits are sold in stores as pack-ages. Or you can buy the components separately.

When the base coat dries, add the glaze to the surface of the base coat. Also brush the glaze on evenly. You will not be able to apply the glaze without brush marks, but don't be alarmed. This is the way it is supposed to go onto the surface.

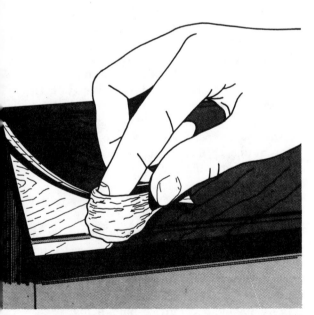

Wipe off the glaze, exposing the base coat. You'll want to remove all glaze from high spots and leave the glaze in the low spots to create the "antique" effect. The glaze could be described as a stain and it acts similarly. Use a soft, lint-free cloth to remove the glaze. Apply finger pressure, not palm pressure.

tice that some of the glaze coloring is still in the dings and dents, the cracks and crevices of the surface. This is exactly the effect you want, so don't try to wipe the glaze out of these spots. In fact, some refinishers prior to antiquing beat the workpiece with hammers, chains, keys and other objects to obtain a distressed look.

The piece is ready to put into service when the glaze completely dries. Give it at least three days, if possible. If you want to paste wax the surface, wait about three weeks.

"Texture glazing" involves the same materials and methods. "Texture" is whatever you want to make it. Here are some tested ideas:

Wad up a piece of newspaper and blot the glaze for a "marble" finish.

Run a fine-tooth comb through a fairly heavy coating of glaze for a lined look.

Cover the glaze with a layer of plastic food wrap. Smooth the wrap into the glaze like wall-paper on a wall. Then pull off the wrap.

A piece of burlap produces a scratched finish that is more pleasing than it sounds.

Patting the surface, when the glaze is almost dry, with a square of fiberglass insulation produces a "leather" look.

You can protect the final finish with a couple of coats of wax. Or you can seal the finish with a coat of clear varnish. Do not sand the surface before you varnish.

The trick in wiping glaze is to wipe the high spots on the surface clean. You leave the glaze in the low spots. This is what gives the wood an antique look.

You can buy an antiquing kit in a paint store, but you probably have some of the stuff in the kit in your workshop: brushes, steel wool, sandpaper and so forth. If you want to buy the remaining materials for antiquing, here is what you need:

Semi-gloss enamel

Glaze

Throw-away paint brush or poly brush. Buy a couple, one for the enamel and one for the glaze.

0000 steel wool

Package of cheesecloth

Medium to fine sandpaper sheets

If the paint retailers in your area do not stock antiquing materials, assemble your own:

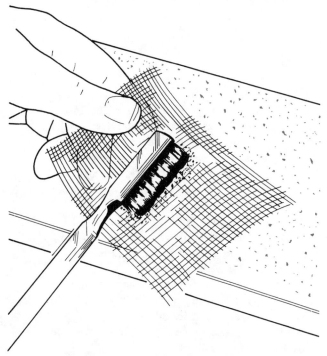

Flyspecking is done by flipping pigments through a small piece of metal wire screening. A toothbrush, flicked with a thumb, "sprays" the flyspecking finish through the screening, which helps distribute the finish where you want it on the surface of the wood. Most of the expensive furniture pieces are highlighted with "flyspecks" of color.

Semi-gloss enamel. Buy a good quality.

Clear resin sealer

Tube colors such as ochre, black, raw sienna, or even colors such as red, blue, green, orange.

Mix the colors with the resin sealer to create the glaze. Let the mixture set for about one hour, stirring from time to time. Then brush it over the base coat of semi-gloss enamel. You do not have to dull the semi-gloss with abrasive before glazing. In fact, it's best if you don't sand it.

Flyspecking Furniture

Go into any expensive furniture store and look very closely at the finish. You'll see tiny globs of color that resemble flyspecks. If you want to create this furniture feature, buy a small can of flat black paint. (If you want colored flyspecks, use a colored paint thinned about 25 percent, or orange shellac.) You'll also need a toothbrush and a small square of metal screening. A home center retailer may have a small piece of screening scrap that he will give you.

The surface that you flyspeck should be clean and free from wax, dirt and grime. If you are refinishing the surface, seal the wood and then flyspeck it. Any clear finish goes over the stain and flyspecked base.

Pour the flyspecking finish in a saucer or flat can and dip just the ends of the toothbrush bristles in the finish. Then, with your thumb, flick the bristles so the finish passes through the screen wire. The flicking action will produce a fine spray while the screening will block out and redistribute the splatters from the toothbrush.

As always with finishes and techniques, test flyspecking first on a piece of scrap wood or even a sheet of plain paper so you can get the hang of the thumbing/screening motion and learn to control the number of flyspecks. You'll probably want an uneven flyspecking rather than a more uniform splatter effect especially at corners and edges.

Gilding Techniques

Gilding means highlighting moldings and trim with gold, silver, copper, bronze, or especially intense colors such as white, red, orange, deep or royal blue, or green. Antiqued pieces are prime candidates for gilding as are mirror frames, picture frames and decorative cabinet hardware.

Time was when gilding material consisted of real gold leaf, i.e., gold foil. The foil was cemented to the surface with a finish called "gold size." Gold foil, of course, has disappeared. The replacement choice is either gold paint or a wax-base gilt in paste form. You may not be able to find this product in home centers and hardware stores. A retailer specializing in paints and finishes probably will stock it; a hobby store (arts and crafts) usually has it.

The gilt paints, which can be gold, bronze, silver or an intense color, are applied with an artist's brush and steady hand. The paste-type gilt is usually wiped onto the surface with a lint-free cloth. Or, you can use a combination of both: the paint first and the paste gilt over the paint.

We recommend that you first prime the surface, after it has been cleaned, with orange shellac. You can use white shellac, but orange is better. Let the shellac dry for two hours. Then brush on the paint. Let the paint dry two days. Then wipe on the paste gilt. You can buff the gilt with a soft cloth to bring it to a shine. Or you can leave it alone and get a duller finish. If the area you are gilding is large enough, you can brush an antiquing glaze over the gilt, then wipe off the glaze, as explained above. This technique produces an antique or old look. It's more effective on large areas than small ones such as the carvings on a mirror frame. You do not have to topcoat the gilded piece.

Working with Stripes

Stripes in different colors and tones add a certain depth to furniture pieces. Stripes, however, are not easy to apply.

The finish used for stripes is semigloss or a high gloss enamel. It should be thinned about 10 percent, because you don't want any brush drag as the paint is applied. The surface to be striped should be clean and flat (no gloss).

You can stripe freehand with an artist's brush. Or you can stripe with tape, which predetermines the border. Hand striping—unless you have a very steady hand—is hard to do. Practice striping a small area first and then graduate to larger areas.

We've found this technique to be easiest:

1. Use a semigloss enamel and buy a very high-quality artist's brush, such as camel hair. The tip of the brush should be pointed like a pencil.

2. Remove wax and dirt from the area to be striped. Household detergent and water is a good mixture for this. Rinse the surface, wipe it dry.

3. With 0000 steel wool stretched over the tip of your index finger, dull the gloss on the surface to be striped. You can control the width of the steel wool swatch with your finger. Don't take off more gloss than about the width of the stripe.

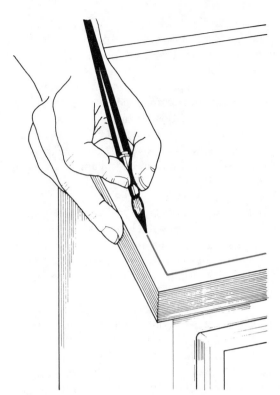

Stripes are difficult to make. A steady hand helps. Use a sharp pointed artist's brush to draw on the stripes, and use a finger along a straight edge to help guide your hand. You can buy mechanical stripers, but the cost—and often the results—may be prohibitive.

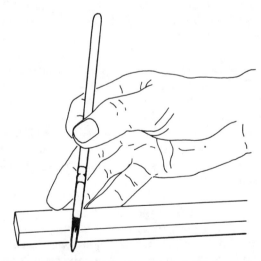

You can run the brush along a straightedge to help cut a straight edge with the point of the artist brush. Or, you can hook your fingers over the straightedge, as explained in the text. Whenever possible, work from the center of the striping area toward the edges of the area, instead of going from one edge completely to the other edge.

The way to do this is to glue two yardsticks together. Then follow the edge of the yardstick(s) with the steel wool-covered finger. The yardstick edge provides a tracking guide.

4. Make a couple of practice striping runs on a piece of paper or scrap wood.

5. Set the yardstick down on the line that you want to stripe. Hold the brush like a pencil, and hook your little finger over the back edge of the yardstick. Then draw your hand and brush along the yardstick guide.

Keep even pressure on the brush as you draw it along the surface. Don't push down or let up on the brush. And draw the brush along fairly fast. Don't stop-and-go; just make a single swipe.

Load the brush with enough paint for a fairly long stripe, but don't load the bristles too much or you'll produce blobs.

As you move along the straight edge, try to roll the brush ever so slightly between your index finger and thumb. This rolling action will help keep the bristles of the brush in a sharp point.

Another way to stripe is with masking tape. The tape, of course, defines the borders of the stripe, and you can dull the finish easily for the stripes with steel wool swiped along the channel between strips of masking tape.

Buy masking tape in ¾ or 1-inch widths for striping. It must be applied to the surface so it is absolutely straight and even. This can be tough to do. Try working with fairly short pieces of masking tape instead of one large strip. You might even draw a guideline on the surface you will stripe with a soft pencil and then follow the line with the edge of the tape. The pencil mark will lift right off with water. Don't over-press on the pencil. You just want a faint guideline.

When the tape is in position, take the edge of a putty knife and press the edges of the tape firmly to the surface.

If plans call for more than one stripe, do just one stripe at a time; don't mask for all of the stripes. This may take lots more time, but you'll get a better job.

With the tape in place, apply the paint with a fairly dry artist's brush. Easy does it. Don't slap on the finish just because you're using masking tape. The paint should be applied very evenly, with no thick or thin spots. When the paint is dry to the touch (run a line on a test board and use it as a guide), strip off the tape very slowly and carefully. If you rip off the tape you can pull away some of the stripe with it, causing a ragged edge.

When striping with either the tape or by free-hand, work from the center of the stripe toward the edges.

Under no circumstances leave the masking tape adhered to the surface more than 12 hours. If you do, the tape can damage the surface, and also the stripe.

Working with Stencils

Stencils are similar to stripes, but easier because you're working with a precut design.

Specialty paint stores stock stencils, and you'll find a variety of designs at art and craft shops. Home centers and hardware outlets may not carry stencils; if they do, the design selection may be limited.

You can stencil over any finish, but the gloss should be removed with 0000 steel wool within the stencil design. This is easy; just wrap the steel wool over your index finger and trace the design.

The finish for the stencil can be almost anything: flat paint or enamel; gilt; paste in bronze, gold, silver, copper or colors.

The very best way to stencil is to apply the stencil finish over a varnished surface that is tacky, but this can be tricky.

The second best way is to apply the finish with

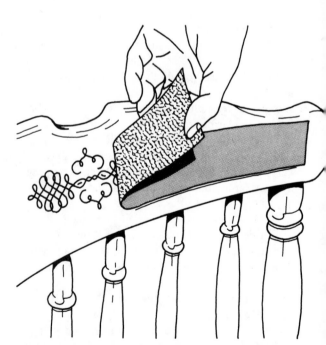

Decals are attached by soaking the decal in water and applying the plastic backing directly to the surface. A paper backing slides off the decal as it is pressed into position. To remove a decal, you can buy a special strip that softens the decal surface.

a spray gun or from a spray can. The third way is to apply the finish with a round stencil brush that you daub on the surface.

The technique for all three is this:

1. Make sure the area to be stenciled is clean and free from wax and dirt. If the surface is glossy, dull the gloss with 0000 steel wool.

2. Align the stencil on the surface and tape it with masking tape. The stencil must lie perfectly flat on the surface. If the surface has been recently finished or refinished, be sure the finish is absolutely dry. If it is not dry, the masking tape will pick it up off the surface.

3. If you use a spray gun, mask the rest of the piece with newspaper to catch the overspray.

4. Apply the paint in very thin coats at right angles to the stencil design. Do not spray or brush into the stencil edges. When you're finished, the paint should be smooth, even, and not too thick on the surface.

5. Let the finish dry to the touch. Remove the stencil, lifting it straight up off the surface.

If you stencil in different colors, let each color dry before you move onto another color. Drying time should be one week.

You also can buy special stencils tailormade to your needs. Look for this service at art and craft centers.

Working With Decals

Decal designs are paste-ons. They are similiar to stencils, but they are usually more refined in design and much easier to apply. Decals are best used on inexpensive furniture, such as Aunt Minnie's attic chairs, garage sale pieces, and unfinished furniture.

Basically, a decal is a printed plastic design stuck to a paper base with a water soluble adhesive. You clean the area where you want the decal with household detergent and water. Rinse. Then soak the decal in warm water until the adhesive gives way and the paper backing peels off. Pick up the decal and slide it into position on the furniture piece. Press down the decal with your fingers, working out the bubbles underneath the plastic film.

If the decal you have just applied is not on straight and you want to remove it for repositioning, wet it with warm water and remove it from the surface. Put the decal into warm water and soak it for a few seconds. You then can reapply the material with your fingers, squeezing out any bubbles as you go.

Decals are easily damaged if not protected. It is recommended that you coat the surface of the decal (and surrounding surface) with a quality clear varnish.

If you want to remove an old decal, don't try to scrape it off because you'll mar or damage the surface. Instead, buy a decal-removing strip. You soak this strip in warm water and press it over the decal. Wait 30 minutes—or according to the instructions printed on the remover strip. Give the strip plenty of time to work, like paint remover. Then peel off the remover strip. The decal will come with it.

Specialty Finishes

Touch-up finishes for chipped sinks, refrigerators, ranges, and so on, are called catalytic finishes. They are sold in most home centers and hardware stores, and by appliance dealers.

For the most part, these touch-up paints are true urethane or epoxy paints and often come in two parts: a resin and a hardener. You have to mix the two prior to application. The cost is not prohibitive, although the finish is expensive when you consider the small amount you get for your money. Once open, the containers are difficult to seal so you can't use the rest of the finish six months or a year later. Plan on just one application and junk the leftover.

The surface to which the catalytics are applied must be clean, rust-free, and dry. You apply the mixed material with a small artist-type brush. The finish is self-leveling, but it's best to feather-in the finish from the still-good surface to the chipped surface.

CHAPTER 19

Removing the Old Finish

■ IN THE EXTERIOR and interior painting sections of this book, we stated that 90 percent of any paint job is preparation of the surface. The same figure holds true for finishing and refinishing projects.

The finish you want will be only as good as the surface to which the finish is applied.

You can, of course, fake some finishes. You can beat the sap out of an unfinished furniture piece with a hammer or chain or a bunch of keys and call the piece "distressed." Or, you can just refinish a piece of furniture that already is distressed and call it an antique.

But for that fine, rich, deep finish on good wood or veneer, you will have to spend much time and effort. That's really the fun of it.

Stripping Off the Old Finish

Old finish—varnish, shellac or enamel—can be stripped off in three ways: with heat; with abrasive; with chemicals.

It's possible you may not have to use any of them. Before you even consider finish removal, try *cleaning* the furniture piece that you want to refinish. Dirt can hide a perfectly fine finish. You can remove this dirt with special cleaners sold at home centers, hardware stores, paint outlets, and some new furniture retailers. Give the cleaner plenty of time to work. In fact, you may have to go over the surface several times in order to remove the grime.

And before you start a refinishing project, ask yourself this question: Is the piece worth refinishing? You can spend a lot of time, effort and money on a piece of wood that really isn't worth it.

Of the finishes, shellac and lacquer are the easiest to remove. For shellac, make a pad of 00 steel wool and dip it in alcohol. Wear rubber gloves, and have plenty of ventilation. Simply rub the shellac surface with the alcohol-soaked steel wool in a circular fashion, and watch the finish disappear and the bare wood come into view. Lacquer finishes are removed in the same way, but you use lacquer thinner instead of alcohol.

Varnish and enamel are more difficult to remove. Before you buy the supplies and go to work, examine the piece carefully; you may not have to remove the finish if it is sound and tight on the surface. Just dull the finish, clean it, and recoat it.

The Strip Joints

If you live in or near a large town or city, you will find in the Yellow Pages a listing for "furniture stripping" establishments. These places are commonly called "strip joints."

The professionals that operate these joints use a chemical such as methylene chloride to remove the old finish. Your furniture piece usually is dipped into a vat of the chemical. The chemical is very powerful. In seconds the old finish is eaten away. The piece is then pulled from the vat and hosed clean. Only the bare wood now is showing.

Your cost for this service depends on the size of the furniture piece; a big piece costs more than a smaller one. The charges, however, are really not prohibitive.

This finish-removal process may be too harsh for a fine piece of furniture. However, the process is great for not-so-good furniture pieces that have multiple coats of finish on them.

There's one drawback: the harsh chemical used to remove the paint also may take the life out of the wood; natural oils that make the wood attractive may be leached out. And the chemical may damage glue joints.

The best approach is to visit a strip joint and watch the process. Then make a decision as to whether the furniture you want stripped will withstand the chemicals. Ask the owner or manager what he thinks you should do. He may well advise against using his service. He may even give you some ideas on how to remove the finish yourself.

Heat Removal

Paint and other finish may be removed with heat from a propane torch or an electric scraper. There are some pros and cons to using heat.

A propane torch will loosen the finish, but it can start small fires in the gobs of finish. The fires are not especially dangerous because you can quickly snuff them out. But the fire from the burning finish and the torch can scorch the wood causing damage that you'll never sand out. If you decide to use a torch, you will need a stiff-bladed puttyknife or 3-inch wall scraper to remove the softened finish. Expect the job to go slowly, and be prepared with a nearby bucket of water.

Electric scrapers or "hot" scrapers work fairly well on flat surfaces but not at all on curved or raised surfaces such as fancy moldings and trim pieces. The heat is not especially dangerous, but it can scorch the wood so lots of sanding is needed.

Most home center and hardware stores stock propane torches and removal accessories and electric scrapers; they are moderately expensive.

Recognize that heat from either a torch or electric scraper may be only moderately effective. Heat really works best on painted surfaces. It can be rated only fair on varnish, enamel, lacquer and shellac.

Lye Removal

To avoid discussion, we almost left out lye as a finish remover. But since you're likely to hear about it, we want to WARN you about using it.

Lye (the same stuff used to open clogged drains) will remove finish. In fact, it does a good job. But lye can also remove layers of your skin, burn your clothing, make you go blind, ruin wood, and kill the grass if it is used outdoors. The grass will not grow again in the area for years.

Ammonia Removal

Ammonia will remove milk paint, which is found on antique furniture. You may not want this paint off the piece for historical reasons.

On other finishes, ammonia tends to slightly soften the finish, but that's about all. It makes a very poor remover.

If you do decide to try ammonia, be sure there's plenty of ventilation, and wear a face mask and rubber gloves. Team the chemical with 00 steel wool and rub off the finish in a circular motion. Plan to spend plenty of time.

Removal by Abrasive

If you have lots of time and energy, you can remove finishes with sandpaper. The job can be done faster with a power sander. But a power sander can damage the wood if you are not extremely careful.

Here are some guidelines:
• If the finish is clear and thin on the surface, the best way to remove it is with paint and varnish remover. Or if the finish is shellac or lacquer (see below) you can use steel wool and alcohol or lacquer thinner.
• If the finish is thick, an orbital type portable electric sander will take it off fairly fast. Disc and belt sanders will take off the finish extremely fast, but *don't use either tool.* They are so fast cutting that you can go through veneers like lightning and ruin the piece. Even solid wood can be ruined by swirls and digs from power sanders.

Paint and Varnish Removers

The best way, in our opinion, to remove old paint and varnish is with one of the quality paint and varnish removers. If you have used these products in the past with limited success, don't be too quick to bypass them for another technique. The past problems probably were not the paint and varnish remover's fault; put the blame on *time*.

Newcomers to furniture refinishing often make the mistake of brushing paint remover on a surface to be refinished, letting the remover work for three or four minutes, and then scraping it off. The chemicals in the remover don't have time to work in this short period. The refinisher blames the product. Paint retailers get this complaint all the time.

Regardless of the type and quality of remover you buy, allow at least 25 minutes for the remover to work; 30 minutes is better yet.

In stores that sell it, you will be confronted by an array of paint and varnish removers on the shelves. All of them will remove paint and varnish to some degree, but there are differences.

Inexpensive paint removers, by and large, will soften paint and varnish, but the mixture may contain paraffin. If so, the paraffin, which is basically a wax, must be removed before any type of sealer or finish can be applied to the cleaned surface. Often, turpentine or mineral spirits will be necessary to remove the paraffin. So instead of getting a bargain paint and varnish remover you are adding to it the cost of a solvent to clean it off.

Make sure you check the label of any paint remover as to its flammability and toxicity. You always need proper ventilation when working with any remover—inexpensive or expensive, water-based or solvent-based.

Some of the more expensive removers also have a wax-type base, which is formulated to prevent the remover from evaporating quickly. This wax, also, must be removed before any finish is applied. Very expensive removers (as compared in price to the cheap ones) usually do not contain waxes. These products are the washable removers. The chemicals in them are especially emulsified so they will mix with water. When the surface is cleaned of old finish, you simply rinse off the debris with water for a clean surface. Well, almost a clean surface. Lots depends on the old finish and the thickness of the old finish as to how much comes off in a single rinsing.

If you do buy the washable removers, keep in mind that water is a natural enemy of wood and adhesives. Dry off the surface just as soon as you have rinsed it with water. We highly recommend that you do not use washable removers over veneered wood or wood that has been inlayed. Water can quickly bubble and warp such a piece, and it's nearly impossible to return it to its original condition. Stick with the solvent-based removers for these projects.

There are basically two types of paint and varnish removers:

1. Liquid removers that are thick—about the consistency of a milkshake.
2. Semi-paste removers that are about the consistency of butter.

The liquid removers are designed for flat, horizontal surfaces. The semi-paste removers are designed for vertical surfaces. Of course either type may be used on either surface.

Here's the way to save money:

Buy cheap paint remover and clean-up solvent for painted surfaces. Buy the expensive spread for varnishes and enamels.

Using Paint Remover

If you follow these rules when using paint and varnish remover you will save yourself some money and lots of scraping and clean-up time:

• Use plenty of paint remover. Don't skimp. Coverages are on container labels, and the figures are usually accurate. So buy accordingly. If you think that one quart will just about handle the project, buy an extra pint and save the cash register receipt. If you don't need the pint, the store will refund your money.

• Work outdoors if you can. If you can't, work where there is plenty of ventilation. Thickly cover the area where you work inside with newspaper. The best way is with newspaper over a plastic dropcloth. Do not use paint and varnish remover over a floor that is covered with asphalt, linoleum or rubber tile. The solvents in the remover, if spilled on these floor coverings, will ruin them almost immediately.

• Shake the remover in the can before you remove the cap. Pour a small amount in a coffee can or wide-mouth container. Do not pour the remover out of the can onto the object to be cleaned.

• Brush on the paint-removing chemical; don't wipe it on with a cloth. Use plenty of remover and spread it evenly with a throw-away brush. Once spread on the surface, *do not brush back over the surface*. Just let the remover set. The brush is used only to distribute the remover.

• After coating them with remover, cover the

surfaces with aluminum foil. Just lay the foil flat on horizontal surfaces and lightly fold it around vertical surfaces such as chair or table legs. The aluminum foil will help retard evaporation of the chemicals in the remover, permitting the remover to do a better job.

• Wait at least 20 to 30 minutes before you attempt to scrape off the softened paint or varnish. A good way to tell whether or not the remover is ready for scraping is to press a gloved finger in the remover and twist the fingertip in the solution. If you can bore down to bare wood easily, the remover is ready to be scraped. If not, let it set awhile.

• When the surface is ready, use a flexible scraper or putty knife for paint or varnish removal. We recommend that you file or grind the corners of the blade so they are slightly rounded. This will prevent sharp corners from digging into the wood as the scraper is pushed across surfaces.

• Use an old coffee can to hold the residue.

• On carvings, you can't use a scraper or putty knife. Instead, use a wire brush, toothbrush, steel wool, suede brush, or even a fiber scrub brush. However, do not scrub the carved surfaces with the bristles. Instead, try to flick off the softened finish. Flicking works better than scrubbing.

• On wood surfaces that have been filled with wood filler—you may have great difficulty removing the filler (and paint) from the pores of the wood. Oak is especially troublesome. A soft wire brush in a portable electric drill sometimes does a fast removal job. If not, you will just have to add more paint remover and use a wire brush or steel wool to clean such areas.

• If you are using a water-soluble remover, don't scrape the surface with a putty knife or scraper. Instead, dip 00 steel wool in clear water to remove the finish from the surface, then rinse the surface with water.

• If you are using a solvent type remover and then decide that you would rather use a water-based remover, finish one entire area with the solvent before you start on another area with the water-based remover. In short, don't mix the removers. One remover may not be compatible with the other remover, with the result that neither one will work.

• If you are using a solvent remover, clean the surfaces immediately with solvent when all of the old finish has been removed. Then put all residue and protective newspapers into a bucket, and place the bucket outside until you can dispose of it. These materials—especially in warm weather—can cause a fire through spontaneous combustion.

20

Preparing the Surface

■ ONCE THE OLD finish is stripped away, the wood will need further preparation before you start wiping, brushing or spraying.

All wood must be sanded after it has been cleaned. A medium to fine grit abrasive is standard, and always, without fail, use a sanding block on flat surfaces. Sand first with the grain and then at a slight angle against the grain.

Removing All Sanding Residue

Now, with a cloth or sponge, lightly moisten the wood with cold water. You don't want lots of water; just dampen the wood. The water will cause the grain to swell slightly. Once the grain is slightly raised, give the surface a final light sanding and apply the finish.

If the surfaces you'll sand are extremely delicate, such as fine inlays, use 000 or 0000 grade steel wool to smooth the raised grain.

Bleaching Wood

Bleaching removes stains. If the wood is not stained with rings and spots, don't bleach it. However, if the wood is blotchy, discolored, or stained with stain or filler, it often can be repaired with bleach.

Do not bleach:

Antiques

Inlays

Cherry

Satinwood

Think twice about bleaching:

Cedar

Bass

Chestnut

Redwood

Elm

Rosewood

Bleaching often helps:

Oak

Ash

Beech

Gum

Light-colored woods such as pine, birch and maple, seldom need bleach.

Bleach you buy in stores has a synthetic base that resembles oxalic acid, which you probably can't buy anymore because of local laws. These new wood bleaches may be in two parts. They are labeled "wood bleach" or "commercial wood bleach." Either is strong. Regular household bleach may do the job just as well as the commercial bleaches; it's worth a test to find out. Use it on a piece of scrap. If you buy a commercial bleach, you should also test it on scrap.

Any type of bleach will work very quickly on softwoods and somewhat slower on hardwoods. The chemicals in bleach are difficult to control. If the bleach is applied unevenly, the surface will lighten unevenly. An uneven surface color made by bleach is extremely difficult to retone.

CAUTION: Bleach like many chemicals can be toxic and harmful to your eyes and skin. When working with any bleach—even mild household bleach—wear rubber gloves and safety goggles. The work area should be well ventilated.

To apply bleach use a synthetic bristle brush (nylon, polyester, etc.). Bleach will ruin a pure bristle brush. Pour a small amount of bleach in a coffee or pie pan and apply it with the grain of the wood. The wood should be coated evenly and thoroughly; don't skimp, but don't drown the wood either.

Watch the surface as the bleach slowly begins to work. You will see dark spots lighten. When these spots are the color you want, rinse the surface with a borax solution mixed in clear, hot water. This will neutralize the bleach. As you bleach and rinse, try to get by with as little of the chemical and water as possible. In rinsing, work fast. When you're through, dry the wood with old toweling or something as absorbent. Get the water off the wood as quickly as you can.

Laundry bleach is a good product for lightening most woods and ridding them of stains. First, laundry bleach is an easy product to buy; you probably have some on hand right now. Second, the chemical is fairly mild so you won't run into too much trouble.

We recommend that you apply the bleach full-strength and evenly over the surface. If the spots or stains are in a small area, just bleach these areas and not the surrounding surfaces. As the stain lightens, wipe off the bleach residue. If, at this time, you still want the area lighter, add more bleach and control the chemical by wiping. With a cloth and bleach, you can almost color-tone the area. When you're finished, go over the *entire* surface with bleach. Wipe it off and neutralize the surface with 1 cup of borax mixed in 1 quart of hot water. Clean off this mixture with clean water, and wipe the surface as dry as possible.

Oxalic acid is poisonous, so you probably can't buy it. But you may find some tucked away on a shelf somewhere. If you do, make sure you wear rubber gloves, safety glasses, and have lots of ventilation. Mix a solution of 1 ounce of powder to 1 cup of warm water. Apply oxalic acid the same way as bleach. Let the acid work for 15 to 20 minutes and then wipe it off with a soft cloth. If the area is not bleached to your satisfaction, repeat the process. Neutralize the area with 1 cup of household ammonia to 2 quarts of water. Rinse off this solution with clean, cool water and dry the wood.

After bleaching with any solution, let the wood dry for about one week. Then lightly sand the wood with medium-grit abrasive, on a sanding block, with the grain of the wood. Then go over the surface lightly with 000 or 0000 steel wool. If there is a gray color on the surface, even (tone) this color with the steel wool. The finish will change the color when it is applied.

Working with Wood Filler

Ask an inexperienced clerk for wood filler and you may get a can of wood plastic, a glazing compound, a spackling compound, or some water putty.

What you're really after is a paste-like filler

Wood Fillers for Specific Woods

Filler not needed	Light filler	Medium filler	Heavy filler
Basswood	Alder	Butternut	Ash
Cedar	Beech	Mahogany	Chestnut
Cypress	Birch	Rosewood	Elm
Ebony	Cherry	Walnut	Hickory
Fir	Gum		Phil. Mahogany
Hemlock	Maple		Oak
Pine	Sycamore		Teak
Poplar			
Redwood			
Spruce			

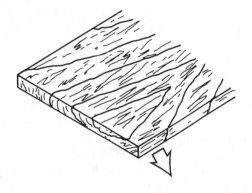

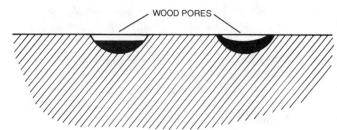

Open-grained woods such as walnut and mahogany and oak often are filled with paste wood filler that you can buy in paint, hardware, and home center stores. But you don't have to fill the pores. The purpose of the filler is to fill the pores so the surface of the wood can be sanded perfectly smooth to accept the finish.

WOOD PORES

Wood filler is brushed onto the surface of the wood across the grain of the wood, as illustrated. All the pores should be filled and the filler should dry before you continue on with the process. Brush the filler on evenly and smoothly—almost like paint. Avoid thick and thin spots, if possible. But most importantly, make sure that all the pores in the wood are filled.

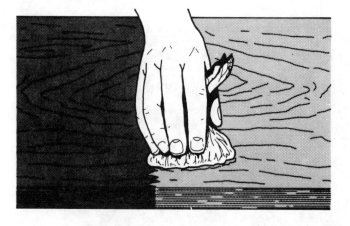

With rough toweling or burlap, wipe away the excess filler after it has dried. Wipe with the grain and then against the grain with the cloth pad. If the filler tends to lift up out of the pores, it is not yet dry enough for wiping. Leave it on the surface for another 10 minutes or so. When the surface has been wiped clean, check the wood pores. You may have to apply more filler.

that is called, simply, "paste wood filler." This material is used to fill open-grained wood: oak, walnut, mahogany and others. The primary purpose of wood filler is to fill the open pores so the surface of the wood is even and level. It provides a smooth finishing job.

Wood fillers are made from a silica base and oil. Fillers are neutral in color. When you open the container it will look off-white and have the consistency of heavy paste. If you apply this neutral color filler to a wood that also is a neutral color, you probably will hide the grain, which you probably don't want to hide. Therefore, on light woods, you may want to color the filler a bit with stain, so the grain is accented.

As a general rule, wood filler is colored with the color of the stain used on the wood. To mix this, use equal parts of filler with equal parts of stain over stained wood. Or thin the filler with equal parts mineral spirits or turpentine for an uncolored filler on wood that has no stain.

Filler is applied with a brush. Or, you may want to use a rubber sponge or squeegee. As the filler is applied it will look shiny. Wait about 10 minutes or so for this shine to dull. When it does, it's time to wipe off the excess filler with a cloth, or better, burlap. Wipe the filler across the grain of the pores. Make a thick pad of the wiping cloth so you have plenty of bearing surface that remains flat. The idea is to have the pores filled and the surface level.

If, after the first application of filler and thorough wiping, you see that the pores of the wood are not completely filled, you probably have not left the filler on long enough before wiping. As you wiped, the still-wet filler was pulled up by the wiping cloth. Go back over the surface once again with the filler and allow more drying time.

Other troubles may include small pinholes in the filler and a hazy-looking, almost cloudy, surface film. Pinholes are caused by the filler being wiped too soon. The hazy surface is caused by not rubbing the surface hard and long enough or rubbing the surface after the filler dried completely. If the filler has hardened on the surface, you can soften and remove it with mineral spirits. Then repeat the filling process.

Let the filler dry at least 36 hours (after it has been wiped and the surface is clean) before you start sanding. Use a sanding block on flat surfaces; a medium to fine-grit paper is about right. After sanding, remove all the residue and apply the finish.

Special Spot Problems

You may notice spots in the wood not caused by water or alcohol. Such spots may be ink stains, grease spots made by a lubricant such as motor oil, or vegetable-oil stains. There are other types of stains, of course, but these are the most frequent.

To remove ink, use ammonia. Spread the ammonia over the surface with a small brush in the direction of the wood grain. Then thoroughly wipe the spot clean with a soft cloth. Rinse with clear water and dry completely.

To remove grease, use either dry-cleaning fluid that you can buy in drug and grocery stores, or mineral spirits. Apply either chemical with a brush in the direction of the wood grain. Then wipe the area dry. Rinse with clear water and dry.

To remove vegetable oil, use acetone applied with a small brush. Wipe up the excess with a cloth; rinse the area with clean water and dry thoroughly.

Cleaning Hardware

Sometimes very expensive cabinet hardware such as brass has been painted over. You don't see its beauty except by accident. Often such hardware is especially designed for that piece of furniture. Before you junk *any* hardware, drop the pieces in a can of paint remover. Let the remover work for 30 minutes or so, and rub the metal with 00 steel wool. You may find a real treasure under that guck.

Wooden knobs and pulls are easier to refinish if you remove them from the piece, soak them in paint remover, and remove the old finish pull by pull and knob by knob. If the hardware is damaged, replace it. Also, hardware that is the wrong style for the piece can spoil the looks of a fine refinishing job.

What Wood Used Where?

Identifying woods is difficult enough when the wood hasn't been refinished. Refinished or finished woods are almost impossible to identify because a stain can make the wood appear to be a species that it isn't.

Below, we've compiled a list of various wood species, some of their characteristics, and where each is commonly used in furniture-making. You never can be 100 percent sure, but the clues may give you some idea so you can make a finishing or refinishing decision.

White ash is a hardwood often used for furniture parts that are curved or bent. The species is open-grained. It takes stain and bleach well, but it also looks good when clear-finished. In the raw, ash is white to gray or has a brownish cast that runs toward the reddish brown in color tone.

Bass. Look for this hardwood species in combination with walnut, mahogany, teak and cherry. Bass is close-grained and straight-grained. It varies greatly in color from white to dark brown or even red. When stained properly, bass can very closely resemble cherry, mahogany or walnut. Even the pros have difficulty identifying it.

Yellow birch is a hardwood frequently used on interior doors. It can and often does pass for maple; the color runs about the same as maple. Birch is close-grained. It takes stain well. Because of its grain pattern, it can be stained and will pass for cherry. Birch is quite hard and can be difficult to work with hand tools.

Butternut. Another fooler, butternut is a hardwood that sometimes is believed to be walnut. Properly stained, it looks like walnut even to the dark and reddish streaks. This species has open pores so it has to be filled—again a characteristic of walnut.

Cedar. This wood is frequently used for outdoor furniture. Inside, it is used as a chest and closet liner. In fact, many home center stores sell it in closet-lining kits. The wood really can't pass for redwood because of the smell. Just nick a piece of cedar with a knife and you'll smell the lead-pencil odor. Cedar is close-grained, and a softwood. Do not bleach or stain it.

Cherry is an extremely valuable hardwood. You won't find it for sale in the run-of-the-mill home center stores or building material outlets. Look for it in specialty shops. Also look for it under a varnish or enamel finish on an old piece of junk furniture at garage sales and in your Aunt Frieda's attic. Cherry in color ranges from a light brown to a dark red-brown. It has a mottled grain. The species is close-grained and doesn't require a filler. The wood, almost without saying, shouldn't be covered with an opaque finish. Rather it should be finished with a clear finish. You can use a *very light* cherry stain on raw wood to help highlight it. Do not bleach cherry.

Elm is a hardwood that the Dutch bugs have almost destroyed. In its heyday it was used for almost all types of furniture, especially where the designs called for bent wood. The species is open-grained; it ranges in color from a light to dark brown with red streaks. The pros often stained elm to resemble mahogany or walnut. Because it is now relatively rare, the species has become somewhat valuable. The grain now is left to show under clear finishes. Elm is another wood—like cherry—that you'll find under coats of paint on furniture considered junk.

Gum is plentiful so it is used as a veneer core for expensive cabinetwoods. It is brown with a slight red cast. The species is close-grained and takes an oak, maple, mahogany and cherry stain very well.

Hickory is as hard as Andrew Jackson. It is an open-grained wood. Look for it in bent woods used for rocking chairs and lawn furniture. It sometimes is used as a cabinetwood veneer. In color, it runs from brown to reddish brown with a very straight grain. You can compare hickory with oak for hardness and durability.

Lauan is a hardwood and often is sold as Philippine mahogany because of its color: tan to brownish and dark red. Its grain pattern is like that of mahogany (ribbonish) and the open-grain pores are usually filled before finishing. You will pay more for red lauan than its white cousin; the wood is plentiful and not too costly.

Mahogany, like cherry, is a rare wood today and it is used only for very expensive furniture pieces. The hardwood is open-grained and varies from brown to deep reddish brown and dark red. Never bleach or stain mahogany, except to lightly stain the wood (very, very lightly) with walnut color. The stain will tend to highlight the grain.

Maple is similar to birch with a light brown color and a red cast. It is close-grained and straight with patterns of curls and waves and "birdseyes." Maple shouldn't be stained, but finished clear. However, sometimes you can get a better grain identification by very lightly staining it with a walnut or mahogany stain. Try the stain on a piece of scrap or where it won't show before you make a full commitment. Maple is used basically in case pieces and tables.

Oak is plentiful, and therefore is a common wood for furniture making. It is open-grained and generally filled, but not always. White oak has a grayish brown tone; red oak has a pronounced reddish cast that you can't miss. The wood is as "strong as oak" and can be difficult to work.

Pecan is a southern hardwood species that is used extensively in furniture. To the untrained eye, it could be passed off as a light teak. The wood is close-grained and varies in color from a palish brown to a red brown with dark streaks. A great deal of pecan veneer is used in office furniture. It is somewhat difficult to work this wood with hand tools, but no trouble with power tools.

Pine. Pine is a staple. There is plenty of it available, so it is relatively inexpensive. Contrary to common belief it is a beautiful wood. It takes stain easily and you can make pine look like the most expensive hardwood. But don't overlook pine as a beautiful wood all by itself. Colonial furniture was fashioned from pine, and pine is used today for most modern furniture, although you may not know it as pine. It varies in color from a cream to a yellowish-brown.

Redwood is similar to cedar in that it resists rot and therefore is used for outdoor furniture. It is a softwood and extremely easy to work. Redwood has a deep reddish color.

Rosewood is a hardwood and is one of the finest species money can buy. But you need plenty of money to buy it: it's very expensive. It is open-grained and varies from red-brown to purple in color. Frequently there are black streaks running through the grain. It usually is filled but never stained. You may find it under layers of paint or enamel in an attic or garage sale but only in furniture pieces such as cases and tables.

Satinwood is a hardwood that is close-grained. It should never be bleached or stained. You'll most likely find it used for decorative inlays and as a veneer on a lumber or plywood core. Satinwood runs from a golden yellow to a dark yellow-brown. It's grain is mottled and ribbon-like. When finished with an oil or satin clear finish, satinwood actually has the look and feel of satin cloth. Hence the name.

Teak went through its popular phase several years ago as a furniture wood from Norway and Sweden. It's still popular, but the cost is almost prohibitive except for veneers, inlays and special applications. If you are looking for solid teak, look for furniture pieces that were constructed in the mid-1950s. Teak is a hardwood that varies in color from a golden-yellow to a dark brown. Its grain, which is open, includes both dark and light streaks. We recommend that you do not stain teak. Finish it with oil.

Walnut has been used for fine furniture for hundreds of years. It's still used, but usually in veneer form because walnut trees don't grow fast enough to meet the current demand. Walnut is a chocolate brown with a dark or purple look—especially in the streaks of the grain.

Sycamore is plentiful and therefore is used often in inexpensive furniture. It also is a popular veneer wood. Sycamore runs from a pink to a red-brown color. It is close-grained. The wood seldom is stained by the pros, but it can be bleached and clear-coated to a rich finish.

Poplar is popular as an inexpensive hardwood used for furniture and unfinished furniture. Furniture makers often use it as back-up for veneers, case piece backs and drawer bottoms. Poplar is brown-yellow with green streaks. It is close grained and takes stain very well. That's why the furniture makers like it: it can be disguised to look like walnut, cherry and oak.

21

Tools and Equipment

■ A DESCRIPTION OF the tools that are available for working with wood, finishing it, refinishing it and repairing it, would fill a book many times this size.

If you are like most woodworking buffs, you'll find yourself actually making tools yourself to do special jobs. There is considerable innovation in the use of refinishing tools. A simple example is using a kitchen food scraper to remove old finish stuck in nooks and crannies. And the end of an unbent paperclip makes a fairly good pick for removing finish from cracks.

In this section we're listing some of the basic tools and materials that you will need. Let it serve as a checklist.

Hammers

For woodworking, a 13-ounce claw hammer is considered "general purpose." It's easier to swing than a 16-ounce hammer and it will deliver strong enough blows for most projects that you will undertake when finishing and refinishing. This hammer definitely should be teamed with a rubber or wooden mallet; we'd opt for the wooden mallet because it doesn't bounce like a rubber one. The very best buy in mallets is a dead-blow or rawhide mallet. The dead-blow mallet is filled with lead shot. It provides a "dead-blow" feeling when struck—no bounce. The rubber mallet is the least expensive, the dead-blow and rawhide are the most expensive. Shop around for these mallets: There are bargains to be found, especially at garage sales and auctions.

Depending on your projects, other specialty hammers you may need will include ballpeen hammers for metal-working and tack hammers for upholstery. A cross-peen hammer is a good replacement for a 13-ounce hammer because it has a flat face for heavy hitting and a little peen face for tight quarters. It may be difficult to locate this hammer, but a good hardware dealer can order it for you.

Saws

For big cutting jobs, such as sizing plywood panels, a power saw is the best buy. For jobs other than this, you'll need just a few fairly inexpensive handsaws, which almost any home center or hardware store stocks. These saws are: backsaw or cabinet saw, hacksaw, coping saw, and possibly a fretsaw, which is similar to a coping saw.

Most of these tools have a power counterpart. But you should minimize the use of power because most of your projects will be small and best worked with hand tools.

A backsaw and cabinet saw are similar. Backsaws are generally used in miter boxes. A backsaw has a stiff metal spline so the saw isn't whippy, and therefore makes straight cuts. The backsaws have a regular handsaw type handle; cabinet saws have a straight grip handle. Teeth on a backsaw or cabinet saw range from 14 to 16 (or more) per inch. This number provides a smooth cut compared to a ripsaw, for example, which has 5 teeth per inch. Back and cabinet saws can be used for both crosscutting and ripping; thin blades permit narrow saw kerfs, which are needed in making and repairing furniture pieces.

A hacksaw is a metal saw but you can use it for woodworking. The blade is very thin, which is excellent for narrow saw kerfs; the teeth produce a fine cut, similar to and sometimes even better

Metal angle brackets for corners are packaged with some strap clamps. With them, you can form a tight grip on boxes and other square objects while the glue dries. The corners are reversible so they can be slipped over corners and held in place while you get the strap part of the clamp wrapped around the object.

Strap clamps are not inexpensive, but they are worth the price when irregular surfaces have to be held tightly while adhesive dries. They work similar to an auto seat belt; a clamp holds the pulled strap tight; a small lever releases the pressure with the flick of a finger.

A ratchet on the adjusting lever of the strap clamp lets you apply plenty of pressure via a wrench, which also comes with most strap clamps. Be careful you don't turn the ratchet too tight. It can produce enough pressure to crush wood.

Spring clamps look like big clothespins and are excellent for clamping down loose veneer while adhesive sets. The spring clamps are available in an assortment of sizes. The large ones produce so much clamping pressure that it takes two hands to open them. Prices vary to the size of the clamp: from inexpensive to expensive.

than a cabinet or backsaw. Hacksaws are designed to cut on the forward stroke, so set the blade in the frame so the teeth point forward. However, this rule is not cast in bronze. The blade may be reversed if pulling the saw through the work is easier for you than pushing it.

For scroll work, a coping saw is the best tool. You'll find yourself making straight cuts as well as fancy ones with this tool. The blade can be mounted to cut either on the forward or the backward stroke, whichever is most comfortable for you. Most woodworkers like the push stroke better than the pull stroke. At the edges of the coping saw frame you will find two pins. These pins can be moved so you can turn the blade once the blade is into the wood and you want to change the direction of your cut.

Handsaw Counterparts

If you opt for power equipment, the counterpart of a backsaw and cabinet saw is a circular saw with a hollowground or plane-type blade. The blades are thick, compared to handsaw blades, so the widths of saw kerfs are always a consideration.

The counterpart of a coping saw is a sabresaw or bench jigsaw. The sabresaw is a hand-held power tool, so accuracy of the cut is only as good as your hand. The jigsaw is a more practical power tool and very closely duplicates cuts made with its coping saw cousin. A bandsaw, also a stationary power tool, makes a good teammate for a power jigsaw. It may be somewhat limited in scroll-type cuts because of the width of the sawblade.

Scrapers

Scrapers are the basic finishing/refinishing tools. And you can buy them almost anywhere tools are sold, including grocery and drugstores. Quality varies, however. But quality isn't always that important in this tool. Some of the cheapie scrapers cost so little that they can be classed with throw-away brushes. They are just as good for removing old finish as the more expensive models.

For general finishing/refinishing projects your

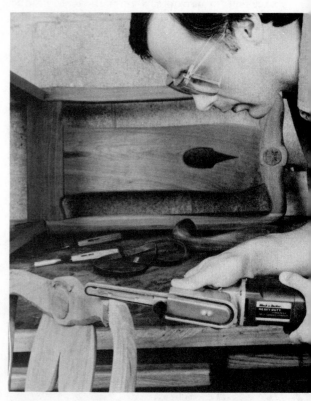

A newcomer on the finishing/refinishing market is a file sander/grinder combination that shapes wood, smooths it, removes old finishes, and so on. It is powered by a small electric motor. Buy this tool for your shop if you are a furniture maker as well as a refinisher. It works wonders and is worth the investment in our opinion. In action, the tool handles somewhat like a portable light-weight belt sander.

tool assortment should include a good putty knife, pull scraper or cabinet-type scraper (they're similar), a double-cut metal file, some pieces of flat glass (window pane), and a box of single-edge razor blades that can be used as scrapers. We recommend that you buy both a stiff and a flexible putty knife. You can use the stiff-bladed one as a scraper in narrow spaces where a wide scraper won't go. The flexible blade is better for pressing fillers into wood.

A cabinet or furniture scraper is a bit different from a regular pull scraper, but both will remove old finish. Since a cabinet scraper is a bit "finer," you'll want it for wood removal, and the pull scraper for finish removal. The key to any scraper is a sharp blade that is not nicked or ragged. To keep the blade sharp you'll need a double-cut metal file. Buy a 10-incher with handle, and use it often. A dull scraper blade can ruin any work. It can also be dangerous.

A broken piece of flat glass makes an excellent scraper to remove finish or wood. In fact, glass, in our opinion, is on par with a cabinet scraper. The only difference is that a cabinet scraper will remove finish or wood from large areas while glass should be confined to the smaller ones. CAUTION: Always wear gloves and safety glasses when using flat glass as a scraper.

Single-edge razor blades can be used as finish scrapers and wood removers, but only in small areas. You sort of flick off finish and wood with them, rather than pulling or pushing them along the surface as you would a regular scraper.

Other scraping tools include almost anything that can be moved over a surface to clean off the finish or remove wood. For example, an old saw blade with the teeth filed off makes an excellent cabinet scraper. So does a kitchen spatula, an old case knife, a paring knife, jackknife, butt chisel, screwdriver, metal-edge ruler, scissor blade—almost anything you can improvise.

Planes

The first one you'll need is a block plane. It is ideal for smoothing end grain and it can be used on edges. A smoothing plane with its long bed is really better than a block plane for edges because it provides a better bearing surface to keep the wood square. We suggest that you buy quality planes and let the inexpensive ones stay in the store. You can quickly see the difference between the two. The more expensive models will keep a cutting edge longer, they are more easily adjusted for thin cuts, they are, as a rule, more accurate.

Other woodworking planes include rabett, dado and jack planes, and drawknives and spokeshaves. These are speciality tools for serious woodworkers; they are not usually sold in home centers and hardware stores, but you will almost always find them in craftsman stores.

Power-tool counterparts of planes are portable electric sanders, molders, routers, planers, jointers, and hobby-type drills with smoothing attachments. The best all-around buy in this category would be a jointer, which is a stationary power tool and fairly costly. The jointer is so precise that you can edge-plane two boards and butt-joint and glue them.

Screwdrivers

You will need two basic ones: a standard slot and a Phillips head. Both screwdrivers come in

Adhesives For Repairing Furniture Pieces			
Type	**Dry Time**	**Use on**	**You Should Know . . .**
Aliphatic resin	Superfast	Wood	It's water-resistant and will withstand the solvents used in lacquer.
Casein	Medium	Plastic, metal, glass, fabrics	It dries clear. Fair to good water and heat resistance.
Animal/fish	Slow	Wood and paper	Gets brittle and weak when old. Little resistance to water and heat.
Thermosetting	Medium	Wood, paper, and most fabrics	Adhesive is stain-resistant.
Epoxy	Medium to fast	Wood and metal	Epoxy has extremely good holding qualities. It won't shrink. Some epoxies are two-part systems that must be mixed before application.
Contact	Fast	Plastic laminates; wood veneers	Generally used to install plastic laminate to kitchen countertops. Two types: water and solvent vehicle. Have plenty of ventilation when using contact. If solvent type, be careful of fire.

A "flap" sander comes in a kit. It has metal prongs that sort of remove finish and wood by "flapping" it off the surface. The wheel does a good job—even a tad better than a wire wheel and is excellent for removing paint and wood from small areas.

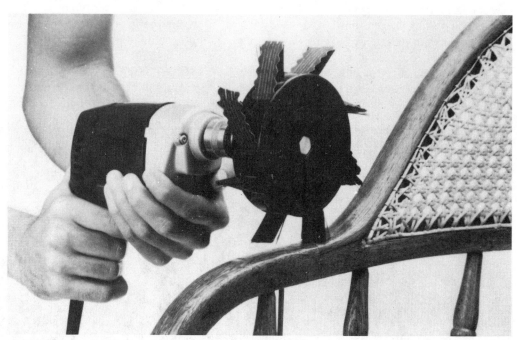

The flapper is teamed with a portable electric drill. The sanding strips are fine, medium, and coarse, and sell for under $5. The kit sells for about $16. Be sure you wear safety glasses when you use this equipment.

Power Sanders: What to Use and What *Not* to Use in Finishing Projects

Type	Recommended?	You Should Know . . .
Belt	No	Belt sanders are fast-cutting and can go through veneer layers like lightning. This tool is best used for removing lots of excess wood. It has a straight-line sanding pattern.
Disc	No	Fast cutting; leaves swirls in wood and on metal. Okay on end grain and removing lots of excess wood. Does a fair job on metal, but watch for swirling.
In-line	Yes	This is a slow-cutting tool which may be used on veneer and solid wood. However, easy does it; it can gouge surfaces and make them uneven if the sander isn't kept in constant motion.
Orbital	Yes	Moves in a circular pattern (orbital). It's faster-cutting than an in-line sander and can produce tiny circular swirls in wood and metal materials. Does a top job, however, when teamed with a muscle-powered sanding block after initial sanding has been completed.

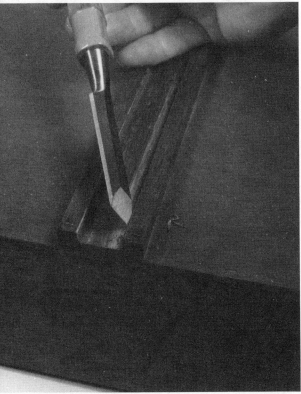

A butt chisel assortment is a must for furniture finishers and for general purpose home maintenance and improvement projects. Sticking drawer guides are very quickly loosened by removing a shaving or two with a chisel. Also include a wooden mallet with the chisel purchase.

A sliding T-bevel tool is really not necessary in your shop unless your projects call for duplicating lots of angles, such as slats that form backs of chairs. By turning a wing nut, you can set the metal straight edge to the angle that you want. The handle serves as the base point. Like a sliding T-bevel, a compass and divider is not often used for furniture repair. But if your budget permits, these are good tools to include. You'll use them.

various sizes and shapes. Since screwdrivers are not too costly you may want to invest in an assortment.

From a power standpoint, you move up to a hand brace with a screwdriver bit; a crank drill with a screwdriver bit; a portable electric variable-speed drill (reversing) with a screwdriver bit that will both drive and draw screws. There is one advantage to the power drivers: Most of them can be outfitted with drill bits and other accessories which makes them multipurpose. But still you will need plain old screwdrivers to start with.

Chisels

Buy an assortment of butt chisels first. You will always use them, if not for furniture repairs and finishing or refinishing, then for many home maintenance and improvement projects. The best all-around butt chisel assortment includes blades of these sizes: ⅛, ¼, ½, and ¾ inch.

Add to this collection:

A firmer chisel with a ½-inch beveled edge. A firmer chisel is designed to go into corners.

An in- and an out-channeled gouge. These tools are excellent for smoothing, planing, removing old finish, and cutting inside and outside curves in wood.

Sandpaper, or abrasive, is as important in wood finishing and refinishing as scrapers and paint remover. To properly cut sandpaper, run an artist or utility knife along the back of the paper, as shown. This produces a sharp edge that you don't get by folding and creasing the paper and tearing it with your fingers. An abrasive chart can be found in the front of the book for selection.

Adhesives play an important role in finishing, refinishing, and woodworking. The store shelves are full of all types (a selection chart on Page 000 will help you determine what product to buy). For all-around gluing purposes, we recommend White Glue which goes on white but dries clear. But be sure to match the adhesive to the job. White glue won't work on all surfaces such as plastic. Most glues are not thermalset, but go on surfaces right out of the container.

A 1-inch butt chisel. The ¾-inch one will do the same job, but it takes longer.

Most chisels, of course, must be driven with a mallet and not a steel hammer. If, however, the chisel has a metal insert in the handle, you can use a metal hammer to drive it.

Power counterparts to chisels are routers and molders, but only in a broad sense. For example, you can cut a mortise with a router and template. You can also cut a groove with a router or molder, which is a stationary router. But as a rule you can't make those fine paring cuts without a chisel.

Clamps

Clamps are as important to furniture-making and repair jobs as scrapers are to refinishing jobs. We suggest that you buy an assortment of C-clamps, and add several bar clamps and at least one strap clamp.

C-clamps fit the name; the clamps are in the shape of a C. There are various shapes and sizes (regular, deep throat, etc.) in a variety of metals (aluminum, steel, alloy). Always buy two of the same size clamps. They often are used in pairs.

A strap clamp is what the name implies: a cloth or plastic strap that is fitted with a clamping device similar to the seat belt in your car or on an airplane. The beauty of a strap clamp is that it goes around irregular objects, such as the splayed legs of a chair. Most of the strap-clamp kits have special metal fittings that go on corners, making the clamp a miter clamp.

Miter clamps have jaws at right angles and work with a turnscrew, similar to a C-clamp. Miter clamps are basically designed for assembling picture frames and small boxes.

Bar clamps are for large objects, such as edge-gluing boards for a table top. You will use them often in refinishing furniture since most case pieces and tops need regluing before the finish is applied. Pipe clamps are similar to bar clamps. Pipes fit brackets (which are packaged separately) in ½- and ¾-inch pipe dimensions. Most hardware and home-center stores sell these brackets, along with large assortments of C-clamps and other clamping devices.

Spring clamps look like big clothespins and are used for light fabrication and gluing down separated veneers on furniture pieces. Like other clamps, you can buy them in a range of sizes. A small, medium and perhaps large spring clamp are useful from time to time.

You can innovate clamping devices. A bucket of paint, for example, can be used to weight (clamp) a laminate to a piece of wood or metal. You can use an adjustable wrench as a clamp; a vise makes an excellent clamping device, but be careful not to use too much pressure. Even masking tape and rubber bands may be used as clamps.

Sanding Equipment

In refinishing and finishing work, sandpaper—or abrasive as the manufacturers like to call it—is a vital tool and one that you will use continually. A complete listing of abrasive types and grits can be found elsewhere in this book.

Sanding devices include power sanders, metal strippers, and even sanding-sealers. For most of the jobs that you'll tackle, you will need just a piece of wood for a sanding block (1×3×4) or a fancier sanding block made of plastic, metal or rubber. You can, of course, use sandpaper without a block, but we strongly recommend that you use sandpaper on a block when sanding flat surfaces. Power sanders will make your work easier, but power sanders cut so fast that you must be extremely careful or you can ruin a piece.

Walk into any hardware store or hardware department of a home center outlet and you'll be greeted with an array of sanding devices, or de-

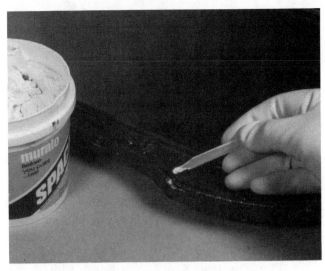

Spackling compound—pre-mixed—is a finishing repair material that can be used to patch many holes and reform fancy moldings. The pre-mixed material is stiff enough so you can form it with your fingers, press it into position, and then sculpture it with a pointed ice cream stick, knife, or artist's pallet knife.

vices that can be used for sanding and smoothing. In some situations, files and rasps can serve as sanders. One manufacturer makes a flat and curved file-like plane that takes off finish fast. There are sanding attachments galore: wheels and brushes for drills; abrasive cones and vertical shafts designed for sharpening metal, but which can be used to remove both wood and finish.

Glue Injectors

It looks like a hypodermic syringe for a horse, but it's really a glue injector that forces adhesive into loose furniture joints and other out-of-the way places. You also can buy glue guns that, through a heating element, melt cartridges of stick glue and direct the adhesive right where you want it without brushing.

Utility Knives

Buy two utility knives and a couple of packages of spare blades.

Pliers

Regular slip-joint pliers are used often in furniture work. So are needlenose pliers and the locking type.

Wrenches

An adjustable wrench is the best buy. It will fit most nuts you have to turn in furniture refinishing. A socket set is nice to have, but not really necessary. Open and box-end wrenches are handy.

Special Tools

Special tools are really not special. They're the ones that we have innovated that may help you, too:
• A plastic credit card makes an excellent tool to remove wood filler. So does the edge of a playing card.
• You can fill edge grain with filler or wood putty with a putty knife. A better tool is your index finger. It does a faster, smoother job.
• A pointed can opener is an excellent crack scraper.
• Apply pumice and rottenstone with a salt shaker.
• A long fireplace match with rosin stuck on the end of it makes an excellent lint picker.
• To strike off the excess finish on a varnish or lacquer brush, drive a nail through a tin can. Use the nail as the strike. The excess finish runs to the bottom of the can and can be poured back into the prime container from time to time.
• A glass pie pan makes a better container to hold paint remover than a coffee can. When you are finished with it, the pan can be cleaned and used for pies once again.
• Artist's pallet knives make wonderful tools for applying wood fillers and some finishes in tight quarters. They are excellent for smoothing melted shellac produced by a shellac stick.

Finishing Materials

The best way to buy finishing materials—varnish, enamel, shellac, and so on—is as you need them for specific projects. However, your shop should contain some staples—those materials that you will use frequently. Some of them will come in handy for chores other than refinishing.
• Household bleach. A good stain remover as well as a wood bleach.
• Plastic wood. A wood patch and also a hole filler for kitchen cabinets, molding and trim.
• Wood putty.
• Masking tape. It's associated with paint, but there are lots of other jobs it will do. Wrapping packages is one of them.
• Glue.
• Denatured alcohol. It can be used for removing some stains.
• Lacquer thinner. A good solvent for cleaning grease and oil.

• Paint remover.
• Linseed oil.
• Turpentine.
• Paste wax for almost all furniture finishes.
• Black wire.
• An assortment of nuts, bolts and washers.
• Abrasives.
• Mineral oil.
• White flat paint.
• Throw-away paintbrushes.

Special Help

You may somewhere along the line in finishing and refinishing projects encounter a problem that this book doesn't answer, or paint-store personnel can't solve. Below is a list of finishing product manufacturers that may be able to help. The manufacturers are picked without preference. They represent a cross section of finish producers that are known to be helpful to the do-it-yourselfer and non-professional. When writing, address your correspondence to the Public Information Director:

Minwax Co.
72 Oak
Clifton, NJ 07015

Formby Products Co.
Richardson-Merril Company
PO Box 667
Olive Branch, MI 38654

Deft, Inc.
Irvine, CA 92714

The Flecto Company, Inc.
Flecto International, Ltd.
Oakland, CA 94608

Watco-Dennis Corp.
1756 Twenty-Second Street
Santa Monica, CA 90404

Roberts Consolidated Industries
600 N. Baldwin Park Blvd.
City of Industry, CA 91749

Illinois Bronze Co.
Lake Zurich, IL 60047

Enterprise Paint Co.
Wheeling, IL 60090

CHAPTER 22

A New Look for Wood Floors

■ WOOD FLOORING went out of fashion some years ago because it cost too much. Carpeting was, simply, less expensive to install than wood, so builders used it to lower housing costs and prices. Indications are that wood floors are reappearing because cost, prorated over many years, favors wood over fabric. If you are installing a new floor, wood-strip flooring is still available, although expensive. If you just pulled back the living room carpeting and discovered a wood-strip floor underneath, you've found a prize indeed.

Wood-strip flooring is only one possibility. A second might be real wood parquet blocks or tiles; most of these products, including some strip flooring, are prefinished at the factory. The overall cost of these materials is usually slightly lower than that of unfinished strip flooring because the manufacturers can use shorter, and therefore less expensive, pieces of wood to fabricate the tiles. And, prefinishing hides wood blemishes (the finish most often is a dark color) that less desirable wood grades highlight. A big advantage of prefinished flooring is that no finishing is required after it is installed. Properly cared for, a prefinished floor will last the life of the house without needing refinishing.

If you buy and install a new wood-strip floor—prefinished tile and strips aside—your basic wood choices will be oak, maple, or pine. Similarly, if your home already has wood-strip flooring, the wood is most likely one of the above.

The finishing and refinishing techniques for all three species are almost identical, and you have a choice of wood-floor finishes from which to choose. Many home center stores and hardware outlets sell floor finishes. But if you have no luck at these establishments, try a flooring contractor who specializes in installing and finishing wood flooring. Chances are that you can buy a finishing product here. You'll find these craftspeople listed in the advertising pages of the telephone book under *Flooring Contractors.*

What's the Best Finish?

We're not trying to be diplomatic when we say that there are several "best" finishes. There are several good ones that rate about the same according to our tests and surveys. Here's what we've learned from our own experience and that of other refinishers.

A quality penetrating wood finish, in our opinion, is the best finish for wood flooring and probably the easiest for the do-it-yourselfer to apply and to repair after it has been scuffed or damaged. As with any wood, the penetrating finishes seal the surface, and, with resin formulas, "harden" the wood to make it extremely resistant to dings and digs. As discussed earlier, in the chapter on wood finishes, penetrating formulas penetrate the wood fibers fairly deeply, whereas pigmented finishes or even some of the clear finishes "lie" on top of the wood surface. Therefore, for floors, the wood has to wear down below the finish line before any bare wood will be exposed, and this can take years and years. A surface type finish, on the other hand, becomes worn-looking fast and damages more easily because the top layers are always extremely thin.

There are other finishes besides penetrating finishes. Our choices, in order, would be the following.

Polyurethane. The manufacturers have done a great deal with this finish over the past few years so the finish is less "delicate" to apply, and gives good results. You can buy this material in several gloss grades (gloss or semigloss, for instance), and application is about as easy as mopping the prepared floor with a roller. You may need several coats to get the results you want. Even so, the work is worth it.

Shellac. Shellac is used by many to finish floors probably because it is inexpensive, dries very quickly, has some penetrating qualities, and is easy to repair if it does become damaged. Shellac, all in all, wears fairly well on flooring, except in very high-traffic or hard-usage areas such as in doorways or on stair treads. The finish is not resistant to water or other liquids, however, and the surface must be waxed continually to protect the shellac base. You shouldn't use it, for example, on a floor that adjoins a swimming pool/patio area. In areas with high humidity, the surface sometimes can become tacky to the touch if it has been misapplied. But in general, shellac behaves about the same on wood floors as it does on furniture: The finish can be rubbed to a deep, rich color that you will be proud to show off.

Varnish. This is still a good choice and really is a toss-up for second place. You can get some penetration with this finish if you thin the varnish slightly before you apply the prime or sealer coat to raw wood. Use about 10 percent turpentine or mineral spirits for thinning. Varnish on floors tends to chip. Even though there is some penetration, a chip usually means exposure to the bare wood and a necessary repair. Patching requires sanding, "feathering" the surrounding finish, spot priming, and finish coating. Some varnishes for floors are advertised as "gym floor varnishes." These products are more wear-resistant than regular varnishes basically because they are thicker on the wood surface. The drawback is that gym finishes (as well as some other varnish finishes) tend to yellow with age (see chapter on finishes). Unlike quick-drying shellac, varnishes take *at least* 24 hours to dry. This brings up an air-borne lint and dirt problem. Drying time of all finishes, however, can vary depending on the temperature and humidity in the room at the time the finish was applied. You can get some idea of drying, curing, and recoating time from the instruction label on the finish can.

Lacquer. Lacquer floor finishes dry like lightning, but they can be very difficult to apply for the same reason. We have found that lacquers wear about the same as varnishes. The finish is easier to patch than varnish, and this is a plus.

Oil-modified. These are really urethane varnishes, and you probably can find them at many paint stores. However, phone first. You may have to go to a store that caters to the floor finishing and refinishing trade. If you are a first-time floor finisher/refinisher, read the labels carefully and check with the dealer. Another finish might be easier to apply and could offer results that are just as good.

Vinyl finishes. The vinyls dry very quickly. However, they are not terribly resistant to traffic, even light traffic. In fact, if you read the paint label carefully, you will probably find that the product is not recommended for flooring. (Or, it may have certain flooring uses only under certain conditions.)

Floor finishes can be high gloss, semigloss, satin, or flat. The flat ones can be coated with floor wax and rubbed to a satinlike shine. Gloss is really a matter of personal taste, although a shiny floor might be easier to keep clean than a flat waxed floor. Another selection factor might be wearability and maintenance of the finish. As a rule of thumb, those floor finishes that have great wearability are often difficult to repair when scuffs appear. The easiest to repair, as mentioned above, are shellacs and lacquers. It's really a trade-off decision.

Changing Wood Color

After sanding a wood floor you will be left with raw wood that has a yellowish-whitish look. Most oaks, pines, and maples are this color with, of course, grain markings such as sap streaks. You can stain the wood a different color, if you want, or just leave it "natural" with the finish you apply. The clear sealers/finishes will deepen the raw wood color only slightly. If there is a change in color at all, it will be to an extremely pale yellow.

You can change the color with:

1. Stain (non-grain-raising) or water stain. This, again in our opinion, is the best stain product to use on floors. It has a permanent, clear tone color and will work with top coats of penetrating finishes, shellac, varnish, or lacquer.

2. Wiping stains. These are pigmented, and work the same way on floors as on furniture woods. You will get some color penetration with wiping stains, but as with all pigment finishes, the stains tend to "lie" on top of the wood. Because strip floors have cracks and grooves involved in their fabrication, the stain can get down into these crevices. Therefore, you should triple the drying time of the stain so it won't work up into any top coat finish you apply—especially lacquer. You can buy stains in different colors or wood tones. The most successful results—again our opinion—are from the dark stains, such as mahogany and walnut.

3. Colored sealers. The penetrating finishes come in colors and work well.

4. Colored varnish. This is really an enamel, and, of course, it works well on floors as well as on cabinets and furniture. But you might not want to hide a beautiful wood floor with color.

5. Antiquing. The process is the same as for furniture: a base coat and a glaze, with the glaze wiped and highlighted (see the chapter on stains and finishes). The floor won't have much wearability, but it will take on a classic look that is both unusual and, oddly enough, rather handsome. If kids and pets are not considerations and you will be using throw rugs in high-traffic areas, you might want to investigate this finish further.

As with all finishes—even the paint on the body of the house—it's a good idea to test the finish on a piece of scrap or in a corner where the experiment won't show if it goes awry. Of course, you can always resand the area to the bare wood, but this could cause an unevenness in the floor surface.

Application

Penetrating sealers and polyurethane can be applied to properly prepared wood flooring with a lamb's-wool roller on a regular cage with an extension pole so you don't have to get on your knees or bend over. Use a roller tray to hold the finish; don't pour it out on the floor and distribute it. The polyurethanes should be very lightly stirred as the finishing process continues, but read the label on the can to determine how much, how often, and with what type of paddle.

Shellac is applied with a brush.

Varnish is applied with a brush or a roller.

Lacquer is usually applied with a brush.

Stains are applied with a brush.

Buy new roller covers and brushes for the finish application. A used brush or roller cover can spell trouble and ruin the job.

Floor Preparation

We've said it before: Almost any finishing/refinishing job requires 90 percent preparation time and 10 percent application time. Floors are no different, unless the floor is in excellent condition.

The step-by-step procedure follows (also see illustration).

Stopping squeaks. Squeaks are caused by the floor boards rubbing against each other or against nails. Squeaks most often are heard during periods of high humidity or when the temperature changes. In damp or humid weather, the wood swells and "tightens" the floor. In dry or cold weather, the wood shrinks. At this time, squeaking may be heard. This may not affect the finish to any degree, but it can sometimes make the floor somewhat tilted. Then, when you run a sander over the surface, you'll have to take a large bite of wood out of the high spot to make it level with the low spot. A quick and permanent repair is easier than sanding.

Locate the squeak by walking over the floor and bouncing up and down on the surface. If you hear the squeak, you may be able to stop it by predrilling pilot holes through the face of the flooring with a drill bit, and driving a nail through the flooring into the subflooring. Drill the pilots at a slight angle. Angled nails hold better.

If you can't locate the squeak from the top of the flooring surface, and your home has a basement or crawl space, go below and have a helper walk across the squeaky area. From below, you will be able to pinpoint it. The squeak-producer may be a small gap between the subfloor and the top of one or more joists. Or, the squeak may be between joists. In this case, the squeak is produced by the flooring pulling away from the subflooring. You can renail it from the top, as described, or you can run short screws from the

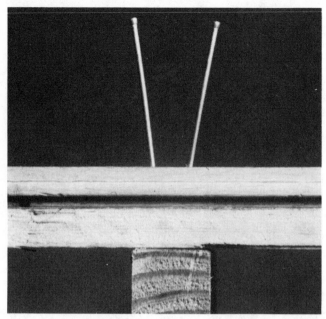

Face nailing down through the hardwood and into a joist is the best way to stop most squeaks. Drive finishing or annular nails at a slight angle, if possible. Then, countersink the nail heads and fill the holes with wood plastic; sand lightly; finish. Nails should be at least three inches long to be effective. Predrill pilot holes for nails through oak flooring. It is super hard and splits.

Shingle shims between joists and subflooring take up slack and stop squeaks. But the wedge must be tight. You also can use wood screws driven up through the subfloor and into the bottom faces of the finish flooring. Make sure the screws don't penetrate through the top face of the flooring. Use 1½-inch screws, if the subflooring is standard ¾-inch-thick material.

bottom through the subfloor into the bottom of the flooring. The screw works like a clamp, pulling the flooring down to the subflooring. If the trouble is at a joist, simply drive a wooden shingle shim between the subfloor and the top of the joist. This usually stops the squeak instantly.

If the problem is really bad, you should add more bridging or blocking between the joists to stop the squeak. Sometimes builders forget to nail all the bridging between joists. It could be that this is the problem at your house, and it's worth checking to make sure.

If the floor is sagging, now's the time to fix it. Buy a jackpost at almost any hardware store or home center outlet. (Jackposts are not expensive.) It should sit on a concrete pad; a two-by-two-foot block usually is adequate. Bridge the joists at right angles with a length of two-by-eight (or a length of timber), and sandwich the jackpost between the wood member and the pad. Tighten the jackpost, and give it one *one-quarter* turn, and no more. Put a level on the floor above and see how much the quarter turn changed the floor level. If not enough, raise the jack just one-quarter of a turn *each week* until the floor is level. Don't raise it level all at once; you could damage the framing or structure of the house with too much lift at one time.

Floor Patches

If strips of the floor are damaged beyond a regular wood-putty repair, you can replace the damaged strips without ripping up the floor. Follow the illustrations in this section for step-by-step details.

Sanding Preparation

There are several ways to get an old floor ready for refinishing:

1. Scrape it clean with a sharp cabinet scraper. This may take months to do, depending, of course, on the size of the floor.

2. Remove the old finish with paint and varnish remover. This may take weeks to do, depending on the size of the floor.

3. Sand off the old finish. This may take hours to do, depending on the size of the floor.

In our opinion, sanding is by far the easiest way to remove old finish and gives the best results.

For sanding, you will have to rent 3 pieces of equipment: a floor belt or drum sander, and a floor edger. You will find these machines at some hardware and home center stores; you'll most likely also find them at rental outlets. The cost of

To remove a damaged piece of strip flooring, drill a series of small holes along the face of the damaged part. For best results, the holes should be close, but not overlapping. Go through the thickness of the flooring just to the top of the subfloor with the drill bit.

With a sharp butt chisel (three-fourths- or one-inch) split out the drilled wood. The drilled holes serve as "bridges" so the entire length interconnects with the chisel. Use a wooden mallet to drive the chisel, and work carefully so you don't gouge the surrounding surface.

Measure and cut the new strip flooring to match the void in the floor. Then, with a butt chisel with the bevel side out, split off the tongues of the new flooring piece and the tongue of the adjoining piece nailed to the subflooring. Work the chisel straight down; the tongues will snap off clean when they are severed.

Slip the new wood strip—sans tongue—into the void; the match should be perfect. Do not cut or sand the end tongues or grooves of the replacement strip; it will fit as the new piece goes into position. Then face nail the new strip to the subflooring. Use finishing nails and countersink them with a nail set. Fill the holes with wood plastic; sand lightly; spot finish.

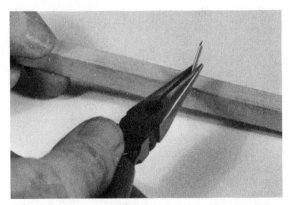

To avoid splitting quarter-round and base molding you remove for floor sanding, pull the nails through the molding from the back side. Any pliers will do; just "roll" the pliers along the wood surface by turning your hand. You can even use the old nail holes to renail the trim when the sanding job is completed.

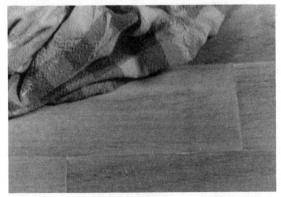

Filler makes some difference in open-grained flooring; you can see the whitish-looking filler in the joints of these boards, but the filler in the grain is not pronounced. If you use filler, thin it to a light paste, let it harden in the grain after you remove any excess, and then rub off the filler haze with old toweling or burlap.

Three types of sealers/finishes are shown here. Top: a penetrating resin sealer; middle: a pigmented stain with no topcoat; bottom: a polyurethane clear finish. The sealer and stain darkened the wood slightly; the clear finish also brought out grain patterns but left the wood surface fairly light. All finishes were on for just five minutes before this photo was taken.

rental is not prohibitive. Almost always, the dealer will be able to provide you with the proper sanding abrasives at an additional cost, and plenty of tips for equipment usage, since his equipment is involved. You'll also need an orbital sander, which the dealer might rent. Otherwise, you'll have to buy this tool, which also is not prohibitive. You can use it in the future for other projects.

Before You Start

Before you rent or buy any equipment or supplies, do yourself a favor and go over the floor with a mixture of boiling water and strong trisodium phosphate (TSP). It could be that the floor is in good enough condition that the detergent solution will clean off the old finish down to the bare wood. It's at least worth a try in a small area. If the detergent works, you'll spend some time and muscle removing the old finish but it could pay off in the end.

If you have just installed a new strip floor, it will have to be sanded level before you apply any finish. To prepare for sanding follow these steps.

1. Remove the base shoe from the bottom edge of the baseboard. The shoe is held by finishing nails. Pry off the base shoe, as illustrated, and pull out the nails from the back to prevent splitting. You may want to number the shoe sections and the baseboard so the pieces are put back the same way.

2. With a hammer and nailset, go over the entire floor and countersink below the surface of the flooring any nailheads you see. We'd suggest you concentrate on three strips at a time, marking them as you go either lengthwise or across the width of the floor. This system will ensure that you don't overlook any area, or go back over the same area several times.

3. Fill all countersunk nail holes with wood putty, smoothing the surface of the putty with a putty knife.

4. Vacuum the floor after all furniture, rugs, and other items have been removed.

The Sanding Technique

Using a floor sander is not particularly difficult, but you've got to get the hang of it before you get down to business. Allow yourself a few practice tries.

The sander is designed so it tips back toward you when you press downward on the handle. This action lifts the revolving sanding abrasive off the surface, so you don't have to continually stop and start the sanding machine with a switch. The sander is balanced so the tip down (and tip up) takes little muscle. We'd suggest that you try tipping the machine a couple of times so you can get the feel of it. When the motor is off, the sander is tough to push; when the motor and the belt are in operation, the machine moves right along, but not so rapidly that you can't be in complete control.

Go to the center of the room or an area that will be covered by a rug or a piece of furniture, tip the machine up off the floor, and turn it on. Now, gently lower the machine (tip it downward) until the sanding belt catches the floor surface. At the same time, move the machine forward. You want to get a "running start" with the sander so the abrasive doesn't dig into the wood cupping it. Move the sander along a short stretch of flooring, then tip it up to remove the abrasive belt from the flooring. Don't stop the machine on the floor and then tip it up. Come up off the floor in a moving motion—again, so the abrasive doesn't dig into the wood.

As you practice, let the machine do the work. You simply steer the tip. Don't force the machine; let it pace itself as you walk along behind it.

When you feel that you've got the machine under control and are comfortable using it, start at one edge of the room and work your way across. Go with the grain of the wood. Have patience. If you don't feel much of the finish is being removed, check the abrasive belt to be sure it is not clogged with old finish. If it is not, try moving the sander *very slightly* in a diagonal direction across the grain of the wood. But don't go at right angles or straight across the grain. Make the angle slight—like a planing stroke.

You will notice that the drum sander won't work when you get right up to the baseboard. This is why you rented the edge sander. But before you do the edges, finish the main part of the floor.

The first sanding pass should be made with a coarse abrasive. The second pass should also be made with a coarse abrasive (the same one or one grade finer). The third, and final, pass should be made with a fine abrasive. As a rule of thumb, the coarse abrasive should be an open-coat abrasive; the final sanding should be done with a closed-coat abrasive. The open-coat abrasive doesn't gum with the sanding residue as quickly as the closed-coat abrasive.

Most sanders have a bag in which most of the sawdust is caught—similar to the one in a vacuum sweeper. However, we strongly recommend that you wear a respirator while using both the drum and edge sanders. Also, try to have plenty of ventilation. If this is not possible, sand for 15 minutes and then leave the room for 10 minutes to let the fine dust settle.

If the floor is new, it may take more than three sanding passes, although three is average. Use a coarse, medium, and fine abrasive, in this order. Or, use two coarse passes, one medium pass, and one fine pass. Remember to go with the grain of the wood, and try going at a slight angle if the sander doesn't seem to be removing as much wood as you would like. If the floor is old and cuppy, you may have to make four or five passes with a coarse abrasive to level it before it can be smooth-sanded.

When you rent the sander, ask the dealer to recommend the type of abrasive and grits you will need for your specific purpose. Many dealers will let you check out extra sanding belts and then return them if you find you don't need them.

The edge sander is a frisky little machine that cuts similarly to a disc sander. Therefore, you have to use it with caution. Make sure it's running before you start the sanding stroke and also as you remove it from the floor surface. Because of the disk's torque, the edger tends to go where *it* wants unless you hang tightly onto the handles and steer. You don't have to move it over the flooring surface; the rotating abrasive will create the movement. All you do is steer and guide the machine as it bites through the old finish to the same wood level you cut with the drum sander. You probably will require several passes with a coarse abrasive to remove the old finish. Complete the job with a finer abrasive. When you're finished, you may want to go over the edge of the room with a regular orbital sander with a medium or fine abrasive. This machine will remove any sanding swirls left by the edging machine.

When you have finished the sanding job, broom sweep and then vacuum the floor area to remove the sanding debris not caught by the bag on the sanding machines. Then carefully look the floor over. If you missed any spots, you can usually take care of them with the orbital sander. If you find any ridging, a sharp cabinet scraper will remove the wood quickly, leveling out the spot and the surrounding area.

Let the room set for 24 hours. Then go back and vacuum the floor once again. By this time, all or most of the sanding residue should be gone. If it is, go over the flooring surface with a tack rag (see section on interior finishing for details on how to make a tack rag) and let the job set for another 12 hours. Now re-examine the flooring. If you find any sanding debris, wipe it up with a tack rag.

Finish Application

Finish, as mentioned above, can be applied with a brush, a roller, or a special finish applicator sold by some retailers. In deciding which to use, one must consider the type of finish and the manufacturer's recommendations, although we would always opt for a roller application because a roller is very easy to use.

The main object, in any case, is to apply the finish to the wood *with* the grain, and level the finish so it is even. Don't pour the finish out of the bucket onto the floor; if you do, it will be difficult to level it properly with any tool.

Wood Fillers

If the floor is oak the wood will be open-grained. Pine is close-grained and maple is also close-grained. You might want to fill oak with a wood filler (see section on interior finishing), but it is not really necessary. We would recommend that you use a filler, however, if the floor will be varnished. The filler helps create the shiny finish you are hoping to achieve.

To apply filler, thin it slightly. Then go over the floor with it, first with the grain, then across the grain, and then with the grain again. Wipe off the excess with old toweling or burlap when the finish starts to dull or when it is dry. Sweep and vacuum the floor. Then, with your fingers, go over the floor feeling for rough spots left by the filler. If you find any, lightly hand sand the spots, using a sanding block and a fine abrasive. You won't need to sand much; just take off the tooth on the surface of the wood.

If the floor will be lacquered, you probably will have to fill the wood after the first coat of finish has been applied to the floor. But check the manufacturer's recommendations.

Floor Finishing

We've assembled several standard finishing schedules for various finishes. Keep in mind that the information is based on a clean, properly prepared and repaired floor. Always be sure to read the manufacturer's recommendations as they could differ considerably from ours.

For penetrating finishes, brush or roll (we still recommend a roller for this one) on the first coat. Let the job set for about 30 minutes. It can take a bit longer or shorter than 30 minutes depending on the temperature and humidity in the room.

Look at the floor. If the finish is dull (dry) in some spots and shiny (wet) in others, recoat the dull spots. Then wait about 3 hours. Examine the finish again. It now should be fairly even in gloss. Give the surface one more thin, but even, coat. Let this coat set for 30 minutes and wipe up the excess with old, clean, toweling. After it dries, you can leave the finish as is for a couple of days, or you can wax it and then buff the wax.

For polyurethane finishes, follow the bucket label to the letter. Generally, the wood first has to be sealed with a sealer recommended by the manufacturer. Then, the varnish can be applied to the flooring surface with a brush. Since these coatings can vary from manufacturer to manufacturer, we will refrain from suggesting a schedule.

For shellac, use a three-pound cut finish. Use a brush to apply the shellac, and even it out with the tip of the brush. It should take about 3 hours to dry, although the temperature and humidity in the room may shorten or extend the time. Check the surface with your fingers. If you decide to use a wood filler, apply it between the first and second coats. The filler will take up to 12 hours to

dry (check the label) so don't go back over the floor with another coat of finish until the filler is hard. After the second coat is applied, sand the surface with 2/0 closed-coat abrasive on a sanding block. We recommend a third coat of shellac for a professional-looking job. After the third coat is dry, lightly sand it with 3/0 closed-coat paper on a sanding block. Remove all sanding residue and then wax.

Varnish ought to be thinned by using one part turpentine or mineral spirits to eight parts varnish. (If the wood has been sealed, do not thin the varnish.) Two coats of varnish are usually enough, although you can apply three or even four coats. If you do, lightly sand with 3/0 closed-coat abrasive between coats and remove the sanding residue with a tack rag. We recommend that you wait at least 24 hours between coats, and 30 to 40 hours if you can.

For lacquer finishes, we recommend a primer or sealer coat before the top coats are applied. You will have to work fast with lacquer, so use a mohair roller or a wide bristle brush to apply the finish. The coating builds up quite easily so be very careful not to lap it or you will have thin and thick spots across the flooring. Let the job set for about 1½ hours. Then, hand sand with 3/0 closed-coat abrasive on a sanding block. Apply the next coat after all sanding residue is removed. If you will apply a third coat, sand the second with 3/0 abrasive, clean up the residue, and brush or roll on the third coat, which should be thinned with one part thinner to four parts lacquer.

All of the finishes recommended can be waxed. We suggest a quality hardwood floor paste wax that is hand applied to the floor surface. You can buff the wax shiny by hand, too, but an electric buffer-polisher is much easier and does a satisfactory job. These machines can be rented, but the cost of buying one is not prohibitive.

Should you buff the finish with steel wool when it is dry and then apply a wax? Some pros finish floors this way, but it is a great deal of work. If you want to steel wool the finish, use No. 000 steel wool and go lightly. Do not wax or polish polyurethane finishes, unless, of course, the manufacturer recommends that you do so.

Should you use porch and deck enamel on an unsightly wood floor? The answer, of course, is yes. But you will have to remove the old finish first. The problem with porch and deck enamel is that it wears fairly quickly in high-traffic areas and is then difficult to patch. Also, colors are limited.

Anatomy of a raised floor looks like this. Squeaks occur when the floor pulls away from the subflooring or the subflooring from the joists. Nails, screws, and bridging can help stop the noise before you refinish.

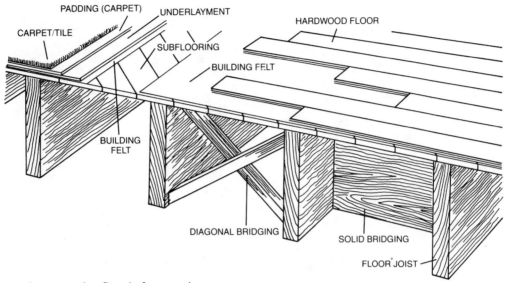

Use a jackpost to raise a sagging floor before sanding the floor for finishing or refinishing. Give the post just one quarter turn every week until the floor is level.

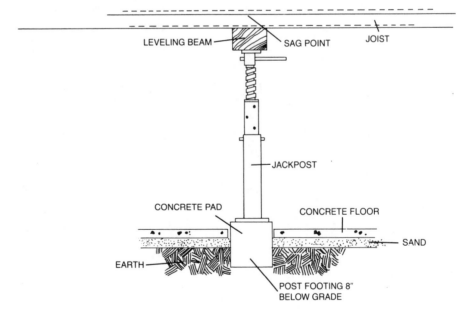

There are three basic ways to sand a hardwood floor for finishing/refinishing. Moving in a straight line is always best, although you can go at a slight angle across the boards to remove old finish and excess wood if necessary.

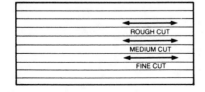
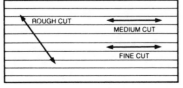
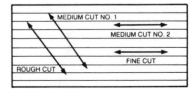

Wallpapering

If the dealer offers them, take home a selection of wall coverings and stick them onto the wall, as we've done with these swatches of burlap and fine woven fabric. You won't get the big picture, but the swatches may help you make a buying decision. We suggest that you stick with stripes or a small patterned wallpaper if you haven't had experience. Big and dropped patterns are somewhat difficult to hang.

Standard backings include prepasted (right), a feltlike backing (top left), and just plain paper (bottom left). If prepasted, buy a water trough, reroll the paper so the back faces outward, and submerge in the water trough. Give the paper enough time to absorb the water, or the paste will not be properly activated; about seven minutes is standard for an eight-foot strip.

CHAPTER 23

Wallpaper: Selecting It, Buying It

■ WALLPAPER IS a term that applies to any flexible paper or fabric that is hung on a wall. That is, the covering doesn't have to be paper. It may be a foil or fabric such as aluminum or burlap—or even a fancy bed sheet. With modern adhesives and more attention being given to the manufacture of wall coverings, wallpapering has been greatly simplified. It is not easy to wallpaper. But it isn't especially difficult, either. Your big problems will be in matching the pattern as you go along and trimming around obstructions built into or out of the wall surface.

Wallpaper is truly a great cover-up. It can hide unsightly walls where paint can't. It is the middle ground between paint and paneling. The width and length of the paper lets you cover lots of area fast. And, once up, very little maintenance is required—perhaps just an occasional light washing with mild household detergent and water or a wallpaper cleaner.

Some home center stores sell wallpaper. A few hardware stores stock it. Your best bet probably is a store specializing in wallpaper, or a retail paint store that sells wallpaper as a sideline. Selection and inventory in some stores may be sketchy. You may have to order the product you want from a wallpaper book and then wait several days for delivery. In specialty stores, you may be able to pick what you want right out of the bin, but the types and designs of the paper can be limited.

Wallpaper Types

There are eight basic types of wallpaper:

1. Lining paper
2. Vinyl wallpaper
3. Standard wallpaper
4. Foil papers
5. Fabric coverings
6. Flocked papers
7. Miscellaneous coverings
8. Prepasted wallpaper

Expect to find bargains during the summer months and from December to February as these are the times when retailers generally put wall coverings on sale.

The vinyl papers are a smart choice for kitchens, bathrooms, hallways, and kids' rooms where moisture, dirt, grease, crayon, and other soiling agents can be a problem. The "soft-faced" papers are perhaps more for decoration than the

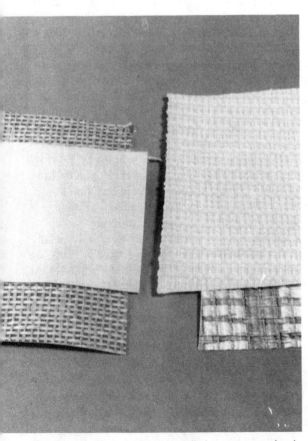

Fabric and grass patterns usually have a paper backing to which the wallpaper paste is applied. If not, paste the wall and then embed the fabric into the paste.

slick-coated papers, although the flocks and fabrics can be used almost anywhere.

Wallpaper can have any design, and some of the patterns almost glow in the dark. If you are a first-time paper hanger, you may want to stick with a plain paper or a paper that has geometric designs that are fairly easy to match. Striped patterns are probably the easiest for a beginner to hang, with little waste and matching involved. You simply cut the paper to the length you want, paste it, hang it, and then trim it at the top and bottom. The fabric-type papers can be fairly easy to match, too, but burlap can be tough since the weave has to be carefully matched where the cross weaves join. On patterned papers, you will see the word "repeat." What this means is that the pattern is repeated at intervals along the roll. Usually, the dealer will know the repeat spacing, or it may be noted in the manufacturer's sample book. For instance: The paper repeats every 20 inches. Your wall is 100 inches from the floor to the ceiling. Divide the 20 inches into the 100 inches and you'll get 5 inches or 5 repeats. In this instance, there will be little or no selvage for trimming; the repeat is a perfect match for the wall. However, another pattern may repeat more often, resulting in substantial waste. To avoid this, you want the number of repeats to closely fit the height of the wall. (See *measuring a room for wallpaper,* this section.)

Following is a selection guide to wallpapers that explains where various papers are best used and which adhesive should be used to hang the papers you are considering. This is a general guide. Be sure to discuss your project with the dealer before making a buying decision.

Lining Paper

Lining paper looks like a roll of regular wallpaper (or even plain newsprint) with no pattern. Lining paper is used to "line" cracked and damaged walls before the decorative paper is installed. Lining paper, which sometimes is called "blank paper," also forms a wonderfully smooth base for the adhesive on the decorative paper and aids adhesive drying. You hang lining paper just like the standard stuff. Use butt joints at the edges of the paper and trim it at the ceiling and baseboard. At jambs, casing, moldings, and so on, leave the edge of the lining paper about ¼-inch from the molding surfaces. This little gap will let the top paper bond directly to the wall surface and help prevent it from peeling back as it might over lining paper in this application. Lining paper also can be used to cover patterns that would otherwise show through the new paper. However, if at all possible, remove old wallpaper before hanging new wallpaper. The less paper thickness on the wall, the better.

Vinyl Wallpaper

Within this classification there are three basic types of wallpaper: vinyl that is affixed to paper; vinyl that is affixed to a cloth backing; and vinyl that has been impregnated into the backing like creosote is pressurized into wood timbers. The vinyl papers are probably the most durable of all wallpapers. You can scrub them with mild household detergents and they are tough to scratch, which makes them ideal for hallways, kids' rooms, and other high-traffic areas.

In the showroom, you may find wallpaper tagged "vinyl-coated." This is not a vinyl paper as such; the paper has been treated with vinyl on its face side and it can be a problem to clean. It is not very resistant to dirt, grime, oil, crayon, or grease. Details about vinyl-coated paper are discussed later.

The vinyls are sold in single, double, and triple rolls in widths from 18 to 27 inches. The length of the paper is always figured with the width so each single roll gives you a total of 36 square feet of wallpaper. Waste on a single roll will be approximately 6 feet, so allow for this in your measurements. You can also buy some vinyls in widths up to 54 inches and lengths up to 30 yards, but this material probably will require a special order, so expect to pay a bit more and wait several weeks for delivery. For the vinyls, we recommend a mildew-resistant type adhesive. The vinyl papers are heavy and, therefore, tend to hold moisture vapor generated from normal household functions. Up to 30 gallons of moisture vapor are generated daily in normal household activities. This vapor has to escape, so it usually goes out windows, doors, and exhaust fans, or through the walls if the walls are not properly insulated. Although blocked by insulation when wallpaper is present, the moisture can cause wallpaper adhesives to mildew (behind heavy papers) and therefore a mildew-resistant adhesive should be used.

Vinyl paper also has another plus. It can be stripped very easily from walls and ceilings in the event you tire of it or want to use it elsewhere in your home. Or, you can reroll it and store it for later use. The vinyl papers are applied just like any other paper, with one exception. Vinyl will not stick to itself. Therefore, the laps have to be double cut and butted.

Standard Wallpaper

This category is made up of vinyl-coated, cloth-backed, and just plain untreated paper. The standards usually sell for less than the more fancy coated papers. However, there is nothing wrong with the standard papers. They are not as durable as the others, so, if you buy them, consider them for areas that won't get hard usage. For example, a hallway wouldn't be a good choice. The standard measurements are the same as for the vinyl wallpapers. For hanging, we suggest either wheat paste or stainless cellulose adhesive. Both types are stocked by most retailers who sell wallpaper. Be careful when hanging the standard papers. The paste tends to make the paper soggy and prone to rips and tears. Also, some *very* inexpensive standard papers may be unwashable or uncleanable. The ink patterns on the surface of the paper can dissolve or run when they become wet.

The Foil Papers

Foil wallpaper comes in two types: a metallike material that has been laminated to a backing, and an aluminum that has been laminated to paper. They look fairly similar. You'll be reminded of aluminum cooking foil with a design printed on one side. Foil conforms to wall surfaces like vinyl sheet flooring conforms to floors. Every little lump and bump will show through the surface, so the wall must be in super shape and sanded as smooth as possible. A foil application is best when done over lining paper. The lining paper will provide the smooth surface you want.

Some papers, like this foil, come in triple rolls with a yield of about 108 to 105 yards. Single rolls and double rolls are standard at most retailers. You sometimes can get a tad more than 30 square feet from a roll if the pattern is a stripe or very plain. But don't skimp in your estimates more than about 2 square feet.

Use the same (mildew-resistant) adhesive for installing the lining paper and the foil. The liner will help speed the drying time of the adhesive. Foil papers will crease—like aluminum foil—so be especially careful hanging them. Also, some foil papers are stuck to the adhesive on the wall instead of covered with adhesive and stuck to the wall or other surface. Ask the dealer about this. Or, check the foil package which usually notes any special handling data.

The Fabric Coverings

Grass cloth, rice cloth, burlap, and hemp are all in this general classification. For the most part, all fabrics are laminated to a paper-type backing, although you can buy the fabric without backing and stick it up as an accent design. The fabrics with the paper backing, however, are much easier to handle than those without the backing.

The fabrics have some "dos" and "don'ts" you should know before buying them. Fabric colors sometimes vary between rolls of the same material. For example, you may see a nice, deep brown roll, but the same covering located in the same bin made by the same manufacturer may be a different color brown and not match the other rolls perfectly. But this doesn't necessarily need to be a problem. A mismatched color can often offer texture and color highlights that are pleasing. As you cut the fabric for hanging, you can lay it out flat on the floor and check any texture or color pattern. Then, interchange the strips and hang them to suit your taste.

We recommend that you line the walls before applying any of the fabrics. You'll get better results and have an easier time of it even though you will spend a little extra time and money. However, if you don't line the walls, the walls must be sealed with a wall sizing. (Use a glue sizing sold in wallpaper departments.) Sized walls will not absorb the water in the adhesive as rapidly, and you can slide the fabric here and there for the proper fit. You generally do not have to match patterns with fabric. Allow about two inches for trimming purposes, however. This trimming figure should be included in your buying estimates. We recommend wheat paste or liquid cellulose adhesive for hanging fabrics. But again, check with the dealer.

Flocked Wallpaper

You can buy this material with the flocking stuck to paper, vinyl, or foil. Paper is the least expensive of the three. There is no special trick to hanging this material but you must be careful not to damage the flocking by rubbing it. If you get adhesive on the flocking (which you will) blot it off with a damp sponge; don't try to rub it off or you will rub off or damage the flocking. We recommend a vinyl or mildew-resistant adhesive for the flocks, but, of course, check with the dealer.

Prepasted Wallpaper

These paper products are what their name implies: prepasted and ready to hang after the rolls are soaked in a special water box provided by the manufacturer/dealer. The selections include "standard" wallpaper, vinyl, foil, and flocked papers. If you haven't applied wallpaper before, the prepasted papers may be your best bet because they save lots of time and eliminate the cleanup you would have with adhesives. However, the prepasting is not always perfect: You may have to add paste to corners and seams as the paper goes up. Use the adhesive recommended earlier for the specific paper type.

Wallpaper squares for accents are also available in prepasted designs. The squares resemble tiles that are twelve-by-twelve inches square. The squares are extremely easy to paste up almost anywhere. However, you must lay out the wall the same way you would lay out a floor or a wall for ceramic tiles. If the first square doesn't go on the surface perfectly, the others will go on askew and the error will compound itself.

Miscellaneous Wall Coverings

Murals and bolt-type fabrics head this classification. Murals can be printed or laminated on paper, vinyl, or foil. The bolt goods are just like those found in dry goods stores, although some wallpaper outlets handle them as wall coverings. Bed sheeting, for example, would be under the bolt label.

Murals are sold in widths up to 36 inches. They can be from 10 to 12 feet long (and even longer), and often have matching paper or "backgrounds" to hang over, under, and at the sides of the murals. A mildew-resistant or vinyl adhesive is recommended for hanging. Bolt goods are laminated to paper backings, and are either ready-to-paste or prepasted. Goods such as burlap come in bolts (sometimes in rolls) 45 inches wide with special-order material measuring up to 54 and 60 inches. It usually is sold by the yard rather than the piece. The adhesive recommended is powdered vinyl or double-faced tape. If the fabric is laminated to a backing, the best adhesive is wheat paste or cellulose adhesive applied with a brush to the wall or the back of the material.

There are still other coverings, including real leather, which are sometimes available in stores, but usually are special-order items. A partial list would include cork, wood veneers, gypsum wallboard with a fabric covering, and Paris tile, a very thin vinyl wall covering that resembles floor sheet goods.

Estimating Your Needs

Before you go shopping for wallpaper, you should know how much you will need, where the product will go, whether or not you'll use a border, and what wall repairs will be needed before the material is applied. Intensive preplanning can save you hours of time and put you in a better bargaining position at the store since you'll be ready with nomenclature, sizes, amounts, and so on. In figuring room measurements, be aware of these considerations:

• Wallpaper comes in different widths. However, regardless of the width, each single roll will contain 36 square feet of wallpaper.

• The width of the wallpaper will determine the length of the wallpaper per roll. If the roll is wide, the length will be shorter. Therefore, you must consider the length needed in order to avoid horizontal joints across the area.

• Although there are 36 square feet of wallpaper in each single roll, the actual yield from the roll will be approximately 30 square feet. This, of course, is an average. The yield could be slightly more or slightly less than the 30 square feet figure. But estimate your needs at 30 square feet.

• Figure the entire room (or wall) when estimating. If there are doors, windows, or fireplaces cut into the wall, you should subtract one-half of a roll of wallpaper per door and window. Each opening is estimated to be about 18 square feet.

Trim or border paper that goes around the walls at the ceiling is usually sold by the yard. Figure the amount, in yards, around the room, and then buy one extra yard of border. For example, if the figure is 10 yards, buy 11 yards. You will need the extra for cutting and fitting.

Wallpaper adhesive usually is sold by the package which can weigh from one to five pounds. You can figure that one pound of dry mix adhesive is enough to hang six to eight rolls of wallpaper. However, you may need more, depending on paper, since some vinyl papers take more adhesive than others. Ask the dealer about this. A good rule of thumb is one gallon of vinyl adhesive for two to four rolls of paper. The lesser amount is for heavier vinyl wall coverings.

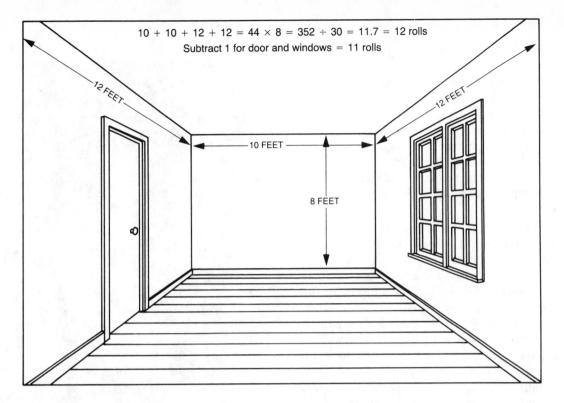

10 + 10 + 12 + 12 = 44 × 8 = 352 ÷ 30 = 11.7 = 12 rolls
Subtract 1 for door and windows = 11 rolls

12 FEET

12 FEET

10 FEET

8 FEET

To estimate a room for wallpaper needs, measure the height of the room and the perimeter around the room. Here is a typical example. Two sides of the room are 12 feet, or a total of 24 feet. Two ends of the room are 10 feet, or a total of 20 feet, for a combined total of 44 feet. The ceiling/floor height is 8 feet. So, 44 × 8 divided by 30 feet (the number of square feet in a roll of paper) equals 11.7. You would need 12 rolls. But there is a door and window. Subtract one-half of a roll for each. Net total for the project would be 11 rolls. This measurement is based on a single roll figure. See estimating chart.

There are two types of wall or wallpaper sizing: wallpaper paste and a product termed "wall" or "wallpaper sizing." Simply, sizing seals the wall surfaces so water from the wallpaper adhesive isn't absorbed quickly producing "dry" voids behind the wall covering. The sizing also is like a paint primer: It gives the surface a "tooth" to which the adhesive sticks better. You can apply sizing with a paintbrush or a roller. It goes on very easily; there is no special application technique. Let the sizing dry thoroughly before you hang the paper.

Tools and equipment to hang wall coverings are readily available. In fact, most dealers sell a kit of tools specially assembled for the job. The tools are not top line, as a rule. So, if you will hang lots of wallpaper, we suggest that you buy professional equipment. The cost is not prohibitive.

You will need the following items:

• Water bucket
• Pasting table
• Wide adhesive brush
• Adhesive bucket

Quick Reference To Wallpaper Rolls Needed

Feet Around Room	Single Rolls/Rooms			Single Rolls/Ceiling
	8 ft.	9 ft.	10 ft.	
36	9	10	11	3
40	10	11	13	4
44	11	12	14	4
48	12	14	15	5
52	13	15	16	6
56	14	16	17	6
60	15	17	19	7
64	16	18	20	8
68	17	19	21	9
72	18	21	22	10

- Tape measure
- Utility knife with lots of replacement blades
- Trimming wheel
- *Metal* straightedge
- Chalk line and plumb bob
- Very sharp scissors with long blades
- Wallpaper smoothing brush
- Stepladder (six feet is a good size)
- Wallpaper seam roller
- Drop cloths
- Wall sizing

You probably have many of these items in your workshop. If not, any necessary additions probably can be used for other types of home maintenance and improvement projects, so the investment can go a long way.

There is, perhaps, one exception: a pasting table. Ideally, a regular table for pasting wallpaper is recommended. You may be able to rent a table. If not, the cost of buying a table for just one wallpapering job would be prohibitive. If this is the case, you can use a regular folding table or even a floor surface (hardwood or tile). The pasting area must be smooth and clean and not covered with newspaper. (The ink on newspaper will float off onto the wallpaper when it becomes damp and wet.) You will overlap the width of wallpaper rolls with adhesive. After each roll, this excess adhesive should be wiped off the pasting surface with a damp cloth or sponge.

Wall Preparation

The walls for wallpaper, as noted above, must be in good repair. The tools needed for this are listed in the sections on interior/exterior painting, and include putty knives, scrapers, spackling compound, sandpaper, and sanding blocks.

You can hang paper over painted glossy walls, but the gloss should be buffed flat with abrasives. Be sure the surface is not slick. You can also hang new wallpaper over new gypsumboard walls, but the gypsumboard covering (a paper) must be sealed first either with wall size or a good flat latex primer. We would suggest the primer; let it dry and then lightly sand the surfaces with medium-grit paper on a block.

You will, no doubt, want to paint the trim molding in the room to match the wallpaper background or design color. If so, paint this trim *before* you hang the new wallpaper.

You can hang new wallpaper over old wallpaper, but it is not recommended that you do so. Any old wallpaper should be removed so you can start anew. Removing old paper is easy to say, but hard to do. There are three methods:

A long T-square makes an excellent straightedge for cutting any wall covering. The tongue of the T is long enough to span the width of most wall coverings. Use a sharp razor knife or utility knife to cut the paper or fabric. Do not use scissors, except for special trimming where you can't use a knife blade. Change the knife blade often. A dull blade will crinkle the covering and skip, causing alignment problems on the wall.

Buy a wallpaper paste brush even though the paper you will hang is prepasted. You will need extra paste on the paper, regardless. A piece of wire coat hanger makes an excellent brush holder. Cut it to fit the bucket and run the wire through the handle bails, as shown. If you leave the brush in the paste, the bristles will become very soggy and moplike.

1. Rent a sprayer and spray water over the wallpaper surface until the paper can be scraped off the wall. Wallpaper dealers sell a solution to add to the water which speeds the softening process. This is a slow procedure, and a wet one, but it is effective.

2. Apply water mixed with a softening solution with a brush. Plan on spending hours.

3. Rent a wallpaper steamer with a steam plate. The steaming method is the easiest of the three, although you will have to pay for the rental equipment. The price, we feel, is worth it.

The steamer will have three parts: boiler, hose, and steamer plate. The boiler is filled with water, which is heated into steam. The steam pressure is forced through the hose connected to the steamer plate. The plate has holes in it through which the steam is forced out and onto the wallpaper. The heat melts the adhesive and softens the paper, which is scraped off the surface. Most steamers are electrically operated; just plug the cord into an outlet and flip the switch.

The best time to operate a steamer is when it is cool—fall, winter, or spring. The machine generates lots of steam heat, so if you use it in the summer months, have plenty of ventilation.

Steamers are so efficient that you may not even have to scrape off the softened wallpaper—or at least not very much of it. The paper actually separates from the adhesive and the force of gravity makes it peel right off. You just have to help the peeling here and there with a slip or two of the scraper. There are also additives you can buy to mix with the water that is used to make steam. In reality, this is more of a gimmick than an aid.

Before you start any wallpaper removal, make sure that the old paper on the wall is not the strippable type. With the blade of a utility knife, carefully lift a corner edge of the paper and gently pull it down. Use an even pressure. If the paper is strippable, it will start to peel off the wall with just a little effort on your part. Pull the paper straight down against itself as evenly as possible. When the paper is off, you will notice "fuzz" stuck to the wall surface. Don't sand this off. It provides a base for the new wallpaper. Of course, if you plan to paint the wall rather than paper it, the fuzz should be removed with sandpaper on a sanding block.

If your walls are lath and plaster (not gypsumboard) you may find "hot spots" in the plaster. These are really alkali spots and they are quite common on new plaster walls and some old ones as well. The spots must be treated before you wallpaper or the adhesive won't stick to them.

You may not be able to see the spots by just looking over the surface. Therefore, coat the wall with glue or wall size, as mentioned earlier. The size will cause the hot spots to color so you can see them. Then, neutralize the spots with a mixture of one part 28% acetic acid, and two parts water. We recommend that you wear rubber gloves and apply the mixture with a soft cloth. Rub the area until the color disappears, which will mean that the alkalis have been dissolved. You may need to go over the surface several times with the acetic acid mixture. When all of the spots have vanished, resize the wall and proceed with the project.

Selection Nomenclature

When you shop for wallpaper, the terms "straight patterns" and "dropped patterns" will fly like the adjectives in a politician's campaign speech. "Straight" and "dropped" sound mysterious, but both are very easy to understand.

A "straight" or "straight match" means that the pattern is the same along the roll. The pattern repeats itself horizontally.

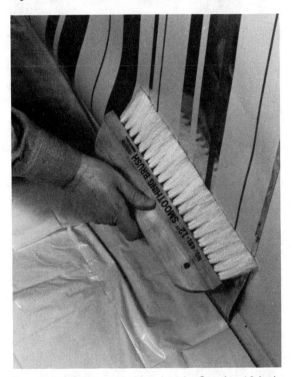

Buy a wallpaper smoothing brush. Get the 12-inch size, if possible. As you hang the paper, the bristles of the brush will tend to fill with adhesive. When this occurs, wash out the adhesive with clear water and rub the bristles dry on old toweling. The best way is to have two smoothing brushes. You can put the second one into service while the bristles of the first one dry. Cost of the brushes is nominal.

Buy a wallpaper seam roller. The roller's surface embeds the wall covering into the adhesive at seams, making a smooth "seam-free" job. Also keep adhesive off the surface of the roller as you work. Use clear water.

For stubborn seams that won't lie flat and adhere, try using straight pins as clamps until the adhesive dries. The tiny pin holes won't be noticeable when the pins are removed. After the adhesive has set for a time, go back over the seams with the roller once again. Then pin down any seams that won't stick properly. You may have to add extra adhesive behind these spots. Be sure to wipe away excess adhesive as you go.

A "dropped" or "drop match" means that the design on the bottom or at the end of the roll matches the design on the top of the next roll—and vice versa.

If the design on the paper is directly opposite the design on another roll of the same paper, the paper is a straight match. If not, it is, simply, a drop match.

Most wallpaper is pretrimmed; i.e., the edges are trimmed at the factory so they can be butt-joined together. This seam is the easiest to do and looks best because you won't see the double-lapped joints when light strikes the surface a certain way. If the paper has a selvage, it must be trimmed off before the paper is pasted. If you will lap the joints, or seams, only one side of the paper has to be trimmed because the trimmed edge then covers the selvage edge.

A "wire edge" refers to a wallpaper seam that has been lapped about one-sixteenth of an inch. Most paper hangers use the wire edge treatment when they can't butt seam edges perfectly. This usually happens on walls that are not particularly straight and level. A wire edge also is the one to use if the paper is noted to shrink. (Ask the dealer about the shrink factor.) The wire edge allows for this contraction so the seams don't form a gap.

Double cutting is an easy way to get all butted seams to fit perfectly. If you have laid carpeting, you know the term. If not, here's how double cutting works: (You will have to add extra wallpaper to your order because of waste.)

To protect outside corners of wall covering, you can buy a clear corner strip of plastic which is tacked into position. The clear strips are hardly noticeable. The strips come in eight-foot-long units; you cut them with a hacksaw.

Paste and hang the wallpaper, lapping the seams. With a straightedge and a very sharp utility knife, cut through both layers of paper—right down into the wall surface. There will be a small strip of paper on the top surface of the cut. Peel this off. Lift the edge of the paper on the wall. You'll see another small strip of paper. Peel this off. Now, butt both edges of paper together. The joint will match perfectly.

Buying a mural takes some planning. First, determine where the mural will go and sketch this wall noting exact width and height. The mural, which is similar to a large wall painting, will have "borders" at the top, bottom, and edges; i.e., it will fit a specific space. Therefore, furniture placement in the room can be critical. You don't want a sofa, lamp, or table to hide the bottom half of the mural.

If the mural doesn't cover the entire wall space, you will need "background" or, more often, a neutral or unpatterned wallpaper to complete the area. Backgrounds specially made for mural patterns are available.

Murals also are available in designs that can be reduced in size by leaving out a strip or two of the total design, or increased in size by adding strips to fill the wall. Ask the dealer about this when you choose your mural. There could be a cost difference. The same adhesive used for the mural almost always is used for the background paper also. Mildew-resistant adhesive often is specified for both.

Cleaning/Protecting Paper

Most wallpapers (but not the "standard" ones) can be cleaned by simply sponging them with mild household detergent and water, and then rinsing away the residue. A commercial wallpaper dough also is available. Ease of cleaning can be an important buying decision. Usually manufacturers and dealers tell you how durable and maintenance-free their products are, but nonetheless, before you buy, ask the dealer about care.

As a word of caution, before you wash or clean paper with dough, test it in an area behind a sofa or chair where any mistakes won't show. Also know that cleaning dough can damage the color and texture of the paper. Be careful.

By estimating your wallpaper needs in advance, you will end up with little or no excess paper. Of course, this is what you want to do—but only to a point. It is a good idea to have a little of the wallcovering left over—half a roll or so—and you may want to take this into consideration when figuring your estimates. The reason is this: Somewhere down the line, an area in the paper may become damaged. This spot can be repaired by patching in a new piece (the double-cut process), but you will need the extra paper to match the patch. The aging process of the paper on the wall and the paper in storage will be about the same. Therefore, the patch won't look as new and out of place as would one that you'd make from brand new paper, if indeed you could even find the pattern still in stock.

Some retailers sell protective coatings for some types of wallpaper. The coatings are clear and are brushed or rolled over the paper surface after the wallpapering job is completely dry. The coatings will not discolor the paper. They are especially good for use in high-traffic areas where the paper will be subject to wear, dirt, or grime.

INDEX

METRIC CONVERSION

Conversion factors can be carried so far they become impractical. In cases below where an entry is exact it is followed by an asterisk (*). Where considerable rounding off has taken place, the entry is followed by a + or a − sign.

CUSTOMARY TO METRIC

Linear Measure

inches	millimeters
1/16	1.5875*
1/8	3.2
3/16	4.8
1/4	6.35*
5/16	7.9
3/8	9.5
7/16	11.1
1/2	12.7*
9/16	14.3
5/8	15.9
11/16	17.5
3/4	19.05*
13/16	20.6
7/8	22.2
15/16	23.8
1	25.4*

inches	centimeters
1	2.54*
2	5.1
3	7.6
4	10.2
5	12.7*
6	15.2
7	17.8
8	20.3
9	22.9
10	25.4*
11	27.9
12	30.5

feet	centimeters	meters
1	30.48*	.3048*
2	61	.61
3	91	.91
4	122	1.22
5	152	1.52
6	183	1.83
7	213	2.13
8	244	2.44
9	274	2.74
10	305	3.05
50	1524*	15.24*
100	3048*	30.48*

1 yard =
.9144* meters
1 rod =
5.0292* meters
1 mile =
1.6 kilometers
1 nautical mile =
1.852* kilometers

Fluid Measure

(Milliliters [ml] and cubic centimeters [cc or cu cm] are equivalent, but it is customary to use milliliters for liquids.)

1 cu in = 16.39 ml
1 fl oz = 29.6 ml
1 cup = 237 ml
1 pint = 473 ml
1 quart = 946 ml
= .946 liters
1 gallon = 3785 ml
= 3.785 liters
Formula (exact):
fluid ounces × 29.573 529 562 5*
= milliliters

Weights

ounces	grams
1	28.3
2	56.7
3	85
4	113
5	142
6	170
7	198
8	227
9	255
10	283
11	312
12	340
13	369
14	397
15	425
16	454

Formula (exact):
ounces × 28.349 523 125* =
grams

pounds	kilograms
1	.45
2	.9
3	1.4
4	1.8
5	2.3
6	2.7
7	3.2
8	3.6
9	4.1
10	4.5

1 short ton (2000 lbs) =
907 kilograms (kg)
Formula (exact):
pounds × .453 592 37* =
kilograms

Volume

1 cu in = 16.39 cubic
centimeters (cc)
1 cu ft = 28 316.7 cc
1 bushel = 35 239.1 cc
1 peck = 8 809.8 cc

Area

1 sq in = 6.45 sq cm
1 sq ft = 929 sq cm
= .093 sq meters
1 sq yd = .84 sq meters
1 acre = 4 046.9 sq meters
= .404 7 hectares
1 sq mile = 2 589 988 sq meters
= 259 hectares
= 2.589 9 sq
kilometers

Kitchen Measure

1 teaspoon = 4.93 milliliters (ml)
1 Tablespoon = 14.79
milliliters (ml)

Miscellaneous

1 British thermal unit (Btu) (mean)
= 1 055.9 joules
1 calorie (mean) = 4.19 joules
1 horsepower = 745.7 watts
= .75 kilowatts
caliber (diameter of a firearm's
bore in hundredths of an inch)
= :254 millimeters (mm)
1 atmosphere pressure = 101 325*
pascals (newtons per sq meter)
1 pound per square inch (psi) =
6 895 pascals
1 pound per square foot =
47.9 pascals
1 knot = 1.85 kilometers per hour
25 miles per hour = 40.2
kilometers per hour
50 miles per hour = 80.5
kilometers per hour
75 miles per hour = 120.7
kilometers per hour